The Cuckoo Clock Owner's Repair Manual

By D. Rod Lloyd

Step by Step

No Prior Experience Required

The following books are also by D. Rod Lloyd are available

The Clock Repairer's Bench Manual: Everything you need to know when repairing mechanical clocks
The Cuckoo Clock Owner's Repair Manual: Step by Step, No Prior Experience Required
The Grandfather Clock Owner's Repair Manual
Happy Anniversary Clock's: 400-Day Owners Repair Manual
A Walk in my Shoes, Biography
The Atmos Clock Repairer's Bench Manual Step by Step
My Clock Won't Run Beginners guide to clock repair

Handbell Ringers Bible
Handbell Ringers Bible Book 2: For the Beginner Handbell Ringer
Build Your own Handbell Tree From Off the Shelf Parts

Laundromat Operations & Maintenance Manual
Money from Mobiles: Mobile Flipping, Loans, Parks, Rentals- A gateway to Real Estate Investing
How to re-hair your Violin, Viola, Cello, or Bass bow
Laundromat Operations & Maintenance Manual
Frederick II - Classic English Narrowboat: A unique Tug / Dutch Barge with a Charming Interior
British to American Dictionary: For Travelers and those who talk to Brits

Home Inspection and Mold Testing Business by an Old Pro
House Flipping for Big Profits by an Old Pro
10% interest
Profitable Rental Property Investing: & House Flipping
How to get rid of MOLD - a homeowner guide
The Care and Feeding of Economy Rental Property by an Old Pro
Toilet Repair or Replacement Without calling a Plumber
Instant Hot Water
To Make End$ Meet: How Not To Be Poor

Contents

Copyright ©

ClockWatchBooks.com

Introduction

There are many excellent books written for the horologist, apprentice, or professional clock shop, but this book is written specifically for a novice clock owner who has an interest in maintaining their cuckoo clock as a hobby and does not own a shop full of expensive and sophisticated tools.

Since I started writing, this book has taken on a life of its own. As I proceed through this writing journey, I discovered that most of the clock repair skills could be broken down into simple steps that the average clock owner can understand and follow.

You probably know of or have heard about ordinary people who have started out with a hobby and become just as proficient at their passion as the trained professional, fueled by passion rather than money or creating a career.

This book assumes the reader has no prior knowledge of the subject and no specialized tools and equipment. Our journey requires minimal initial outlay.

As a member of NAWCC chapter 31 [National Association of Watch and Clock Collectors, Portland], I was persuaded to take over as an instructor of a local hands-on clock class. It turns out by teaching this class, I have learned a lot from my students. I discovered clock hobbyists are an incredible sharing group. Each member coming from a different background and experiences. Each willing to provide suggestions and tips, more of a roundtable pooling of information.

I owned many many clock books and found myself searching through several to find the answers to even the most basic student tasks. This book attempts to pool all the necessary information you need in one place.

I decided to turn this book into a class workbook aimed at the new students that walk in at the start of each term with no prior experience but a loving clock project in their arms. With each project, new questions arise. I decided to document each question/problem and their solutions in this book, so all may learn from them.

The skills I have learned on my clock journey have turned out to be useful in a surprising number of times and places in my life outside of clocks. Repairing my wife's glasses, washing machines, jewelry music box, etc, etc.

Caution, when you start working on clocks, time seems to stand still, in more ways than one. Before you know it, an hour or two has passed by as you get absorbed into your project.

I write this book as an average working man, not an English major. Please forgive any spelling or grammatical errors. However, I would be happy to hear from you if you do find any, so I can make corrections for future editions. rlloyd@clear-lake.com

About the Author

My grandfather died when I was seven. We lived in Southport, England. He had owned three grandfather clocks. About a year after he died, I asked my mother what happened to the grandfather clocks. She said they were distributed to the grandchildren. I said, "where is mine?" She said I think Auntie Florrie got one.

The next time we were visiting Auntie Florrie, I said to her, "you got my grandfather clock," in a way only an 8-year-old could without being disrespectful. I caught her off guard, but she replied, I could have it when the time was right.

As a kid, whenever I saw an old clock at a jumble sale or going cheap, I would buy it and take it apart to see how it worked. I don't think I ever got one back together again, but I enjoyed tinkering with them.

Twenty years later, when I was getting married, now living in the USA, Auntie Florrie wrote to me saying I could now have the clock.

I arranged to have the clock shipped over, and it was proudly placed in the entrance hall to my home. It was built in about 1880 in Maghull England by a local clockmaker [before the electric light was invented], had a stately mahogany case, hand-painted dial, and ran nicely.

After a few years, it stopped. I was frustrated that I didn't know what was wrong with it or how to get it going. I ended up having it serviced by a local repair shop, and it ran again. I was fascinated with the clock.

In 1995, my family decided to spend a year in England, including putting the kids in school. It was a big challenge to arrange to swap houses with an English family. Finally, we were settled, and the kids started school, my wife was volunteering at a local charity shop, and suddenly I had time on my hands.

I read the paper that morning and came across an ad for a clock course starting nearby at Manchester City College. I called the college, and they told me it was a three-year course, one day per week. I explained that I was only in the country for one year, so I persuaded them to let me take the course, coming all three days.

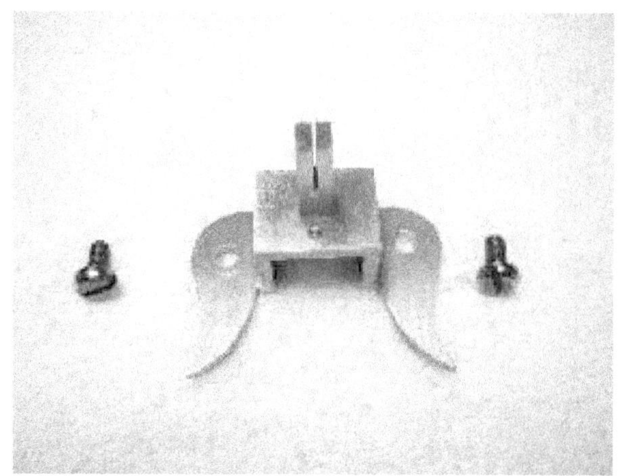

I enjoyed the course and did very well. The final exam took several weeks, making a 'suspension bridge' from scratch to exact specifications, restoring several old clocks and watches. I documented the process and took the extensive final written exam all set by BHI [British Horological Institute]. I did pass the exams and became a Horologist.

Twenty-five years later, I taught clock repair classes and 'passed it on.' This manual is the class workbook for cuckoo clocks.

SECTION ONE

The Cuckoo Bird

The Cuckoo Bird

The cuckoo bird is known to be a brood parasite. This means that they do not raise their young, instead, they depend on other birds to do it for them. They are classified under the Cuculiformes order and fall under the Cuculidae family. They aren't big nor small birds. They vary in length, depending on the species. And they can live up to almost 13 years of age.

Habitat

The cuckoo bird is lives pretty much anywhere with trees. They mainly inhabit deciduous and coniferous forests, woodland areas, meadows, scrubs, moorlands, lowlands, and even wooded steppe. They are therefore distributed on a global scale all over the world except for Antarctica. They also refrain from dry or very cold areas like northernmost parts of North America, dry parts of Africa, the Middle East, or Australia.

Since the cuckoo depends on other birds to raise its young, they inhabit close to their hosts. There are over 100 species that the cuckoo uses as hosts. They generally choose insectivorous songbirds like warblers, wagtails, flycatchers, buntings, or chats. Sometimes they will also select fruit-eating birds. This is because the cuckoo is an insectivore itself.

Cuckoos are migratory birds. They fly south for the winter. From Europe, for example, they fly down to India, Southeast Asia, the Middle East, and parts of Africa. The exact locations of their migration depend on their species. They generally live solitary lives [except the breeding season].

How Cuckoo Clocks are Built

Traditionally, cuckoo clocks were handmade by a team working together to create distinctive timepieces. Each person has their part and skills: case, decorative carvings, bellows, hands, dial, bird, weights, pendulum, etc. When the clock is finally assembled, all the parts must work together in harmony.

Much of its development and evolution was made in the Black Forest area in southwestern Germany [State of Baden-Württemberg], the region where the cuckoo clock was popularized.

Linden wood is used for the carvings. It needs to dry and cure for years before it can be crafted. Only the best pieces are used for the decorative parts.

The outer worked wood case is usually made of beautiful dark wood that is intricately carved with folk and forest scenes. The clock itself is made in the premier clock-and-watch-making area of the world. When the tiny wood cuckoo emerges to call the hour, two small pipes attached to two miniature bellows make his call.

The figures that appear on the cuckoo clock are hand-carved and painted, as well.

The movement [or clockworks] is then installed and tested to complete the clock.

Cuckoo clocks are one of the most popular items that come from Germany. These clocks that are manufactured in Germany are made by six renowned manufactures in the world. All these manufactures are members of the Black Forest Clock Association. The productions have to be certified.

These six companies include Rombach & Haas [also known as Romba], Hubert Herr, Anton Schneider, Hönes [also known as Hoenes and Hones], Hekas [or Helmut Kammerer] and Trenkle Uhren. All these manufacturers are members of the Black Forest Clock Association, and all their clocks have the certification of the VDS.

Left, early [1987-2006] and right, modern [post-2006] VDS seals on clocks originating from a manufacturer in the Black Forest Region registered with the syndicate. [Designed by artist Benno Gasche from Schonach].

The Lötscher company, based near Zurich, can boast it makes the only genuine Swiss cuckoo clocks in the world.

Three hundred years ago, Germany's farmers had no means of generating an income during the long cold winters. They decided to make clocks to survive the season. They were very simple wood clocks with wooden gears, but they were very popular.

More and more farmers started to make clocks, so to compete, they started making more attractive and appealing clocks. They began painting black forest scenes and decorations, creating "shield clocks."

Next was added a cuckoo bird that came out of a door at the top of the face. The birth of the familiar cuckoo clock.

In about 1850, wood carvings were added, and the next generation was born. A wood case became in demand, and animations were added. The modern cuckoo clock was created.

Today, there are many cuckoo clockmakers, but 90% of the clocks are made by Regula and Hubert Herr.

Styles of Cuckoo Clocks

There **two general designs** of cuckoo clocks.

A) **Chalet** cuckoo clock [house style]

B) Traditionally **carved** cuckoo clock

Chalet Cuckoo Clock

The chalet clocks look like Alpine or Black Forest houses. These days, they are more popular than traditionally carved cuckoo clocks. The chalet cuckoo clocks range from traditional Black Forest house to Tudor Style framework houses. The clocks show traditional scenes of everyday life and often have moving elements/figurines.

Traditionally Carved Cuckoo Clock

Traditionally carved cuckoo clocks look back on a longer tradition than chalet cuckoo clocks. The most popular are hunting and forest scenes. They are equipped with large hand carvings of scenes from nature like leaves, birds, or deer.

The repair and servicing of cuckoo clocks is much like repairing any weight or spring-driven mechanical pendulum clock. For information about more detailed cuckoo clock repair, please see the comprehensive **Section Two** of this book. **Section One** deals specifically with the general procedure to service cuckoo clocks.

Taking cuckoo clocks apart is quite simple. The challenge is to put them back together again, **so it will run correctly**. This book will teach you the simple process that will allow you to re-assemble the clock, so it runs successfully.

There are, of course, unique points to consider when servicing cuckoo clock movements. First, they are, in general, rather rugged mechanisms intended for long wear under very dirty conditions. The teeth on the wheels and the trundles on the pinions are seemingly over large or not finely enough made.

The arbors seem too short between the plates and the pivot holes a little sloppy. Usually, the clock was supplied with weights heavy enough to run the clock despite dirt, wear, and neglect. We want to remember these are not defects. They allow the clock to keep on ticking in their drafty and dusty cases.

Cuckoo clock repairers should, therefore, try not to eliminate this excess end shake or bush pivots too closely. Be careful to watch that pins on wheels that interact with levers will still do so no matter which way forward or backward between the plates, the arbors are pushed.

Most likely, it is because the works are excessively dirty, need oiling, or most likely both. When the clock stops, think of it as "a cry for help," "the oil light is on." Without oil, the metal parts grind on each other, causing severe wear and damage.

Oil also attracts dust, which can make the oil "gummy' or congealed and adds drag to its operation until it can no longer overcome the friction.

If a clock is oiled regularly [every three to five years], chances are you will only ever need to re-oil your clock.

If the clock is allowed to run until it stops, the only sure way to service it is to remove the works from its case, dismantle the parts, clean, service and put the movement back together with fresh oil and correct adjustments. This book will teach you how to do all this.

As you go through this text, please refer often to the schematic on the next page.

Regula Cuckoo Clock Schematic

Werk 25-232

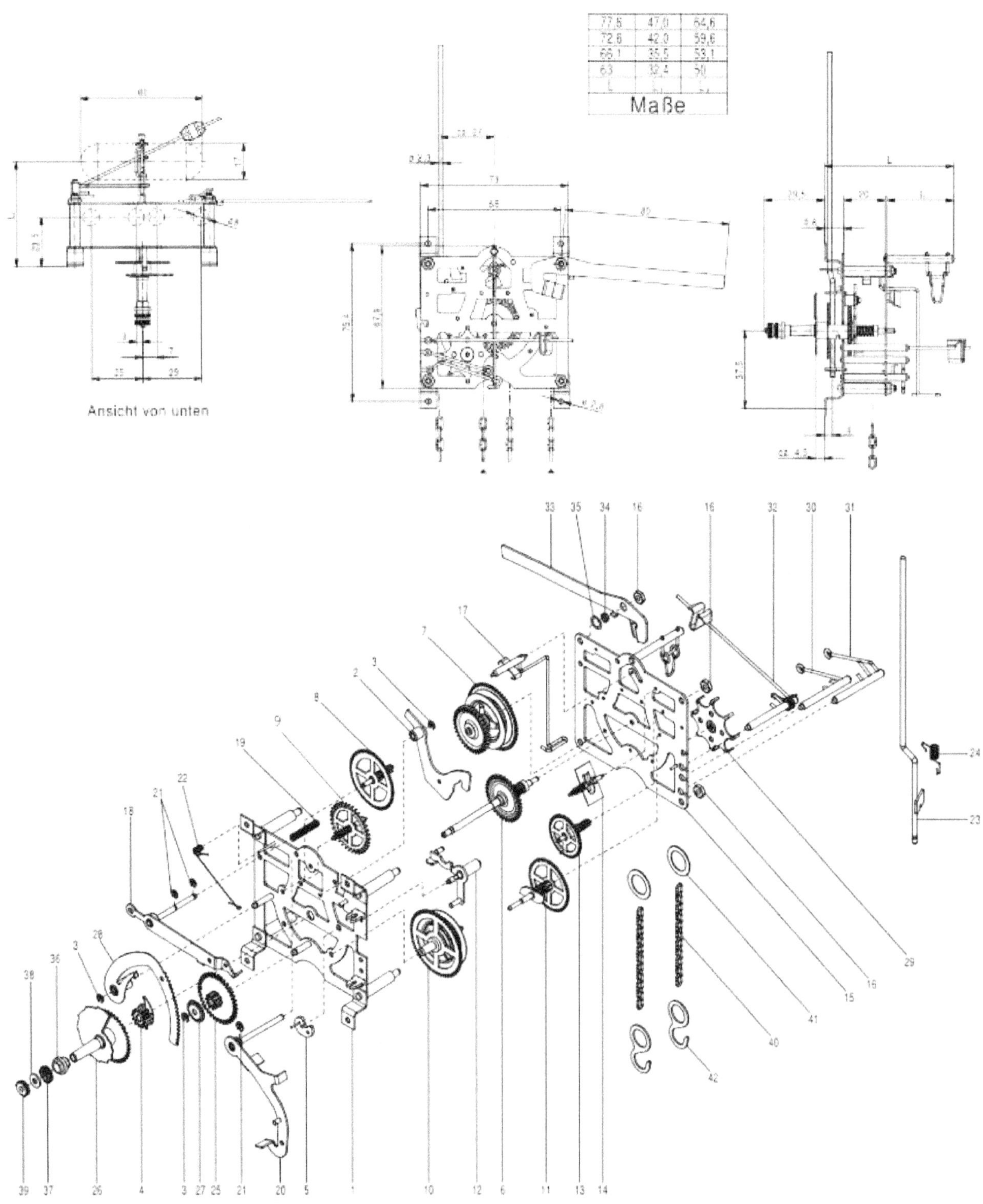

Item	Description
1	Front [top] Plate
2	Locking Lever
3	Safety Washer
4	Cam Gear
5	Gathering Pallet
6	Minute Wheel Shaft
7	Great Wheel Gear
8	Center Wheel
9	Third Wheel
10	Great Wheel
11	Gathering Pallet [2nd] Wheel
12	Release Lever
13	Third Wheel
14	Fly
15	Rear [bottom] Plate
16	Hex Nut
17	Anchor Escapement Assembly
18	Warning Lever
19	Pressure Spring
20	Fallen Lever
21	Safety Washer
22	Spring for Trap
23	Birdstock [perch bar]
24	Birdstock [perch bar] Spring
25	Changeover Motion Wheel
26	Snail
27	Washer
28	Rack
29	Bearing Disc
30	Bellows lift wire
31	Bellows lift wire
32	Gong Hammer
33	Shut-off Lever
34	Socket
35	Washer
36	Hand Socket
37	Hand Socket
38	Disc ø2.6
39	Hand Nut
40	Chain 70" Long
41	Chain Ring
42	Chain Hooks

Some terms you need to know to follow this text.

In the clock world, we call gears **Wheels**.

A set of connecting wheels is called a **Train**. One train for the time operation and one train for striking or cuckooing.

Time wheels are numbered **T1, T2, T3,** etc. starting with the **Great Wheel** that is driven by the chain.

Similarly, striking wheels are numbered **S1, S2, S3,** etc. starting with the Great Wheel.

The wheel is connected to an axial we call an **arbor**.

At the end of the arbor, it has **pivots** which are supported by the clock frame called **plates.**

The clock operates the animations using **wires** and **levers.**

The levers have flat arms called a **flag** or **detent** that control pins.

Some wheels include **cams** that control the levers.

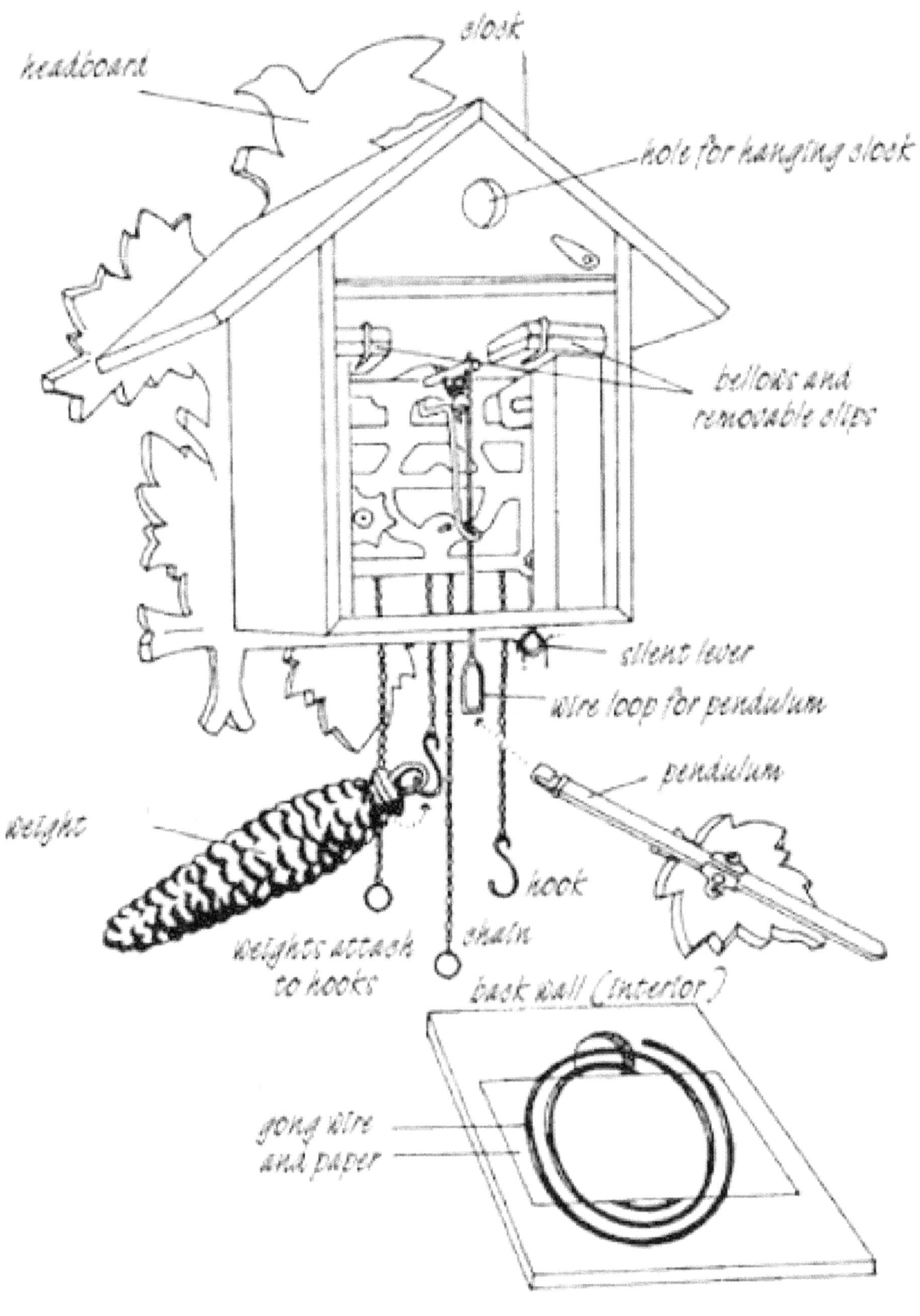

headboard
clock
hole for hanging clock
bellows and removable clips
silent lever
wire loop for pendulum
pendulum
weight
hook
weights attach to hooks
chain
back wall (interior)
gong wire and paper

You have a nice clock, and even though it might not work, at least it looks great, and even though it is not working, it has value. Once you start taking it apart, the widespread concern is you will not be able to get it back together again. In other words, you are worried about ruining a valuable and or sentimental item.

Believe it or not, this is a very healthy attitude. My worst students are the ones who are fearless in taking a clock apart without following the correct and logical procedure, as described in detail in this book.

Example-
A neighbor came to my house one Saturday evening in a panic. He asked me to help with a repair to his toilet. It was his only toilet in the house, and he had a wife and children at home.

The toilet was "running" and needed adjusting, and he decided to take the whole thing apart. But he did it after the hardware store closed, and he did not have the correct tools or parts on hand.

Luckily I had the tools, parts, and knowledge needed to get his toilet back working.

Lesson learned. Never embark on a project without

- understanding what you are getting into
- the tools to complete the work
- the parts or access to the parts that might be needed

Of course, a clock is not one of life's necessities, but it does illustrate the point.

We will go through a systematic checklist, starting with the easiest items first, and proceed on until we find the problem. There is no point jumping into a full servicing if the problem is something simple, which is often the case.

Step 1
Are the weights attached? The clock will not run without power. The weights provide the power to run the clocks. Are the weights the correct weights for the clock – the correct size? If you are unsure, check the later chapter called "Weights". Try adding something to the weight to see if the clock then runs. Anything heavy that you can hook onto the chain will work, as long as it does not catch on anything. If it runs with a little more weight, it is most likely there is some problem with the movement itself like needing oil or worn parts.

It is also important all the weights are installed. If it uses two weights, both need to be installed. If it uses three weights, all three need to be fitted.

Step 2

The next thing to check [forgive the obvious] is if it is wound up.

Contrary to popular belief, you cannot overwind a clock [or watch]. If it is fully wound and does not run, something else is wrong.

Your cuckoo clock most likely has weights. You might need to pull the chains to wind up the clock. Pull the loose chain that does not have the weight attached. Hold the clock against the wall as you pull the chain, so you don't pull it off the wall. I have had to repair many a clock that has fallen during winding.

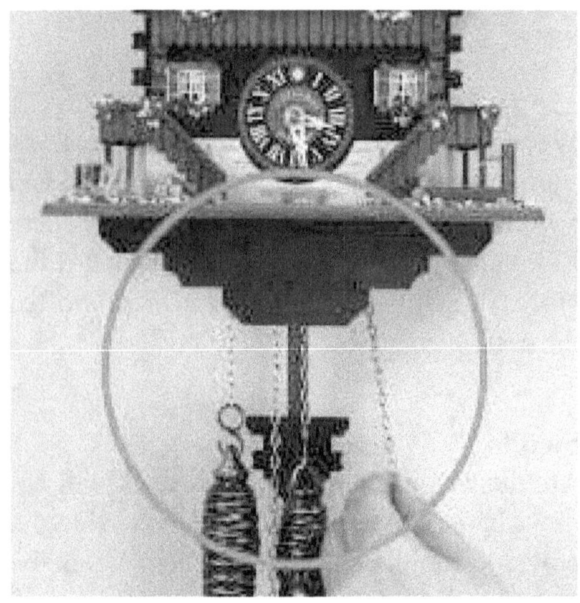

If the chain will not pull, it has likely come off its sprocket and needs reattaching, a tricky maneuver which I will explain later. Pull all the chains, usually two or three sets, so the weight is just below, but not touching the bottom of the clock case. Some people like the weights all in a row, others like the middle [time] weight just a little lower than the other two. However, you like it is okay.

Step 3

Now the clock is wound up. Give the pendulum a little push and listen to what the clock tells you. Listen to its ticking. It will most likely start ticking but might slow down and stop.

If it has an uneven tick-tock, you need to adjust its "beat." It is most likely a little out of level. It takes a lot more power for a clock to run when it's out of beat, extra power your clock

can't supply, especially if it has not been serviced recently.

If the tick and the tock are not even, your clock is out of beat. This is its 'heartbeat.' Move the bottom of the clock a little to the left, say ¼". If the tick-tock is worse, try moving the bottom ¼" to the other side. Experiment by moving it left and right until the tick-tock is even.

Your clock will need to be level from front to back and side to side. This is critical.

Step 4

Check if the chain has come off its sprocket. If the chain does not pull for winding, or its pull is not smooth, the chain has most likely come off its sprocket. Check the section later in this book called "Installing the Chain".

Step 5

Bird caught on the door. Check that the bird door opens and closes easily, and nothing is catching during its operations. Advance the minute hand to the hour and observe if the door opens, the bird pops out smoothly, retreats and the door closes without any interference.   Study how it operates and correct any problems.

If the clock will run without the pendulum but not with the pendulum, the clock either needs oiling, totally cleaning and/or repair. These items will be covered later.

If the clock will not run without the pendulum, there is a more serious problem and the clock will need to be dismantled and fully serviced, as described later.

Step 7

Try running the clock without the hands installed, by unscrewing the nut. See later chapter for more information on removing the hands.

Step 6

Run the clock without the pendulum attached. Just unhook it from its perch [wire loop]. It will most likely start ticking [very quickly] but if not give the perch a nudge.

If the clock will run with the hands removed, you know the problem is with the hands. The hands might be catching on each other, rubbing on the dial or they might be fitted too tight. Study what is happening and make the corrections.

Step 8

If the clock still stops after checking all these items, there is one more basic task to try. Advance the minute hand to about five past the hour, pausing to allow any striking to complete, then remove both hands. Take off the pendulum. The strike might be causing an issue. If it runs, put them back, one at a time, until the problem returns, and you have likely found the problem.   Study this area, track down the problem, correct it, and retest.

If it Still Stops

If you still have no luck, we will need to go to the next level. Most likely, the clock will need oiling. The fact that the clock stopped is a good thing. It is trying to tell you something. If it continued to run with no oil, it would cause a lot of wear and damage the clock seriously. Consider the clock stopping as

"The oil light is on."

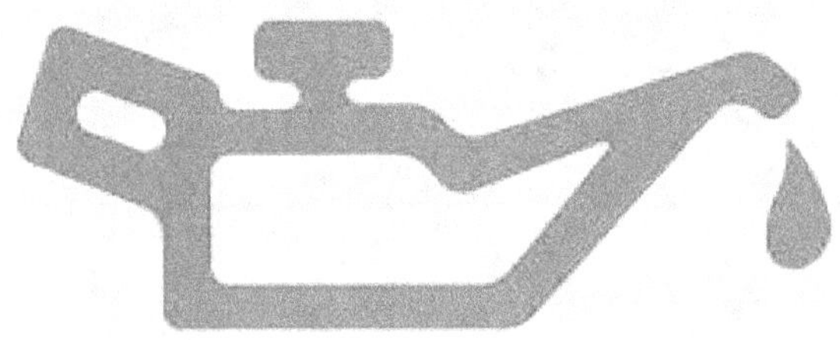

Installing the Chain

Check if the chain has come off its sprocket. The winding chain is like a bicycle chain. If it comes off its sprocket, the bicycle will not work.

Unfortunately, putting the chain back on a cuckoo clock is a little trickier than a bicycle, but I will walk you through the procedure.

First, identify which way the sprocket turns on its ratchet by rotating the sprocket where indicated by the arrow in Diagram 1.

With the clock upside-down, thread the chain through the hole in the bottom of the clock and let it rest on the side of the sprocket. Diagram 1

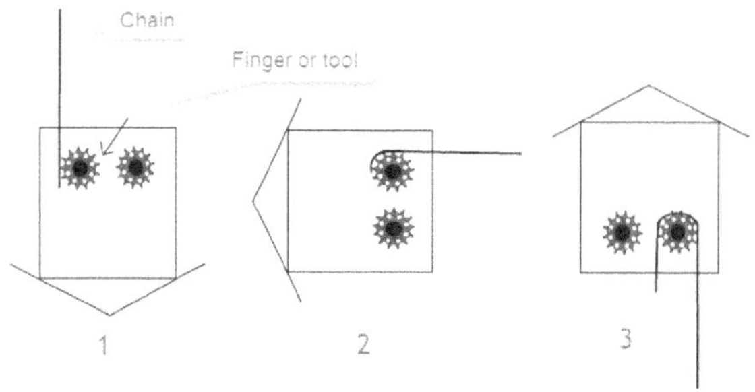

Use your finger or a screwdriver and advance the sprocket as indicated by the arrow. Diagram 1

Rotate the clock one quarter turn clockwise and advance the sprocket to pull the chain onto the sprocket, using gravity to keep it on the teeth of the sprocket. Diagram 2

When it is past half-way, rotate the clock one quarter turn again so the clock is the correct way up, and continue to advance the sprocket to pull the chain all the way around and comes out of the second hole in the base of the clock case. Diagram 3.

Do the same for the second chain if needed.

Oiling the Clock

We can try to oil the clock first without removing the clockworks from its case. You will only be able to oil the rear of the works but you will have a 50% chance this will correct the problem.

The most important thing to remember is to ensure that you only use clock oil. Using substitutes like WD40 can damage your movement.

Just like regular oil-changes extend the life of your car's engine, regular clock oiling extends the life of your clock. Oiling your clock every five years will prevent expensive clock repairs and ensure that your clock will last for generations to come. Imagine never changing your car's oil; it wouldn't take long for the engine to seize. Without regular oiling, your clock will end up requiring a major service or possibly a new movement.

We can start by oiling the movement while it is still in its case. You will only be able to lubricate the rear side of the clock, but that is better than nothing, and it is easy to do. Remove the back door.

You will notice multiple oil sinks on the surface of the clock plate. Oil sinks are located where the ends of the steel arbor meet the brass clock plate. Please refer to the picture and diagram showing an oil sink.

To oil a clock, apply ONE drop of oil to each oil sink. Use a magnifying glass to see better. Don't try and fill the oil sink, because the oil is held in place by capillary attraction and surface tension.

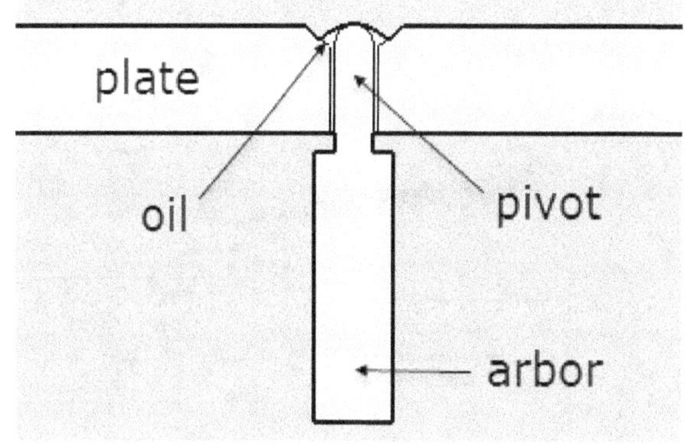

If you apply too much oil, the surface tension will not hold, and the oil will run down the plate, leaving the bearing dry. Repeat the oiling process for all visible oil sinks.

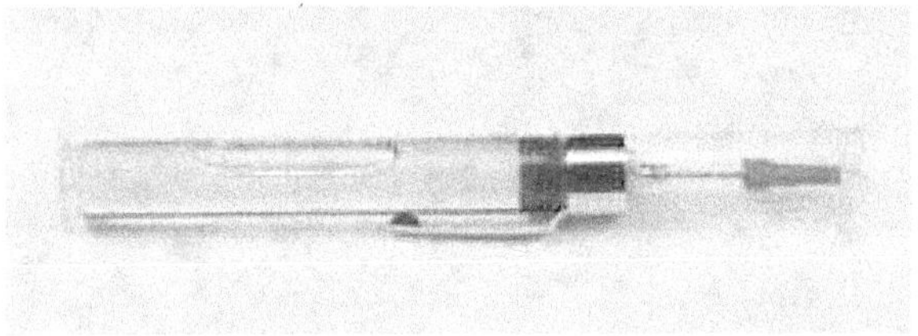

Do not oil the wheel/pinion teeth during this process; they need to stay dry to maintain an efficient working condition.

The eye of a very small sewing needle will usually carry the right amount of oil. Just wet the pivot.

It is not normal to oil the teeth of the wheels, but the escape wheel is the exception, as the teeth slide on the impulse face of the escapement.

Place one drop of oil on one of the escape wheel teeth and advance the escape wheel about 5 teeth, [by moving the pendulum left and right], then add another drop. Continue this until the escape wheel has made one full revolution. This will ensure each tooth and the escapement impulse face has a small film of oil on it.

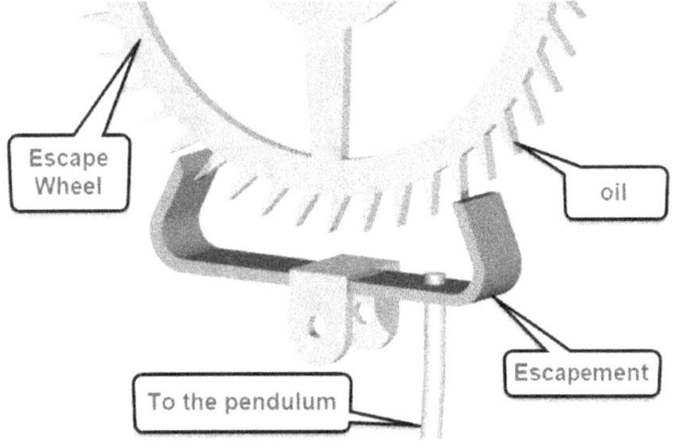

The escape wheel is sometimes located outside the plates and is easy to access.

However, in some movements, the escape wheel is between the plates and is harder to access.

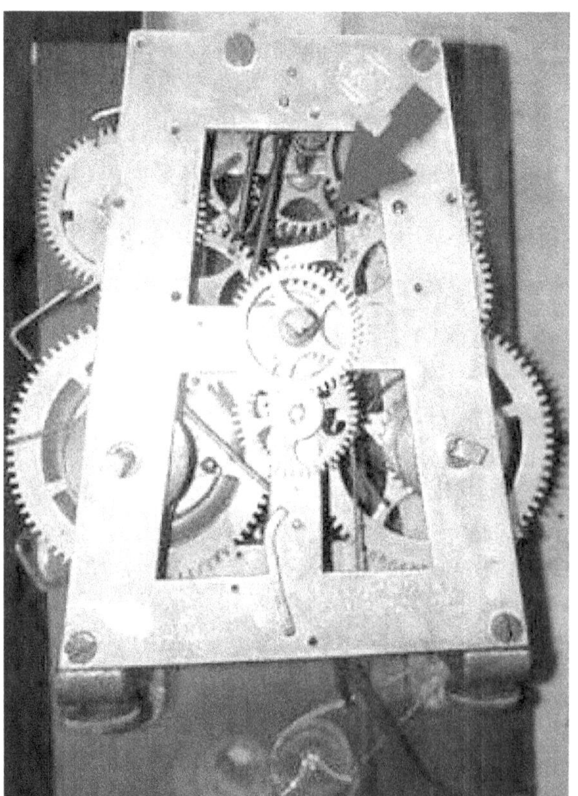

Movement with the escape wheel inside the plates

Regula is by far the most used cuckoo clock movement, for clocks made after 1950, so this will be used for this first explanation.

Remove the weights noting which goes in which position [left and right]. Remove the pendulum. Put some tape around the leaf so its position will not change on the pendulum stick [making regulating its time easier on reassembly]. Remove the clock from the wall.

To remove the movement from its case, first, remove the hands.

Unscrew the hand nut counterclockwise while holding the minute hand. You might need to use pliers on the nut while holding the hand with your other hand. Carefully note any washers that are fitted, their location, and even which way up they sit.

Next, remove the hour hand. It is friction fitted and will just pull off.

If the hands are broken, replacement hands are available from the supply houses. Some filing and fitting is usually necessary to make new hands fit the clock arbor.

Now open the cuckoo door and disconnect the bird wire that is connected to the inside of the door [open its loop]. If the loop of the wire is longer than 3/8", reduce its length now to 3/8" for easier assembly later.

At this point, turn the clock over and remove the chains. You need to remove the weight hooks by twisting the last link with needle-nose pliers, and then the chains can be pulled out of the movement.

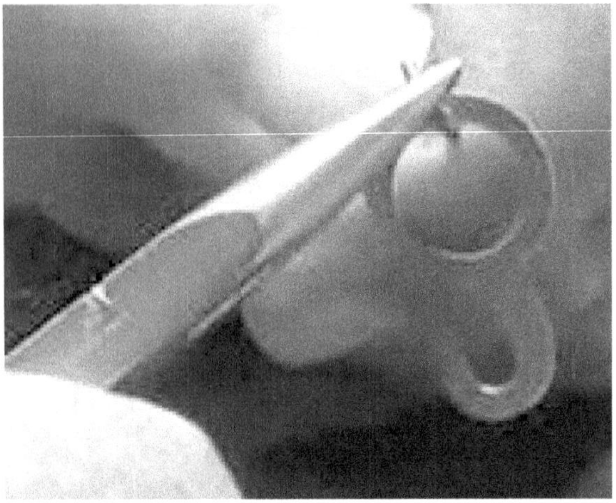

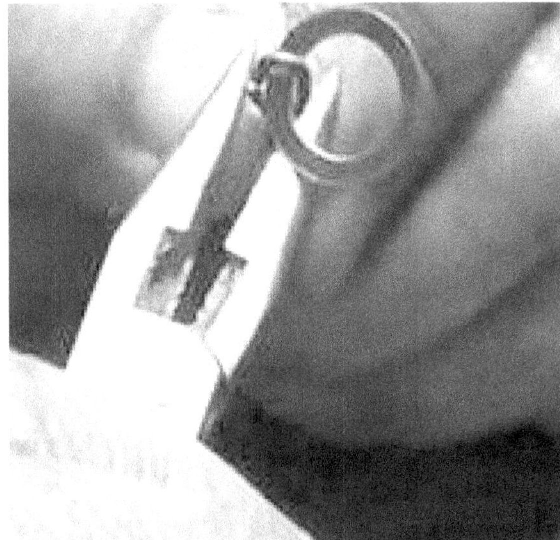

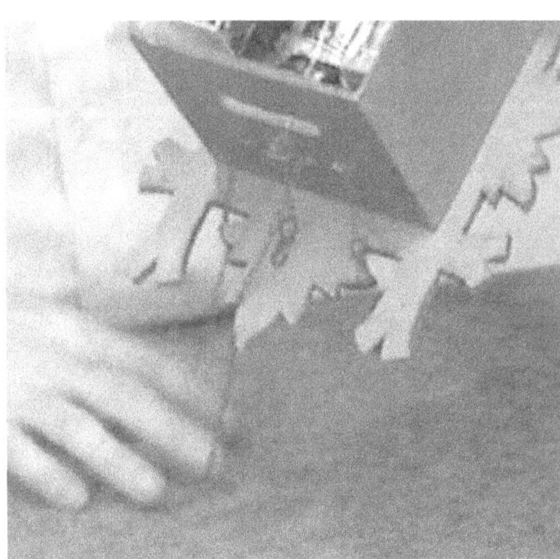

Now the bellows and windpipe need to be removed to gain access to the movement. They are held in place with a screw and brad from the side. It is a good idea to mark the location with a pencil on the side of the case before you remove them to make reassembly easier.

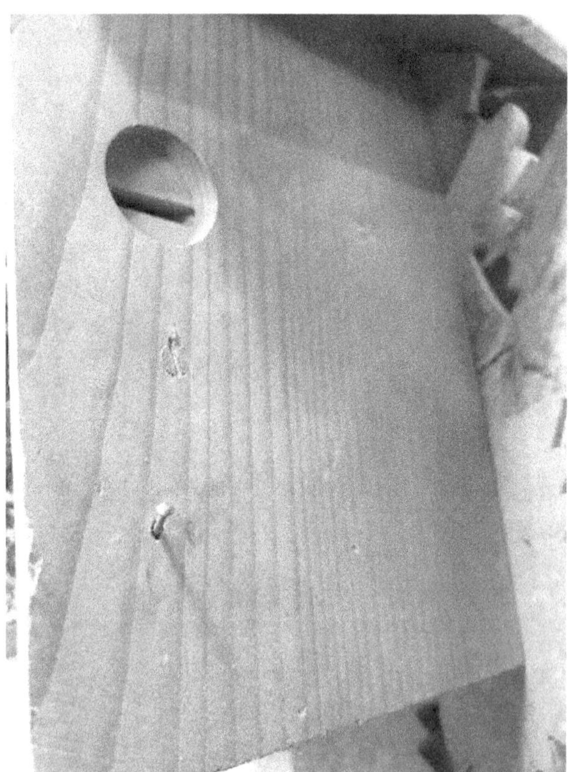

If you find a spot of glue holds the windpipes, they can easily be pried off with a putty knife.

As you remove the bellows from the case, disconnect the bellows lift wire at the bottom of the movement. Some rotating of the bellows might be necessary. Do not bend the wire to disconnect it unless it is a closed-loop and must be opened. Resist bending wires at all costs. The two wires are not the same length, so make a note of which one is which. Make a diagram of exactly how it is connected before disconnecting it. Remove the bellows and lift wire all in one—Mark on the hidden side of the bellows, which is the left and right for easier reassembly.

Now the movement can be removed from the case by removing the four screws in the corners.

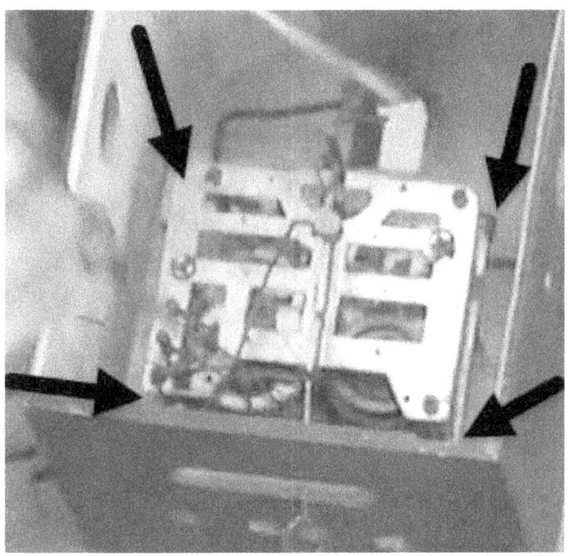

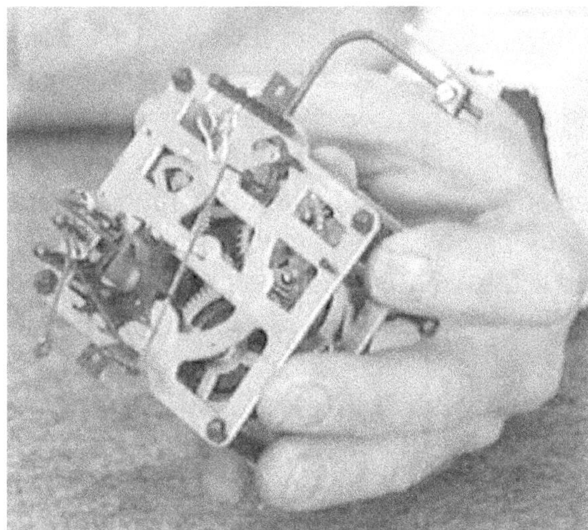

Next, remove the pendulum hanger by opening the top loop a little and snake it out. Use a container to keep all the small parts safe as they are removed.

Look at the movement for any apparent defects. Look for three springs and check they are present, how they are fitted and in good working order.

1. Return spring on the perch bar.
2. Return spring on the gong hammer.
3. Return spring on the rack stop lever.

Repair/replace any broken springs. That might be all that is needed to correct the problem. If it is, oil up the movement, test on a test stand for one full cycle [30-hours or 8-days], and if all is OK, return it to the case, and you are done. If not, proceed.

At this point, we can now start disassembling the movement. First, mark on the perch the location of the bird, then remove the bird by loosening its screw.

Next, remove all the striking levers and motion idle wheel from the front. Start with the rack by removing the split washer.

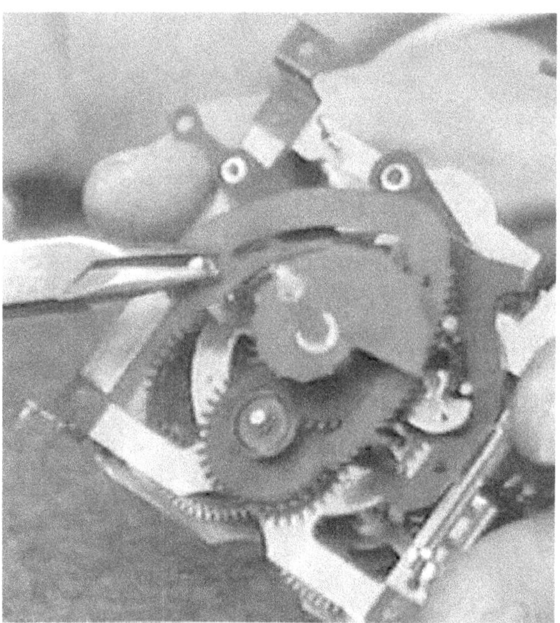

Remove the idle wheel split washer and larger washer.

You might need to advance the snail around to gain access to this clip. Insert the minute hand and slowly advance until the small part of the snail is over the clip, giving better access.

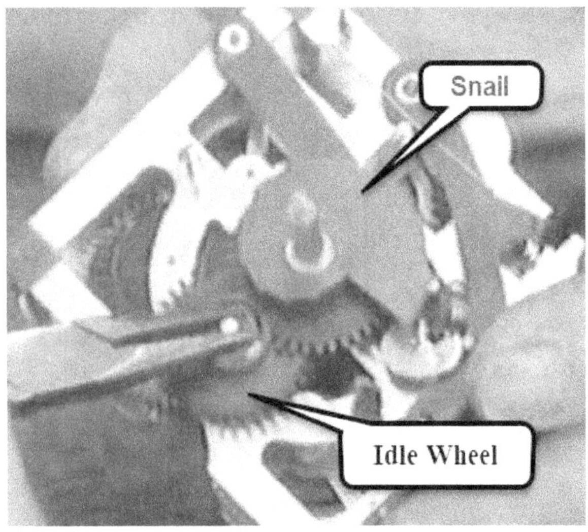

Remove the snail and idle wheel. The larger washer stops both the snail and idle wheel from coming off.

Scribe a small line on the snail and the tooth it mates with for faster, more accurate assembly later.

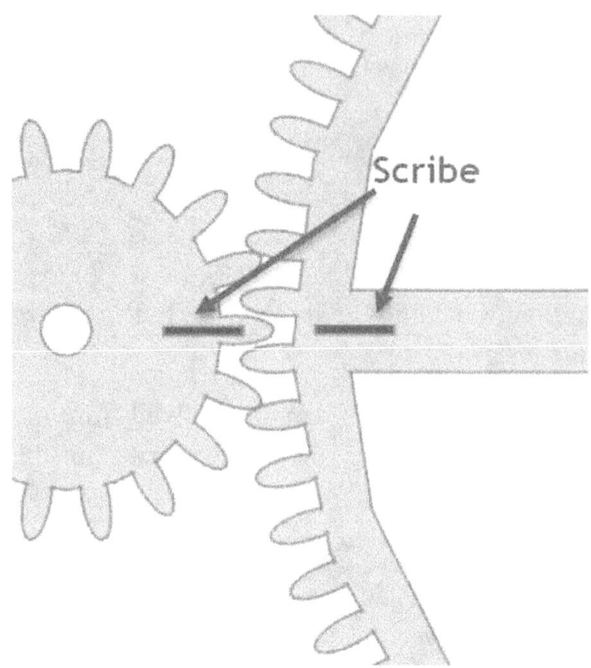

Remove the snail and mark the same way, the minute pinion and mating idle wheel tooth. The arrows show where the scribe marks are made.

Now remove the idle wheel.

Next, remove the Warning Lever and Fallen Lever by removing their E-Clips [safety washer] located either on the inside of the front plate or on the outside of the backplate. They can be very tricky to remove. Use a sturdy pair of pliers on the open end and post. If this does not work, slide a pocketknife under the open end and twist up a little to make room to get a sturdy pair of needle nose pliers on one open end and twist off. Do not even try to reuse the E-Clip. On reassembly, I use new 7/64" split washers.

Another option is to try a hand puller if you have access to one.

The clip might be located on the inside of the front plate instead.

Leave the spring on the plate that holds the upper strike lever. Hook it back over the top of the plate for now.

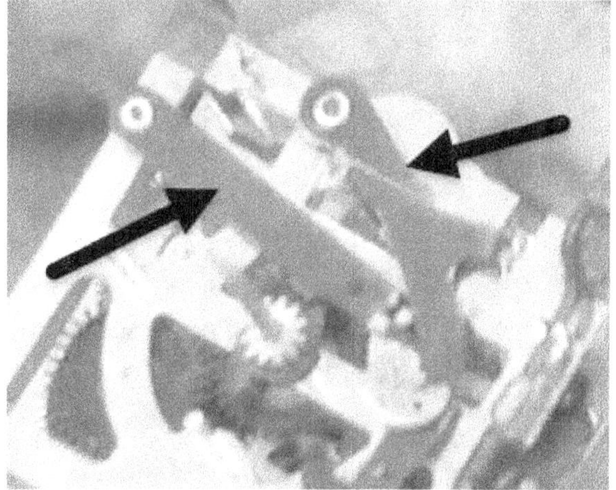

Lastly, remove the gathering pallet. It is friction fit on S2 arbor and will come off using a gear puller or pry bars, pulling it straight up from the movement.

Homemade prybars made from old screwdrivers or paint can openers.

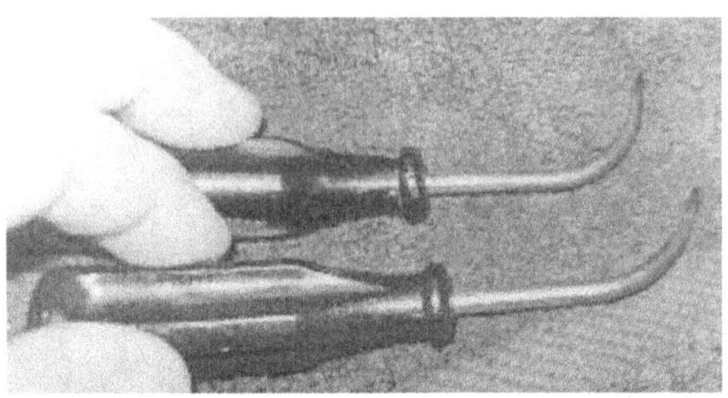

Now turn the movement over to the back and remove the Bearing Disk [also know as the Actuating Wheel] by loosening it's set screw, and it will just slide off.

On newer movements, the Bearing Disk is a machine press-fit in place and, in some cases, impossible to remove. Without removing this disk, reassembly and correct setup is almost impossible. To best overcome this, with the strike in the lock position, scribe a small mark

on the backplate at several points on this disk the location of the points. On reassembly, you will install the disc points back on these marks.

Now disconnect the gong hammer. Disconnect its spring from the hole in the plate and rotate the hammer one-half turn counterclockwise and it will pull out. Leave the spring on the hammer.

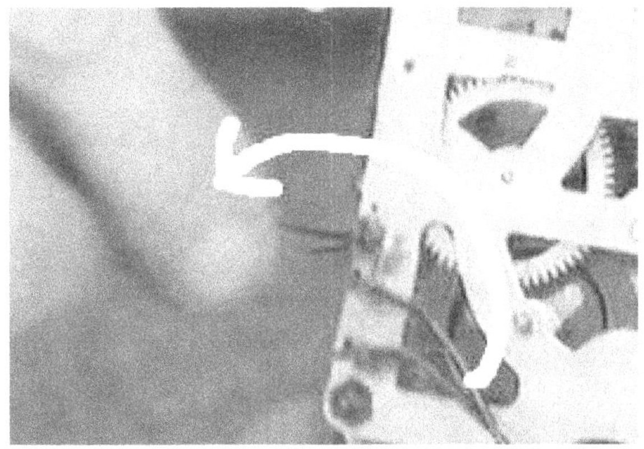

Now remove the bellows lift wires the same way. Make a note about which position the long and short wires go. There is no spring on these.

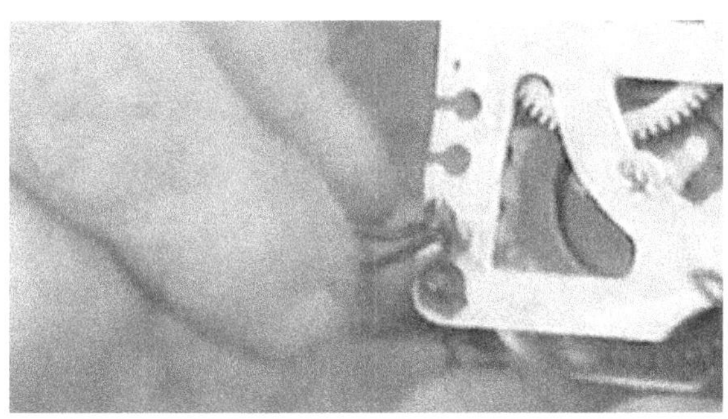

At this point, we are almost ready to take the movement apart.

Make detailed diagrams, notes, and photos of all the wheels and levers to help reassembly.

Support the front of the movement with movement assembly legs or set it on a box with a hole cut into it or use a toilet roll.

This is the critical point to identify wheel relationships. With the movement in its locked position [at the end of striking] we need to make some timing marks. Scribe a small mark on the second wheel where it meets the third wheel pinion.

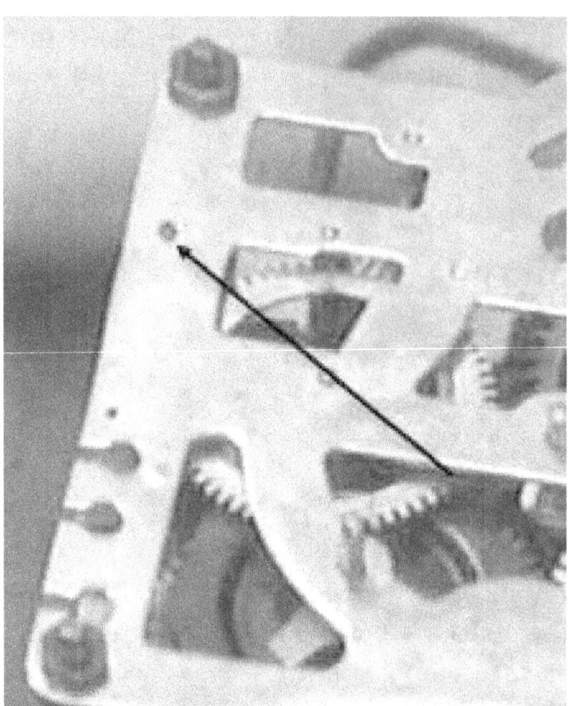

Also note the position of the strike second wheel cam, located between the plates. It should point to the Fallen Lever post.

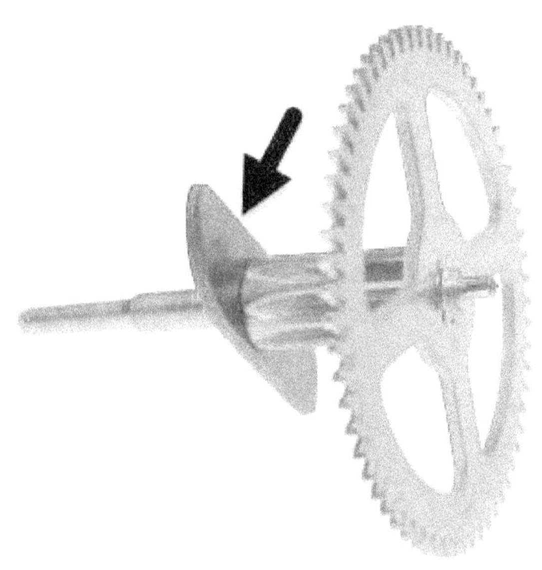

At the same time, the striking third wheel pin must be at the top of the movement – 12 o'clock position.

DO NOT SKIP THIS STEP. Scribe a small make on the top place where this pin is located.

Only after noting the above, you can remove the four corner hex nuts and very carefully lift off the top plate so as not to disturb any of the wheels at this point.

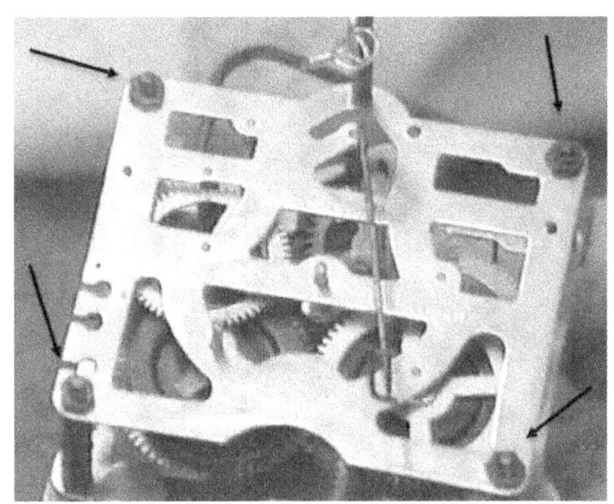

Make more diagrams, notes, and take good photos at this point. Take special note of the location of the release lever [i.e., passes between S2 and S3 arbors].

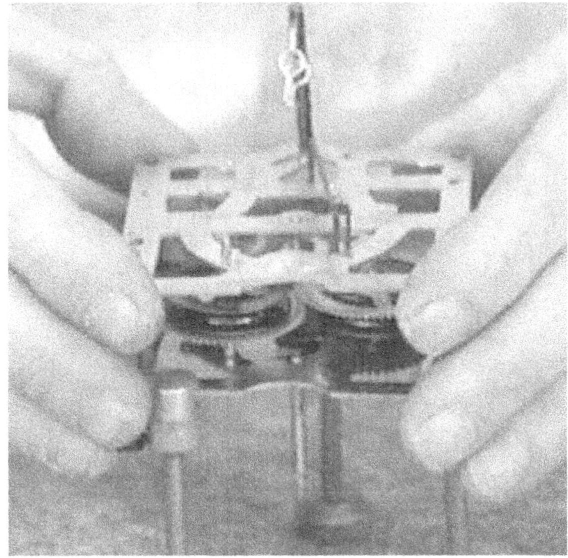

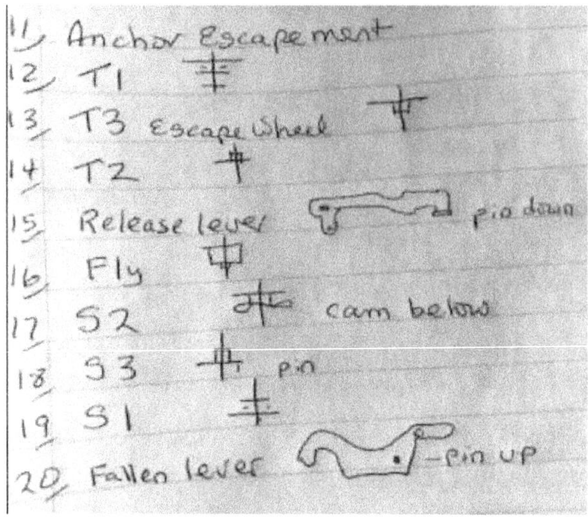

At this point, the internal parts can be removed. I strongly suggest they be removed one at a time, in the order of ease of removal, AND keep a log of what order they are removed for fast, efficient, and accurate reassembly.

The following is my log as an example [your clock might be a little different]. I make a stick diagram of each wheel. The vertical line is the arbor, the horizontal line is the position of the wheel [high or low], and the box is the position of the pinion [high or low]. Also, note any pins and cams.

Do not try to remove the center arbor as the cam gear outside the front plate is very hard to remove and even harder to reinstall.

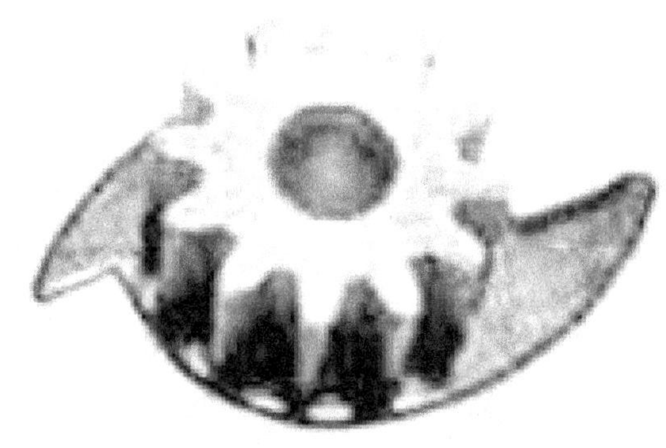

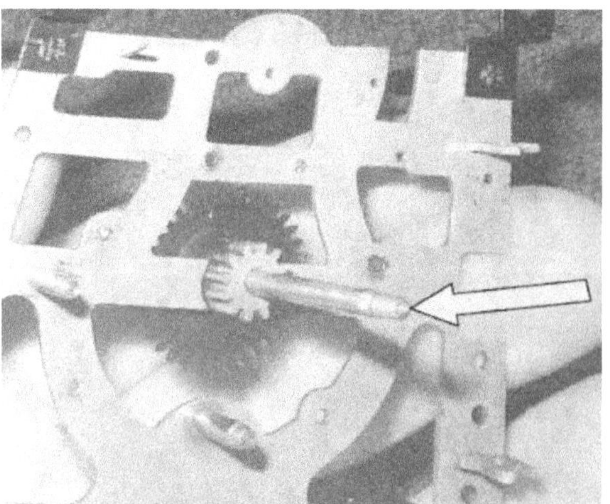

I usually push the wheels, in train order, into a piece of Styrofoam, so I can keep track of what goes where.

Check the pendulum hanger for wear and replace if needed.

These levers control the bird arm, rotating it to open the top door and popping out the bird at the correct sequence and closing it again.

Remember to install S2 with the cam pointing to the Fallen Lever, and S3 pin at the top 12 o'clock.

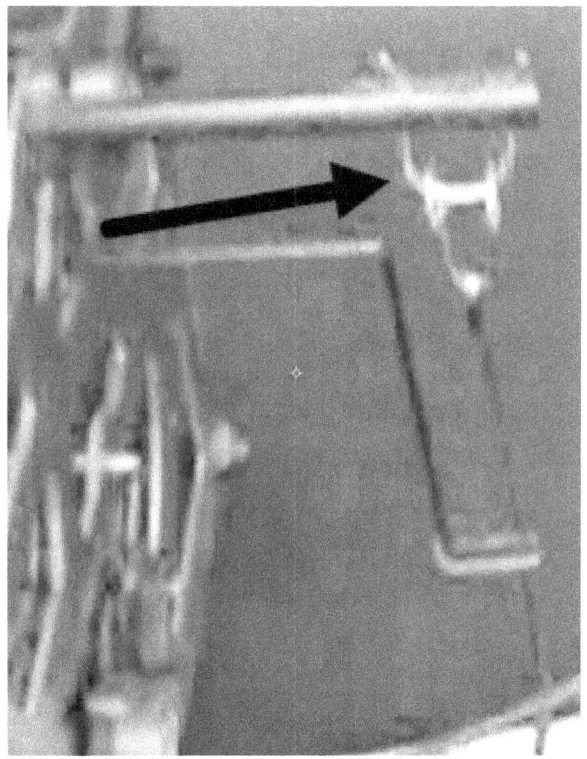

After cleaning and making any repairs [see section two of this book], the movement can be reassembled in the reverse order. Because of your preparation in the disassembly, this will be the fun part. Start with the inside levers.

It does not matter the orientation of any of the other wheels between the plates.

Fit the top plate, orientating the parts correctly. Test its operation by applying pressure to the Striking Great Wheel with your finger and observe the strike runs successfully and stops precisely. If not, open the plates a little and make the necessary adjustments and retest until it is correct.

For detailed instructions for cleaning and making repairs to the movement while it is open, please see section two of this book.

When the movement is back together and before you reinstall the front Rack, Snail, Levers and Bearing Disk, oil up the movement [see section two]. It is harder to oil the pivots after the striking equipment is installed. Do not put any lubricant on any of the levers.

Install the rack and snail, so the rack tail acts at the two o'clock position. Make sure the rack tail flag acts in the center of the 2 o'clock flat.

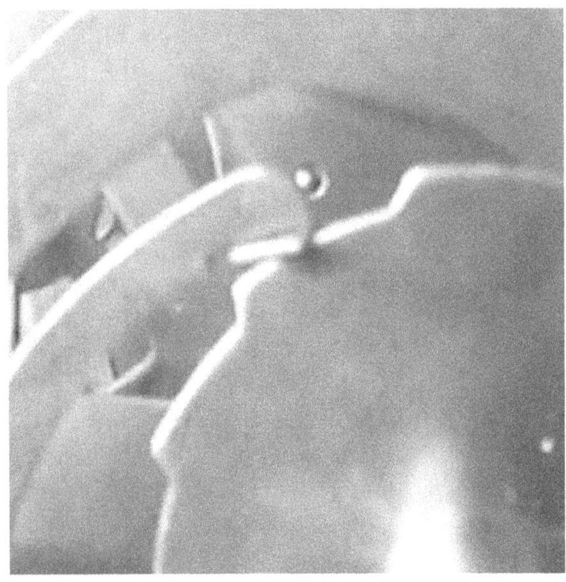

Now you can install idle wheel and install the washer and clip without the snail being in the way.

Install the gong hammer and its spring, and the bellows lift arms.

The last item to install is the Bearing Disk. Set it in place and rotate [in its run direction], watching the sequence:

- gong hammer
- high note [cuck]
- low note [koo]

As soon as the low note lever drops off the point of the bearing disk, tighten the screw.

This is the end of the cuckoo sequence. Stopping it immediately after the drop, will allow some run of the bearing disc so it gains momentum for the next sequence.

Remove the high and low note bellows lift arms again for now.

Double-check its operation one more time. It is best to do the testing and adjusting with the time set to about two o'clock, so you do not have to go through a long striking sequence each time.

Install the chains on the Great Wheel Sprockets and place it on a test stand with the weights and pendulum fitted. As the movement runs, advance the minute hand and carefully observe the striking function. It is essential testing be done BEFORE you put it back in the case.

If everything checks out, run the movement for one full cycle [30 hours or eight days depending on the movement] before putting the movement back in its case. Re-install the chain hook and rings with the opened links, and carefully close the links up again.

You will know everything is working if all weights come down at the same rate over a few hours. If the time weight is lower than the striking weight, you know there is a problem with the striking.

Before installing the movement back into the case, clean the case both inside and outside.

To put the movement back in its case, rest the minute arbor in the rear case hanging hole so you can feed the chains through the holes in the bottom of the case.

Use a screw-holding screwdriver to install the movement screws.

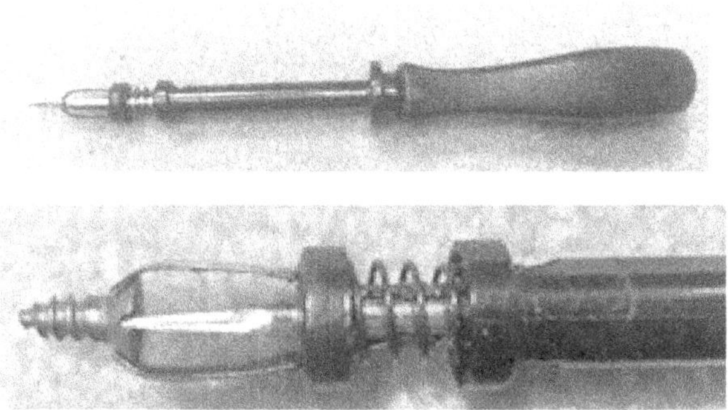

While putting everything back in its case is the reverse order, it is recommended you do one item at a time and make a short test run before moving on to the next item, in this order. If a problem occurs during one of the steps, it will be easy to see the problem and how to correct it.

1. Reinstall the bellows lift arms. TEST.
2. Install the Bearing Disk. TEST.
3. Install the movement in the case and put it in beat with the case level. TEST.
4. Install the bird on the bird arm. TEST.
5. Install the low note [left side] bellows and lift wire. TEST left bellows and bird tilt.
6. Install the high note [right side] bellows and lift wire. TEST.
7. Install the music box and wires. TEST.
8. Install the back door and adjust the gong. TEST.
9. Test run everything again for one full cycle [30 hours / 8 days].

Regula 25-35 Movement Specifications

<pre>
                            Platform
R25   2 wt   1 day
R25L   2 wt   1 day
R25XL   2 wt   1 day
R25/24   3 wt   1 day   19.1 24 mm from top
R25/24L 3 wt   1 day   23.5 24 mm
R25/41   3 wt   1 day   23.5 41 mm
R25/41S 3 wt   1 day   19.1 41 mm
R25/41BL 3 wt   1 day   23.5 41 mm
R25/51   3 wt   1 day   23.5 51 mm
R34   2 wt   8 day   19.1
R34 LP   2 wt   8 day   19.1 long post 45mm
R34ASO 2 wt   8 day 23.5 long post, 1 weight inside
R34LASO 2 wt   8 day   28.5 as above
R34XLASO 2 wt 8 day   40.0 as above
R34/44   3 wt   8 day   28.5 47 mm
R34/46   3 wt   8 day   23.5 47 mm
R34/59   2 wt   8 day   40.0
R34/63   2 wt   8 day   23.5
R34/66   2 wt   8 day   28.5
R35   2 wt   1 day   28.5
R35S   2 wt   1 day   20.5 Replaces Hubert Herr
</pre>

If all else fails in your quest to repair an old cuckoo clock movement, you can always buy a new replacement movement. Externally no one will see any difference and it will give decades of new life to your favorite clock with minimal work.

Case Decorations

The most visible parts of a cuckoo clock are the case [house] and its carvings. Often the carvings become damaged or lost. Fortunately, replacement carvings are readily available for the supply houses.

The following are some examples of items for sale at Time Savers. These items come in many sizes and styles.

Cuckoo Bird

Description: Grey and white plastic cuckoo bird has stationary wings. Comes with metal mounting hardware. 3" long.

Item # 10457

Condition: New

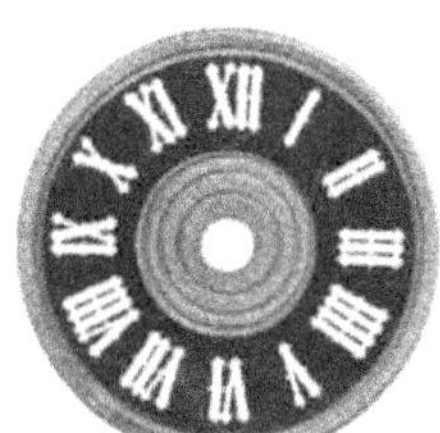

Cuckoo Clock Dial 4" Diameter

Description: Made in Germany. 4" (100mm) edge to edge diameter wood cuckoo dial. Dark brown with white roman numerals. Numerals are painted on, not raised.

Item # 10508

Condition: New

12mm Cuckoo Dial Wood Numerals

Description: Made in Germany. Complete set of 12mm tall wood numerals for cuckoo clocks.

Item # 19307

Condition: New

12" Brown Cuckoo Hunting Top

Description: Hand carved wood hunting style cuckoo top with deer head, antlers, rifles and leaves. Measures 12" from end to end. Made in Germany. Stained walnut brown.

Item # 16929

Condition: New

20 X 25mm Brown Cuckoo Door

Description: Cuckoo clock wood door is 3/4" wide x 1" tall and is stained walnut brown.

Item # 17759

Condition: New

Square Hole Cuckoo Hands For 70mm Dial

Description: White plastic cuckoo hands with 3mm square mounting holes to fit 70mm diameter cuckoo dials. No bushings. Made in Germany.

Item # 19562

Condition: New

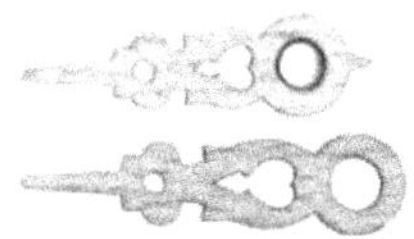

Wood Cuckoo Hands To Fit 110mm/120mm Dials

Description: Wood cuckoo hands with round mounting holes to fit 100-110mm diameter cuckoo dials. With a 4.6mm brass bushing in the hour hand. 5mm round mounting hole in the minute hand. Made in Germany.

Item # 19315

Condition: New

Cuckoo Clock Top 8-1/4" Brown

Description: Hand carved wood cuckoo top with birds and leaves. Measures 8-1/4" from end to end. Made in Germany. Stained walnut brown.

Item # 10404

Condition: New

14-1/2" Brown Cuckoo Hunting Top

Description: Hand carved wood hunting style cuckoo top with deer head, antlers, rifles and leaves. Measures 14-1/2" from end to end. Made in Germany. Stained walnut brown.

Item # 16928

Condition: New

1.20mm x 48 LPF x 70" Brass Plated Steel Clock Chain 8-Day Cuckoo

Description: Brass plated steel clock chain is 70" in length, has 48 links per foot and is made of 1.20mm wire. Used on Regula #34 8-day cuckoo clocks.

Item # 19614

Condition: New

350 Gram Cuckoo Weight

Description: Sold individually. 350 Grams cast iron. 454 grams = 1 pound.

Item # 36011

Condition: New

Brown Maple Leaf Cuckoo Pendulum 2" x 7"

Description: 2" wide x 2-1/4" tall maple leaf with a 7" wood rod. Brown finish.

Item # 10243

Condition: New

Horizontal & Vertical Bellows

Description: Made in Germany for cuckoo clocks. One horizontal and one vertical bellows are sold in pairs. One horizontal bellows is 2-3/4" long and side opening. One vertical bellows is 4-3/8" long and back opening.

Item # 18411

Condition: New

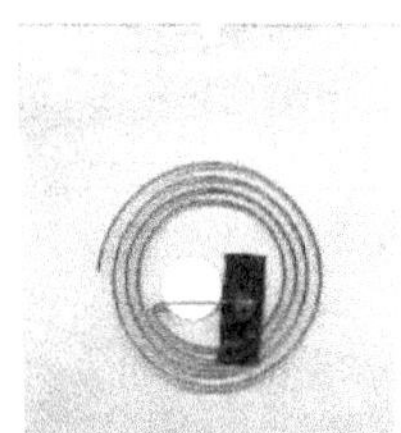

Cuckoo Back Cover 4-3/4" X 5-1/8"

Description: Made in Germany. Walnut stained wood back cover is complete with the appropriate size gong and base. 4-3/4" wide x 5-1/8" tall.

Item # 20506

Condition: New

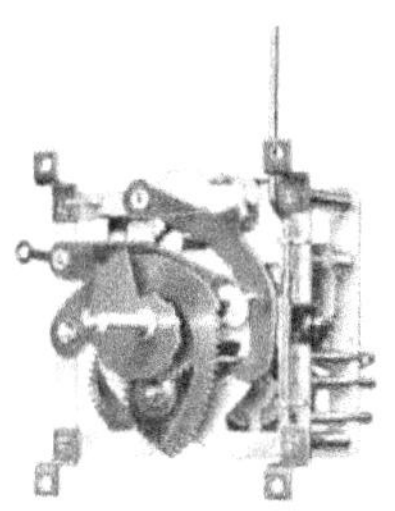

1-Day Regula 25 Cuckoo Movement 9-1/4" Drop

Description: Made in Germany. Regula 25, 1-day movement includes chains, hooks rings, hand nut and hand bushing. Weights, pendulum and bellows are not included and must be purchased separately. 1-1/8" Hand. More Details »

Item # 23508

Condition: New

1-Day Regula 25 Cuckoo Movement With 2-1/4" Dance Platform 7-3/4" Drop

Description: Made in Germany. Regula 25, 1-day time, strike and music 3 train movement includes dancing platform, chains, hooks, rings, hand nut and hand bushing. Weights, dancing figures, pendulum and... More Details »

Item # 16409

Condition: New

Count Wheel Striking

It is essential to have a good understanding of the correct striking setup when you put a time and strike movement back together.

After all the wheels are set between the plates, some adjustments are usually necessary for the striking to work correctly and in sync.

The count wheel system uses a large extra wheel on or driven by the winding arbor on the strike train. The count wheel has a series of regular teeth and some extra deep slot teeth. The deep slot allows the count lever to drop deeper at the end of the striking sequence. At one o'clock, there are two deep slots next to each other, so the clock strikes once and stops. At two o'clock, there is a shallow slot and then a deep slot. This allows the clock to strike twice before stopping. Etc. The speed of the train and thus the striking is controlled by a fly which acts as an airbrake to slow the strike train and ensure a measured beat. There are

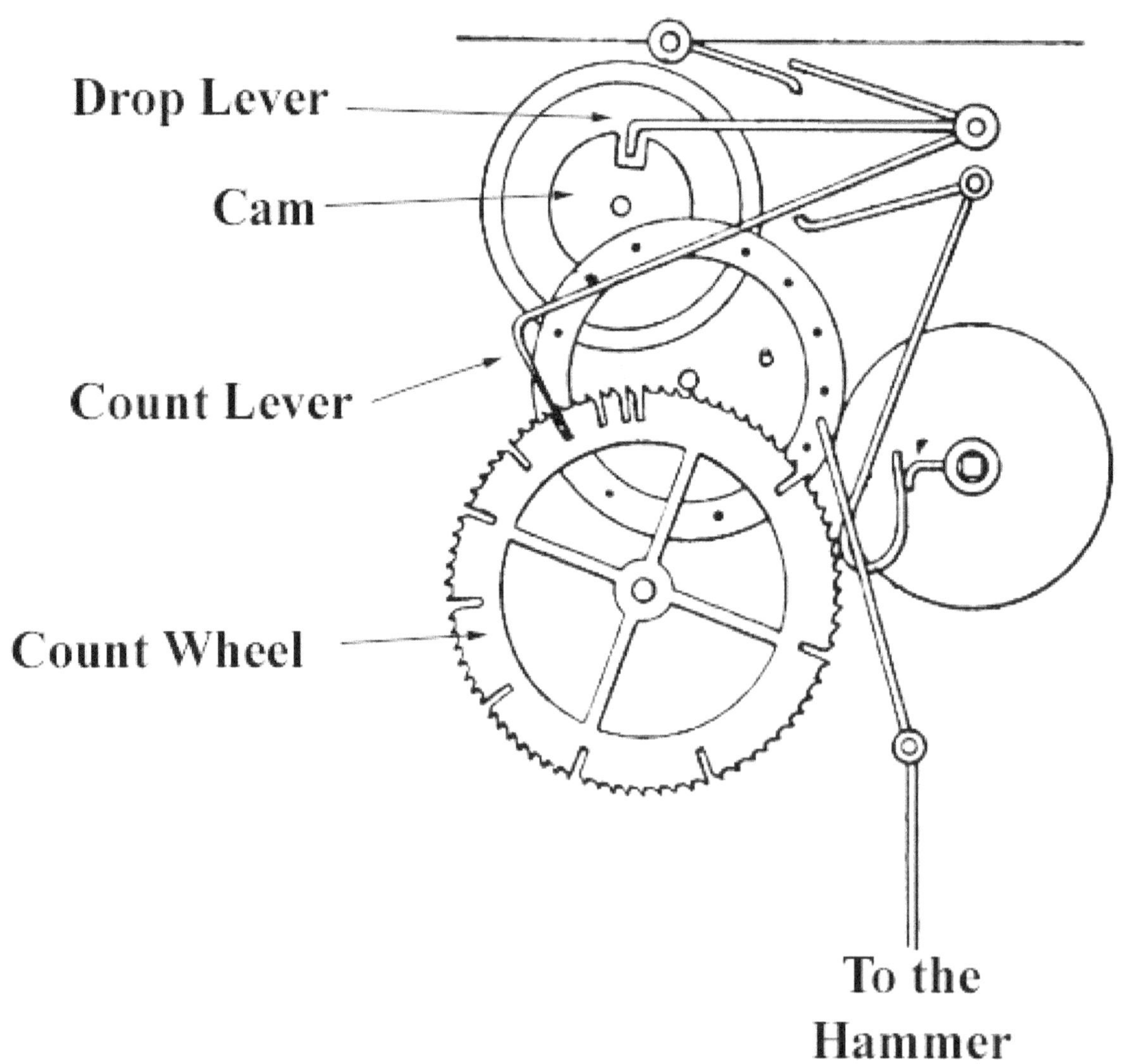

usually two combination levers. One raises the other, and both combine to set up the warning run, hold it until the proper time, release it, and then count the strikes.

First, make sure the **Count Lever** points directly to the center of the count wheel. Adjust it if necessary.

These three items must all be correct at the same time:

- The Count Lever must be in a deep slot.
- The Drop Lever must sit in the slot of the Cam.
- The Locking Lever must be engaged with the Lock Pin.

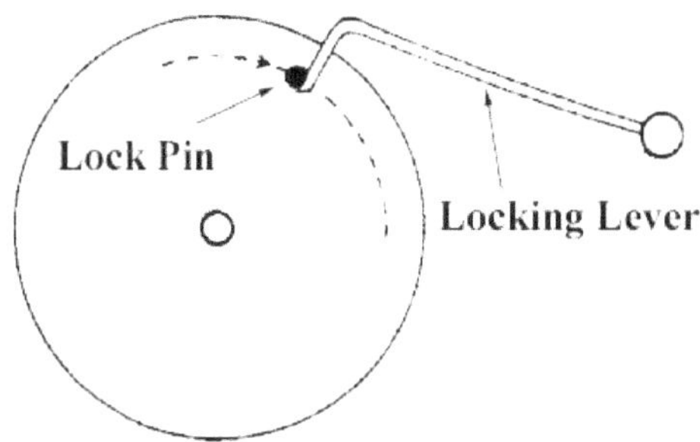

If the Locking Lever is not sitting next to the Lock Pin, you may need to open the movement

and adjust the meshing of the teeth, so it does sit next to the Lock Pin, while the Count Lever is still in a deep slot **and** the Drop Lever is still in the Cam slot.

You only want to advance the wheel that is in the incorrect position [usually the locking pin wheel], leaving the rest in the same location. This is easier said than done. To help, press a small amount of Rodico into the wheels you want to stay the same, allowing you to focus on the incorrect wheel. Capture the mainspring before making any adjustments.

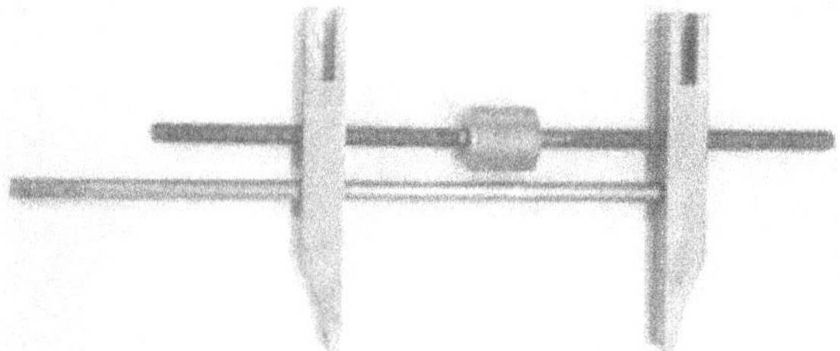

A plate spreader is a very useful tool. It allows you to spread the plates just enough to make minor gear meshing adjustments without dismantling the whole movement or disturbing the other wheels in the train.

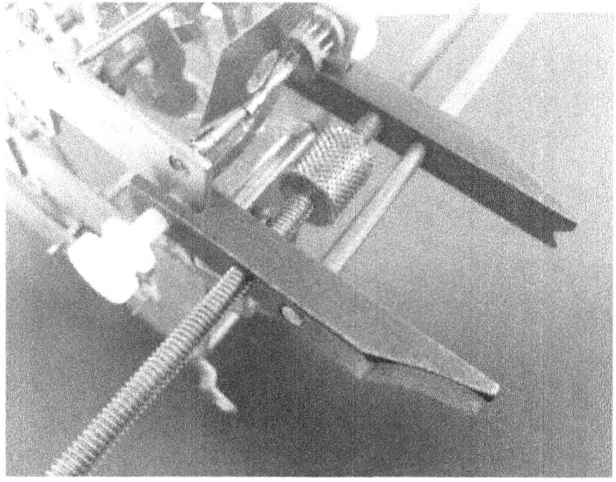

Test it over at least a 24-hour period to make sure everything is working correctly.

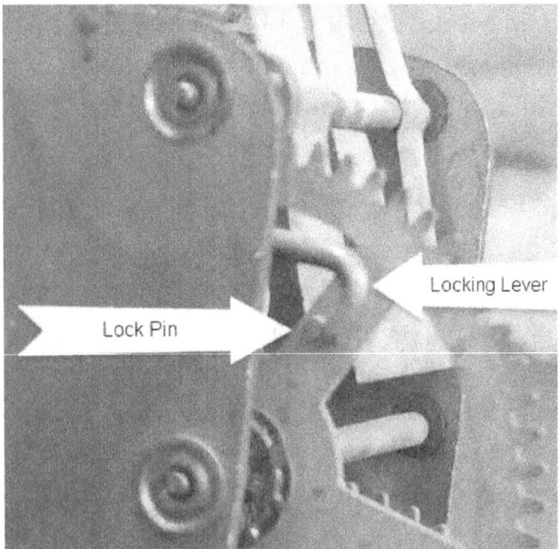

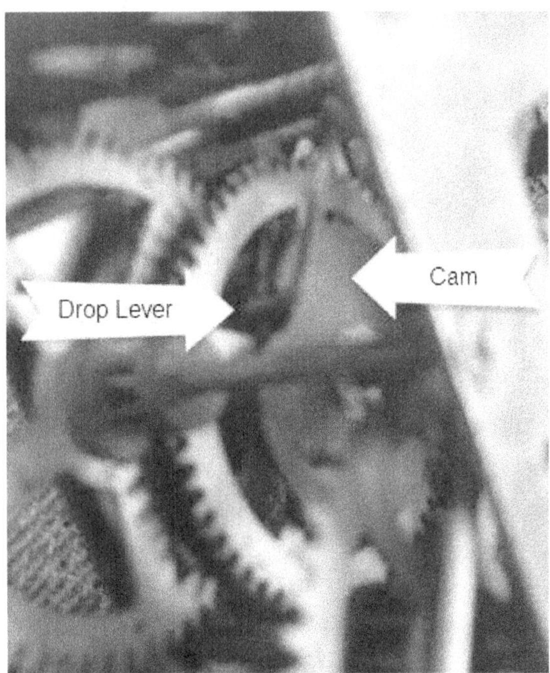

in such a manner that the lifter falls exactly when the minute hand is upright [exactly at 12]. Put the minute hand on the square of the cannon pinion and see that it does so, or move the cannon pinion a few teeth in the minute wheel until right.

When assembling the movement, the cannon pinion, and minute wheel must work together

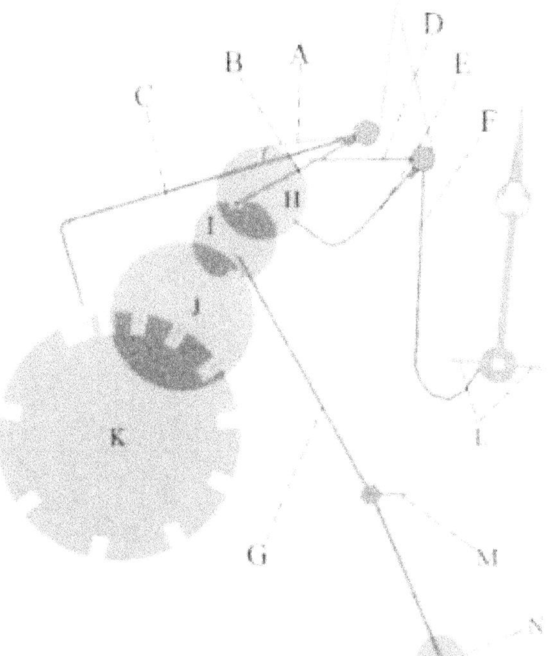

A- Stop Lever
B- Maintenance Lever
C- Count Lever
D- Lift Lever
E- Warning Lever
F- "J" Lever
G- Hammer Lever

H- Stop/Warning Wheel
I- Maintenance Cam
J- 2nd Wheel
K- Count Wheel
L- Strike Release Pins
M- Hammer Detent
N- Hammer

Before you dismantle the movement, look carefully at the setup. You will likely see three sets of levers. Each set is attached to an arbor between the plates.

- Upper Lifting levers
- Lower Lifting levers
- Hammer levers

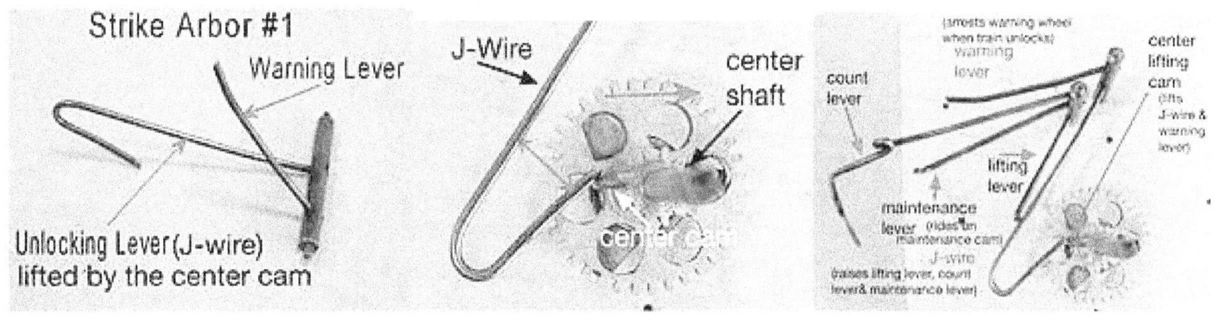

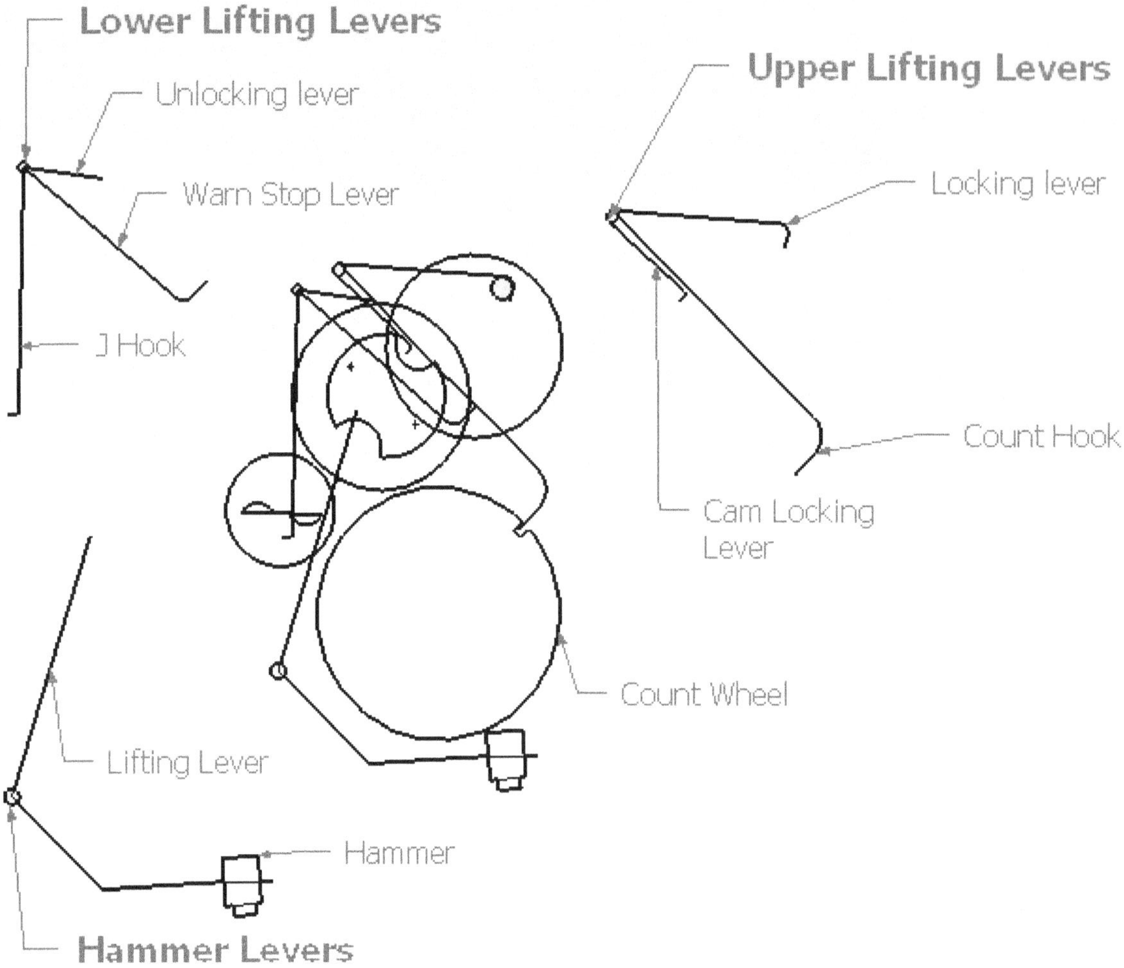

Lower Lifting Levers
Unlocking lever
Warn Stop Lever
J Hook
Upper Lifting Levers
Locking lever
Count Hook
Cam Locking Lever
Count Wheel
Lifting Lever
Hammer
Hammer Levers

Striking Levers

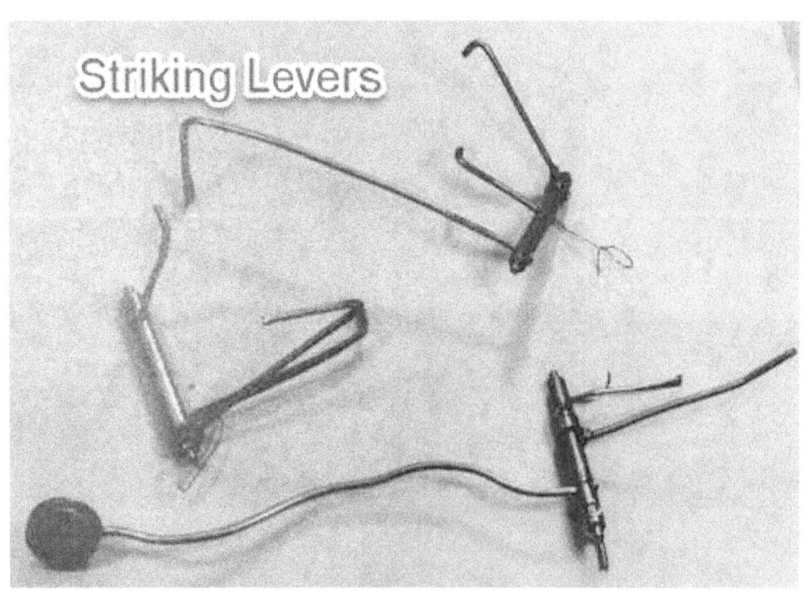

Rack & Snail Striking

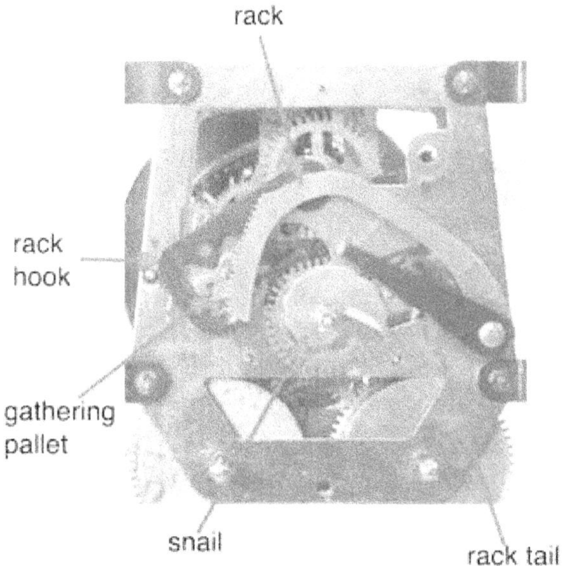

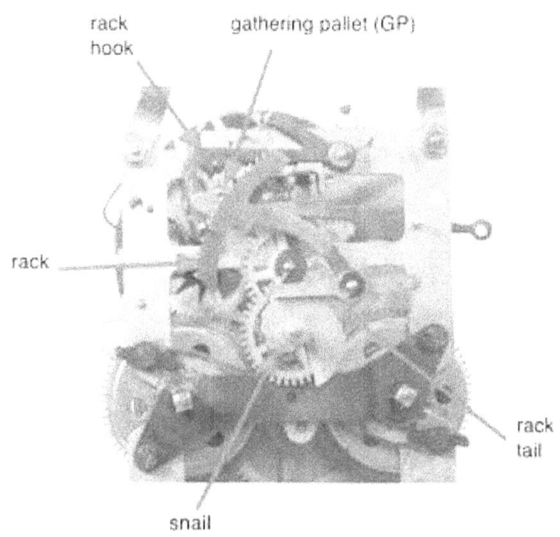

These are two common examples of Rack & Snail striking movements. This is a modern upgrade from the older more primitive count wheel system which is prone to getting out of sync.

The main mechanical components of every rack-striking clock are:
- saw-toothed rack, with a tail
- nautilus-shaped snail, with 12 steps that turn with the hour hand.
- rack hook, to support the rack
- gathering pallet, to engage the teeth of the rack

The snail, with its ever-enlarging radius, determines the number to strike and is indexed by the rack tail. The rack counts off the strike.

- When the rack hook is fully dropped beneath the rack,
- The warning pin is resting against the locking stub; and
- The projection on the rack hook is nestled in the dent of the bean cam.

That means the rack hook is synchronized with the warning wheel.

The cam is a pressed fit on its arbor. It can be adjusted either by twisting it on the arbor or by prying it off and repositioning it with its recess against the rack hook pin. Do this while the warning pin is against the locking flag. Observe the position of the pinwheel. There should be a little run before the next pin lifts the hammer.

Things are properly adjusted when...

Identify these parts. Each Rack and Snail striking movement will have some variation on this concept.

The Lift Cam on the minute arbor lifts the Hour Warning Lever.

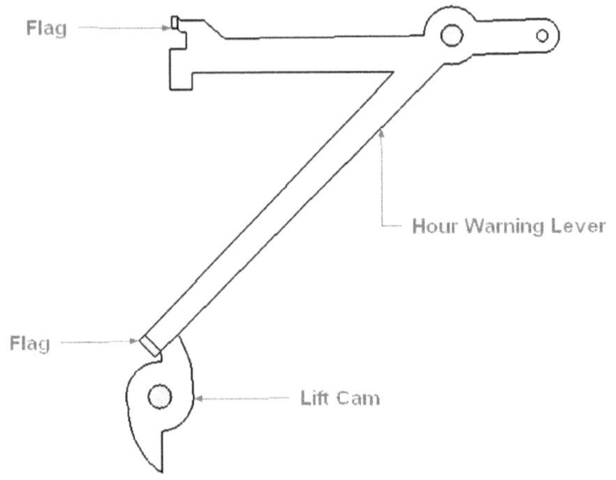

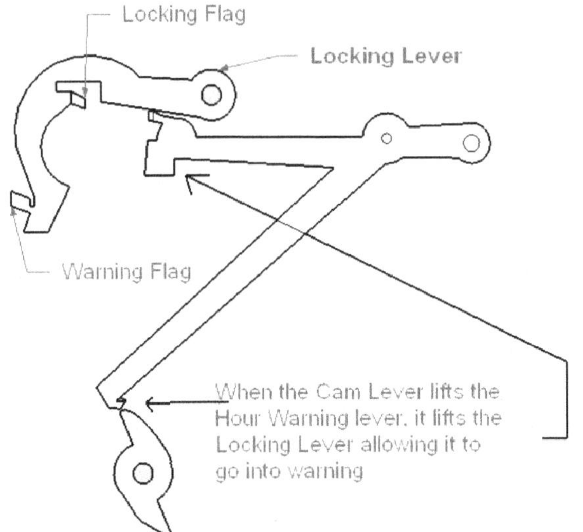

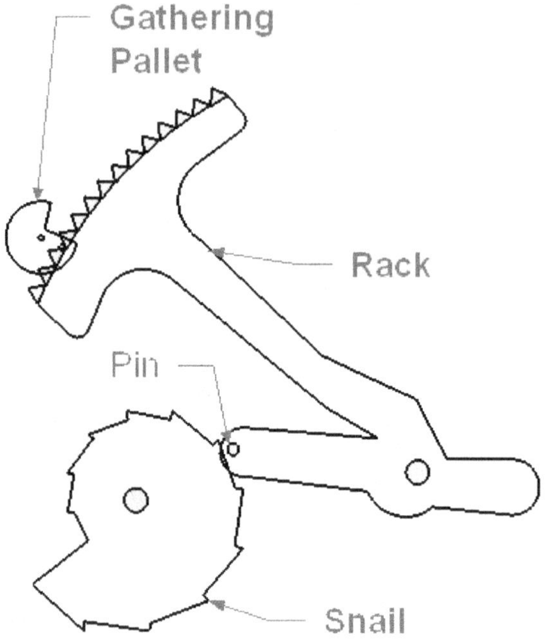

When it goes into warning, the pin on the Rack lands on the Snail to determine how many times to strike. The Gathering Pallet advances the Rack until the correct number of bell or gong strikes have sounded.

The advantage Rack & Snail has over the Count Wheel system is the striking stays synchronized with the hour hand, so it always strikes the correct hour. The Count Wheel will get out of sync if the hands are advanced without allowing the strike [and Count Wheel] to stay synchronized.

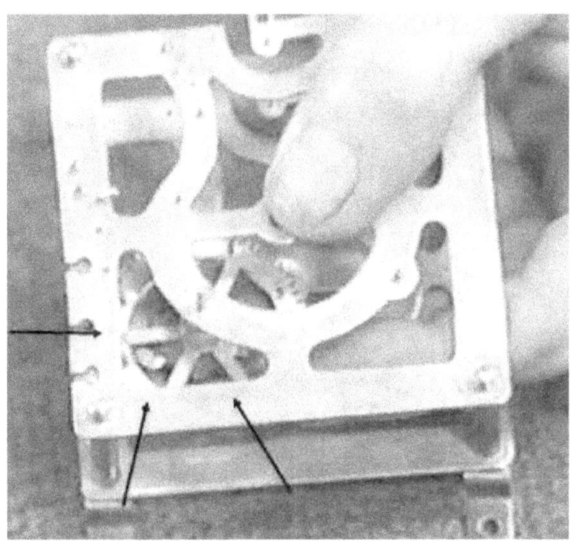

Before disassembling the movement, with the striking in the locked position, scribe small marks on the top plate to mark the location of the points of the S1 hammer pins. Do the same to indicate the pin on S2 and the pin on S3.

To set up the Herr Movement, first install the center arbor and time train.

Install S1

S2 place the pin closest to T1 arbor at the 3-O'clock position.

S3 place the warn pin at the top at the 12 O'clock position at the fly.

Install the locking lever between S2 and S3 with the flag just above the S2 pin.

Add the top plate, locating the S1 hammer lift pin scribes on the plate marks and keeping S2 and S3 pins in the correct locations on their scores.

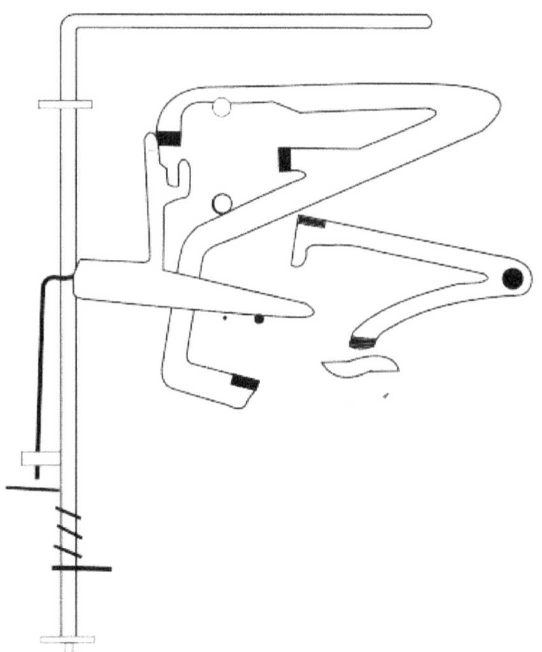

Rear View

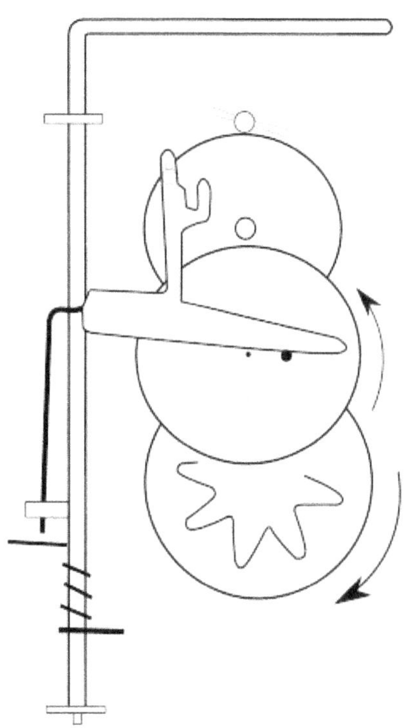

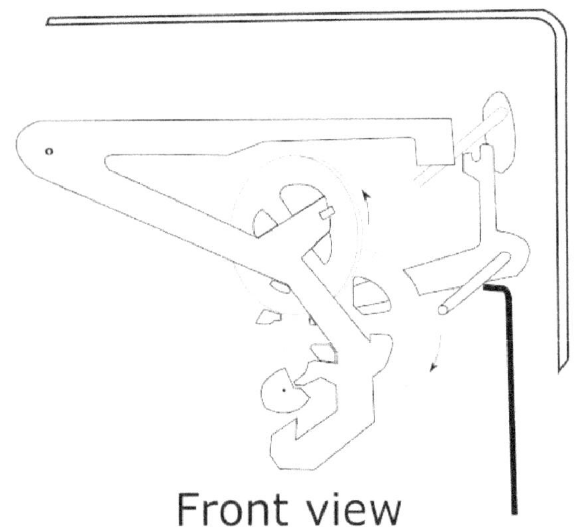

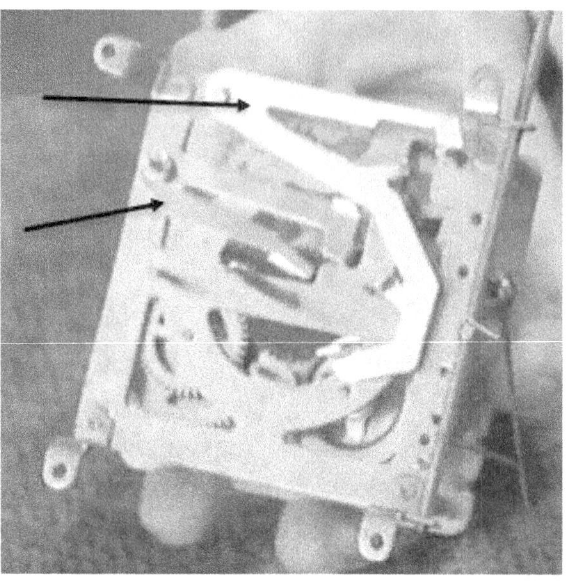

Install the gathering pallet so it locks correctly. Finally, add the snail and rack,

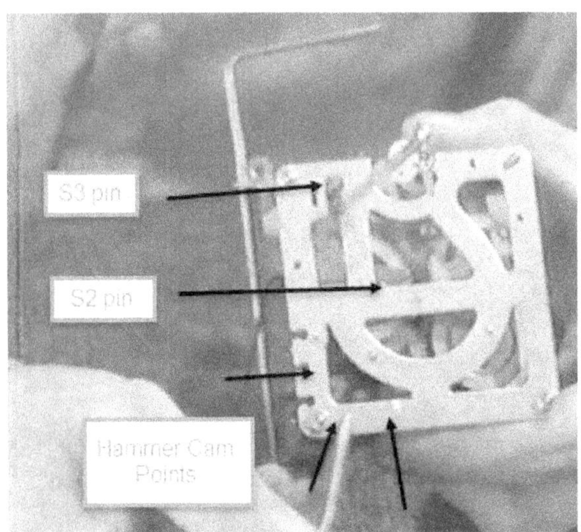

After the plate hex nuts are tightened, add the sliding bar next to the fly, held in place by a split washer. Make sure the sliding bar has room to slide after the split washer is installed.

Oil the movement and add the striking levers on the front, held by split washers and test the action is correct.

the gong hammer and strike levers.

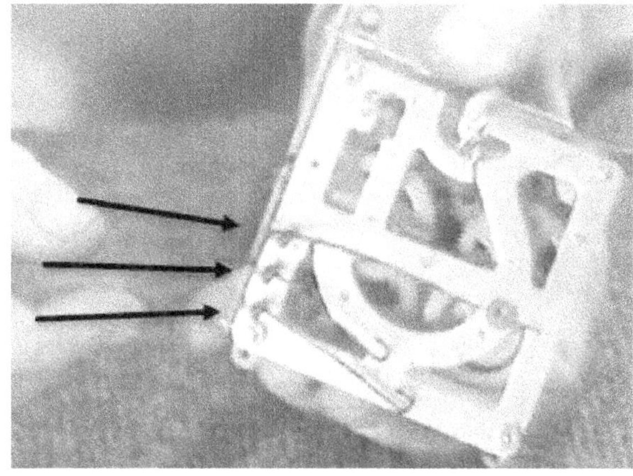

Now do a final test of the correct operation and shutoff.

Test for at least 24 hours on a test stand before putting it back in the case.

This is the inside of an 8-day Hubert Herr movement. Note it has an extra wheel on each train, and the hammer pins are on S2.

Hubert Herr Movement Specifications

KW60	2 wt	1 day	
KW 60/1M	2 wt	1 day	2 bird wires
KW 80	2 wt	8 day	
KW80/1 Clock	2 wt	8-day Used in New England	
KW 80/RM 65 mm from HS	3 wt	8-day	dancer table 2.5" or

The Baduf Movement

Badische Uhrenfabrik AG.

The plates are usually stamped Cuckoo Clock MFG CO.

Oil the movement. Note the correct position of the front levers.

Add the gathering pallet in the locked position.

Before disassembly, mark the position of the S1 cam points, and the S2 pin on the top plate.

Reassembly

With the perch pulled around, insert the locking bar, then install S2 with its pin at the 12 o'clock position, S3 with the warn pin at 12 o'clock, then the great wheel with its cam points set to the scribe marks.

Then install the time train. Bring down the top plate and make sure each wheel is still in the correct position as they drop in place.

Make sure the locking bar is on the correct side of the perch flag.

Below is the front fully assembled.

The back fully assembled. Note the hammer is located at the bottom of this movement.

Add the gong hammer and strike levers.

Now do a final test of the correct operation and shutoff.

Test for at least 24 hours on a test stand before putting it back in the case.

The Schatz Movement

"Schatz" means, "sweetheart"!

The movement is marked "Jahresuhren Fabrik Germany" manufactured during the 1950's. They are all 8-day movements with no music box additions. The rack and snail time and strike trains are revered than normal, with the strike train on the right as looking from the front.

From the rear, the strike train is on the right, the hammer and bellow levers are on the upper right side with the hammer the lower of the three. Also, note the bird shape in the backplate.

The door opening/closing and the bird operation is different than other cuckoo clock movements.

When the bird is cuckooing, the bird pops out and returns inside between each strike. Most other cuckoo clocks, the bird comes out and stays out for the complete cycle.

The weights are 2.766 pounds [or 1,255 grams]. The chains have 42 links per foot. The pendulum is 13.8 inches.

A hoop is attached to S3. An L shaped lever is lifted by the rim of the hoop which in turn lifts the door and bird levers causing the door to stay open but the bird pops in and out.

Before disassembly, mark the position of the S1 cam points, and the S2 pin on the top plate.

The hands are secured by an S shaped wire passing through a hole in the minute arbor with a very thing washer below.

Before disassembly, scribe marks on the top plate, the location of all pins and cam points.

The gong hammer and bellows lift wires can only be removed when you open the plates.

When assembling this movement, the L shaped lever must be in the gap of the hoop, while the stop pin on the 4th wheel must be at the top 12 o'clock position.

Test the movement without the gong hammer and lift levers in place. Once you are satisfied all is correct, install them using a plate spreader, going from the bottom [hammer] to the top [long lift wire].

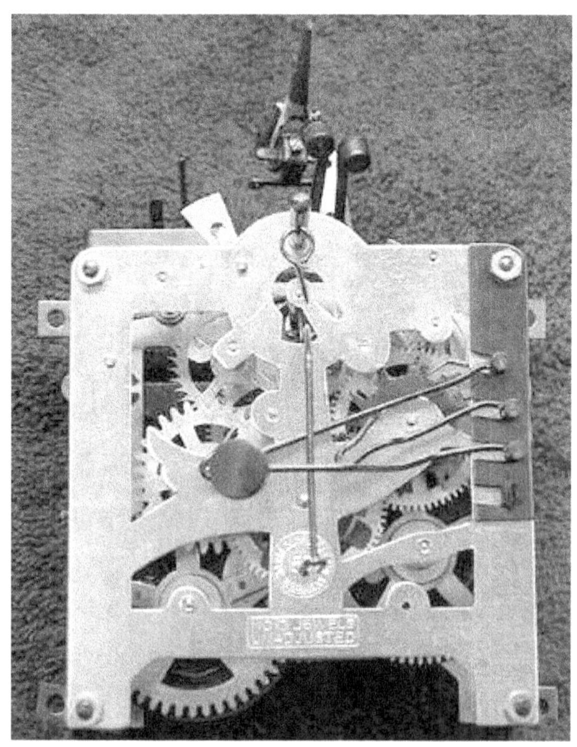

NIG. SCHATZ & SOHN
KU 50
GERMANY

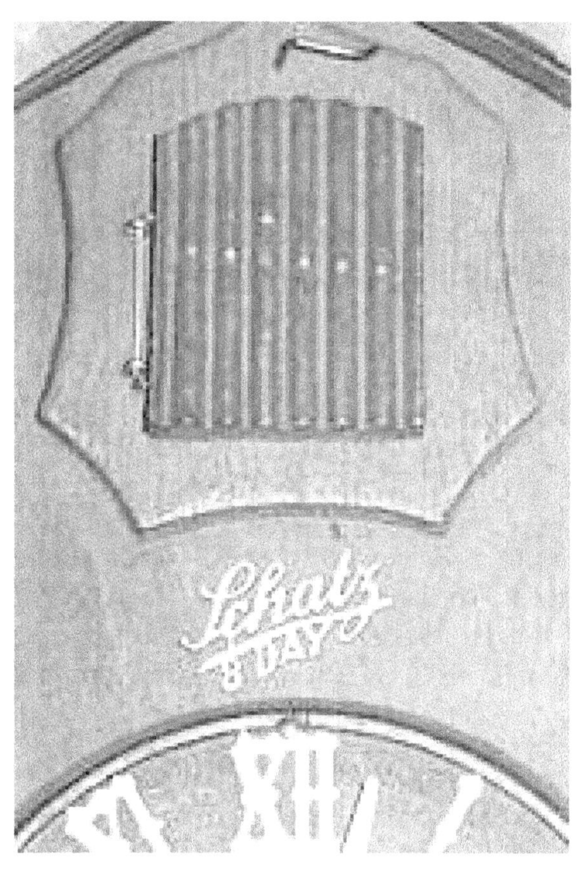
Schatz
8 DAYS

The Music Movement

Music movements, often referred to as music boxes, can be installed either to the inside roof or the walls of the case. The music movement itself is not very loud until it is secured to the case, which acts as a soundboard or amplifier, making it much louder.

The dancers will move with the music [not with the cuckoo].

The most common problem encountered is the governor. This is the part that controls the speed. Replacements are available mainly in two sizes, 18-tooth, and 22-tooth. Often some mounting adjustments are needed to mount the replacement.

A 3rd train is provided to operate the music movement with a third chain, weight and control is by wires. Of the two added wires, the first one releases the lock of the action, ready to start playing. The second starts the music after the striking has finished and stops the music at the end of the tune by controlling the fan.

Never run the music movement barrel through the cleaner.

You can ruin the music movement by turning them backward, which snaps the teeth off from the comb. Repairing broken pins and tines is just about impossible.

The music-making parts are the pin drum and the comb. As the pin drum turns, its pins flick the tines of the comb, producing musical notes. The pin drum is turned by the chain pulley. The gear on the end of the pin drum powers the fan fly.

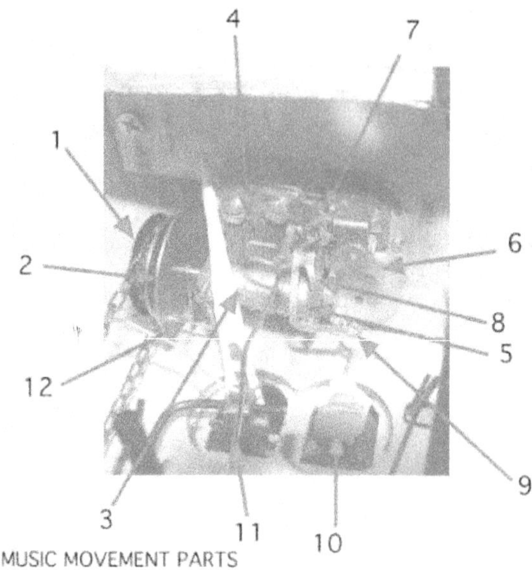

MUSIC MOVEMENT PARTS

1. chain pulley	7. fan lever
2. music man cam	8. drum lever
3, pin drum	9. pull lever
4. comb	10. music man
5. pin drum gear	11. warning wire
6. fan fly	12. music man wire

MUSIC MOVEMENT PARTS

1. chain pulley	7. fan lever
2. music man cam	8. drum lever
3, pin drum	9. pull lever
4. comb	10. music man
5. pin drum gear	12. music man wire
6. fan fly	13. spring leg

The most ingenious part of the mechanism is a four-pronged lever, all one piece of metal. I have labeled the prongs- the spring leg, the fan lever, the drum lever, and the pull lever.

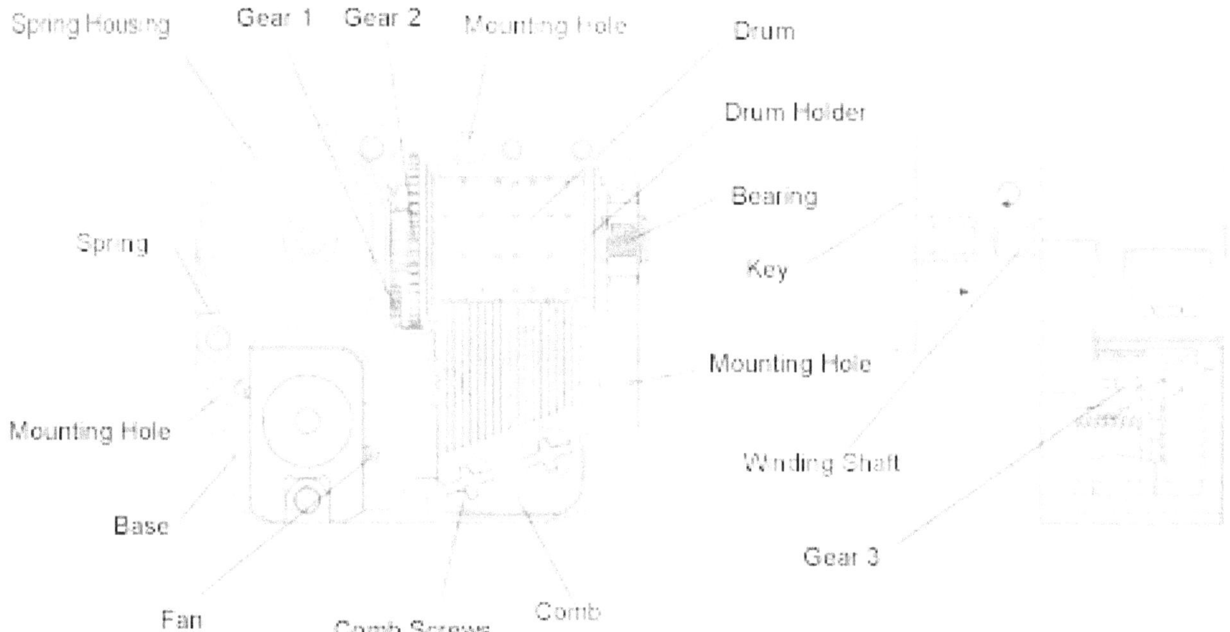

The drum lever rides on the side of the pin drum gear, held against it by the spring, attached to the spring leg. The end that touches the gear, is a pin or projection sticking out sideways from the lever. The side of the gear has a hole, into which the end of the drum lever can drop.

When the music box is at rest, the drum lever is resting in the hole of the gear, pulled to the left by the spring. That way, the fan lever is pulled to the right, just barely blocking the blade of the fan from turning and preventing the music from playing.

The fan lever blocking the fan is what locks the mechanism at rest, NOT the drum lever.

The clock movement has two levers that interact with the music unit to allow it to play when it is supposed to --right after the cuckoo has announced the hour.

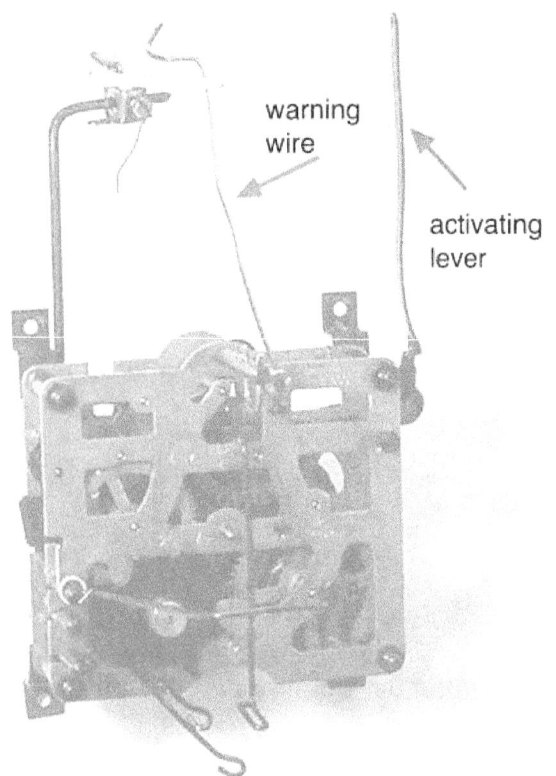

One is the music activating lever, on the same arbor as the lifting lever that's raised by the center shaft cam to enable the cuckoo. The other is the warning wire, on the same arbor as the rack hook. A wire runs from the activating lever to the pull lever on the music unit.

When the lifting lever is raised by the center cam to put the strike into warning, the attached activating lever pulls on the pull lever, which pulls the pin drum lever out of its hole AND thereby backs the fan lever away from the fan, allowing the fan to turn and allowing the pin drum to start turning.

If it continued to turn, it would play its music at the same time the cuckoo is sounding. But as the strike goes into warning, the rack hook rises to allow the rack to drop. That moves the warning wire attached to the rack hook arbor into the path of the fan fly on the music movement, halting it after it has barely started to turn.

That little bit of a run before the warning wire stops things is very important.

At the end of the strike, the rack hook falls beneath the rack, and the warning wire moves away from the fan fly. The spring on the spring leg has pulled the pin drum lever back against the side of the gear, but the lever pin doesn't go back into the hole, which would let the fan lever block the mechanism from running. It doesn't go back into the hole because the hole has moved a little bit during the warning run.

Since the pull lever is no longer being pulled, why doesn't the fan lever just drop back into the path of the fan? Because the drum lever, riding on the side of the gear, prevents it from reaching into the path of the fan. It won't be able to reach the fan until the drum lever falls back into the hole in the gear.

When the warning wire falls away, the pin drum turns, and the music plays. The hole in the side of the gear is situated at the end of the tune, so that when the last note is played, the spring forces the pin drum lever into the hole, moving the fan lever into the path of the fan and bringing the mechanism to a halt.

Next to the chain pulley is the music man cam—basically a disk with a vee-shaped notch in it. The music man perches on one end of the music man wire. The other end of the wire is bent into a crank, sticking into the notch in the cam. When the pin drum starts to turn and play, the cam rotates, the crank rides up the side of the vee, and the music man pops toward the door. At the end of the music, the crank falls back into the notch, and the music man retires.

Here is the sequence of events.

1. The center cam raises the lifting lever to put the strike into warning.

2. The activating lever pulls the pull lever, putting the music into a warning run.

3. The rack hook rises to release the rack.

4. The warning wire moves into the path of the fan fly, halting the music unit.

5. The strike train runs; the cuckoo counts the hour.

6. At the end of the strike, the rack hook falls beneath the rack.

7. The warning wire moves away from the fan fly.

8. The music plays.

9. At the end of the tune, the pin drum lever snaps into the hole in the gear.

10. The fan lever moves into the path of the fan fly.

11. The run is over.

ADJUSTMENTS

There are three adjustments that are crucial to the proper operation of the music. One is the activating lever. Another is the fan lever. The third is the warning wire.

The activating lever has a sliding connection to the pull lever. The connecting wire passes through a hole in the activating lever and is bent down at a right angle on the end. This allows the activating lever to pull against the bent-down end of the wire, but not to push it.

When the activating lever snaps back forward [as the lifting lever drops off the center cam], it just slides along the wire rather than pushing it.

The activating lever must be adjusted to pull the pull lever far enough to release the fan lever. And it must do it as close to the end of the lift as possible, to reduce the time between the release of the fan lever and the lift of the rack hook and activation of the warning wire. Too long a warning run will allow the music to start playing before the warning wire can interrupt it.

The fan lever must be adjusted so that, when the pin drum lever is riding on the side of the gear [not in the hole], the fan lever just barely misses the fan.

This is accomplished by gentle bending. We're talking thousandths of an inch. It's essential that the lever misses the fan during the entire run, but that it blocks the fan the instant the drum lever falls into the hole.

Otherwise, the drum can continue to turn just enough for the drum lever to ride back up out of the hole, moving the fan lever back away from the fan and letting the music continue to run.

The warning wire must be adjusted so that it blocks the fan before the first note of music plays. This, too, is accomplished by gentle bending.

It must continue to keep it blocked until the strike is completed. This is complicated by the fact that it doesn't stand still while doing its job. As the rack hooks bobs up and down, gathering the teeth of the rack, the warning wire will bob back and forth. Getting it to continue blocking the fan while bobbing back and forth can present a challenge.

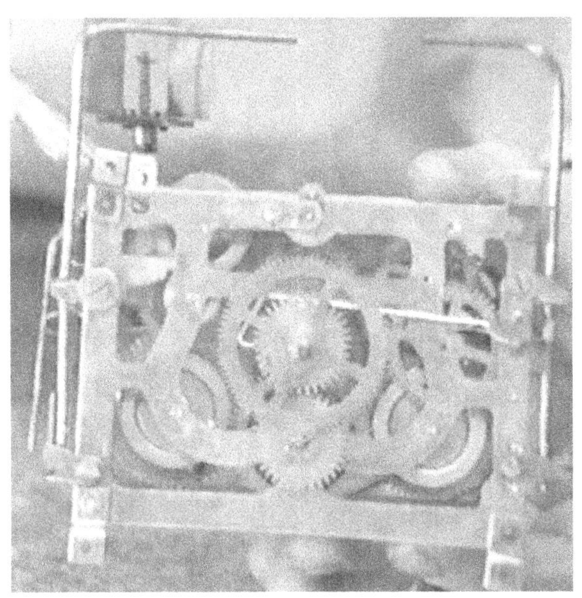

Dancing Platform Movements

There are two types of cuckoo dancers. The one with the platform attached to the movement or the platform attached to the case. If it's connected to the case, it's usually driven by an auxiliary wheel mounted on the music movement.

Dancing platforms come in different heights above the movement. The 25 measures either 2.25", 2.875" or 3.375" measured from the minute hand shaft to the top of the platform. The 34 height is usually 3.1875".

The dancing platform operates at the same time the music box plays and is operated by the same wires and levers.

Other animations may also be present that utilize the existing operation of the striking train by extending arbors.

Before dismantling, take lots of CLEAR photos AND, more importantly, make lots of detailed diagrams of the wires and components. The act of making diagrams adds to the understanding of the actions more than taking photos.

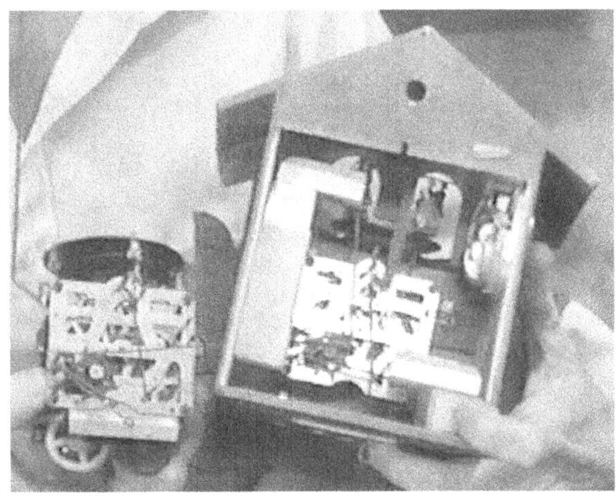

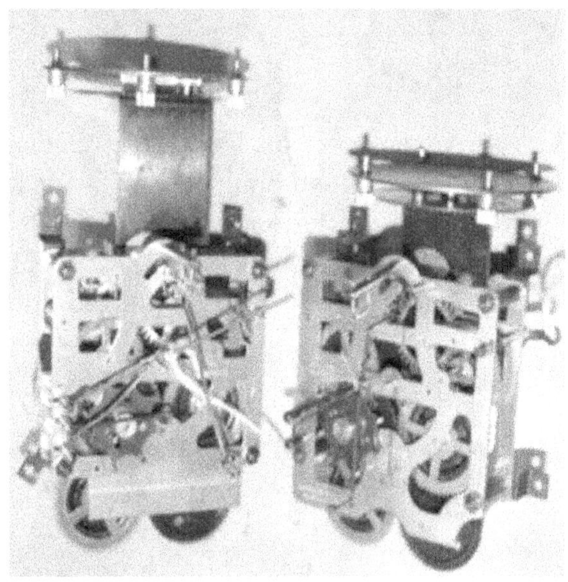

The gear on top of the platform often cracks and needs replacing. Available from Black Forest Imports.

The Quail Movement

The Quail cuckoo clock has three weights, three bellows, and two bird doors. The quail sounds on each quarter-hour. Once for the 15, twice for the 30, three times for the 45 and four times for the hour plus the normal hour cuckoo strike.

The modern Regula movement.

Four pins on [Quail] Q2 to lift the bellows to make the quail sound every fifteen minutes. Toot-D-Toot.

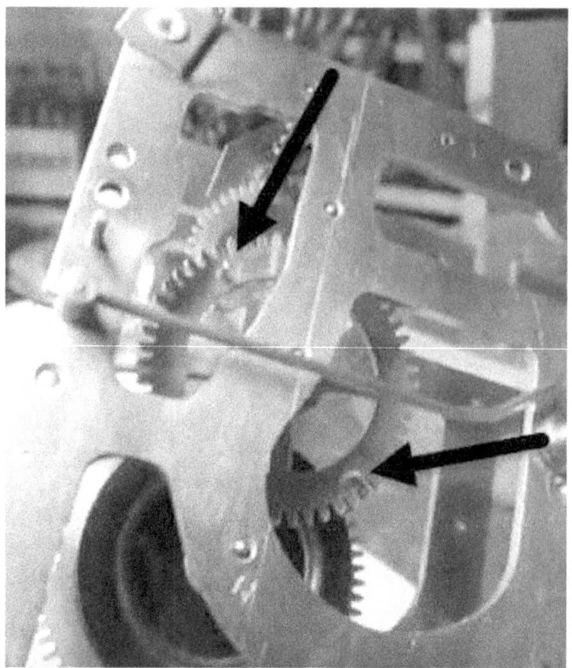

Brass Cam also on Q2

Then Q3 has a stop pin on one side and the warning pin on the other side.

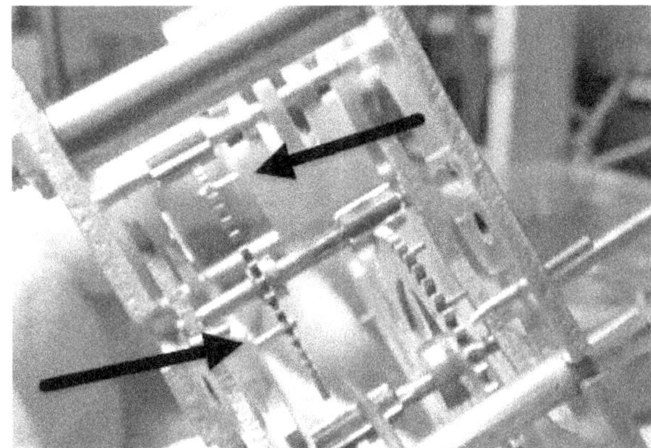

The Quail count wheel.

The pin activates the cuckoo on the quail count wheel at the end of the quail cycle.

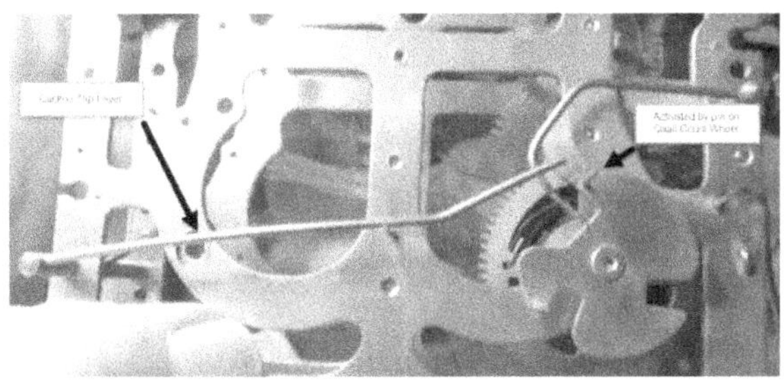

The correct cuckoo train setup is the flat of the cam on S2 must point to 12 o'clock, next to the flag on the lever. The pin on S3 is at 5 o'clock, next to the second flag on the lever.

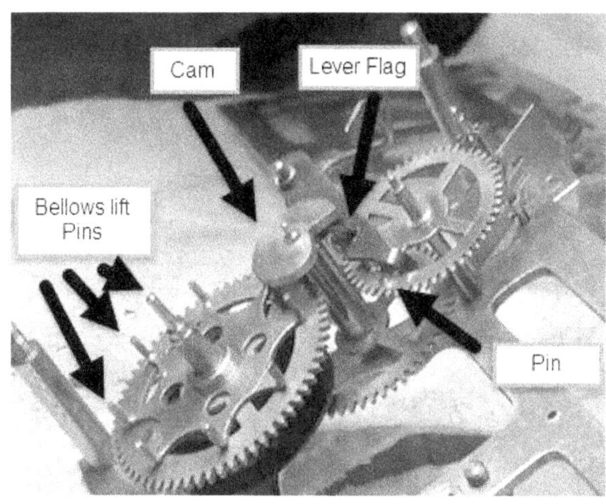

The cuckoo count wheel.

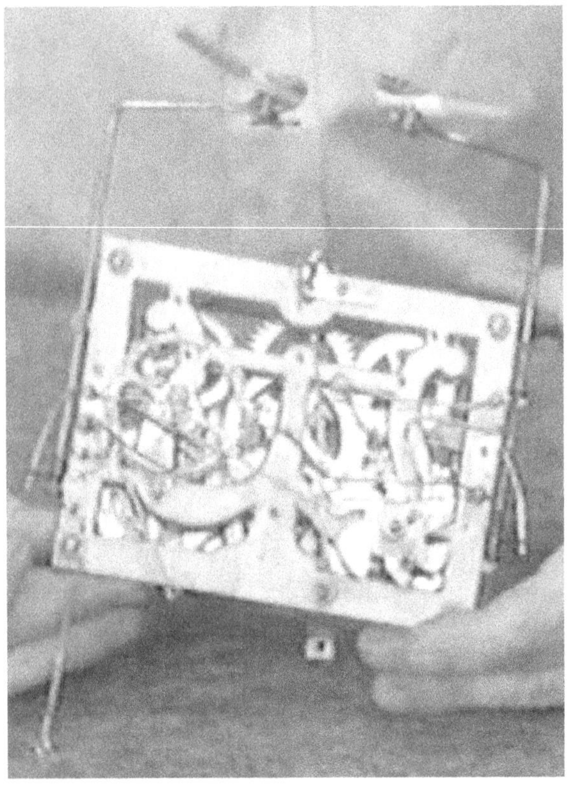

Then open the door on the right side and press a similar lever until the cuckoo call is correct.

Resetting the Quail if it gets out of sync with the hands is easy. First, open the door on the left side and press the lever until the call is correct.

Many of the case parts are readily available from the parts houses – carved bird, bellows, pendulum, dial, hands, weights, chain, etc.

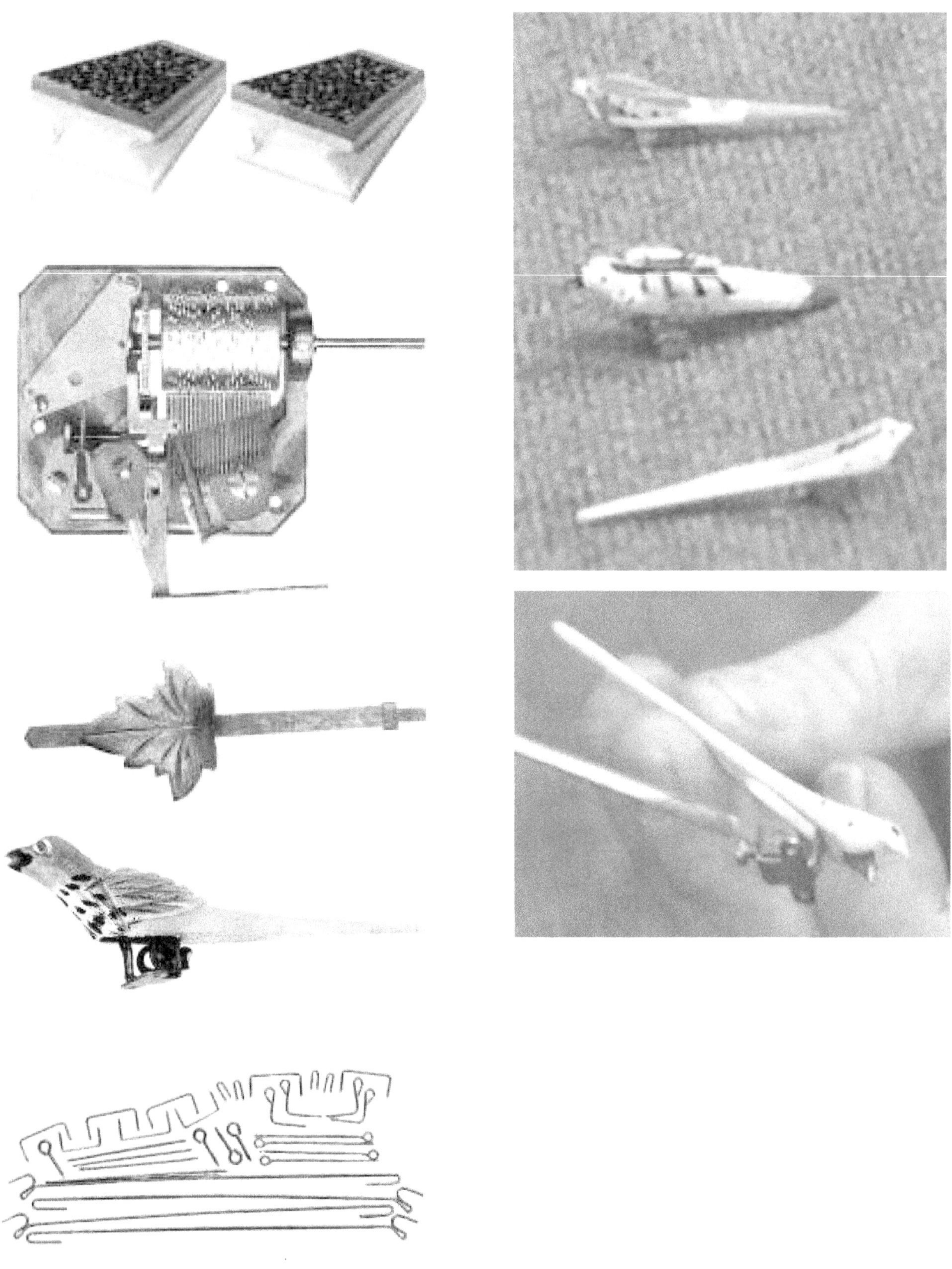

Sometimes the bird wires need adjusting, or
the bird paint needs touching up.

You must make detailed notes of each wire and how they fit. Also, take several GOOD photos from several angles.

The dancers and water wheel operate with the music movement.

This clock has a cuckoo, rotating dancers, rotating water wheel, moving brolly of the peddler and music box.

The music box is driven by a pinion meshed with the dancer weight pully,

The umbrella moves as the second note of the cuckoo sounds. It is connected by a second wire to the lower note bellows.

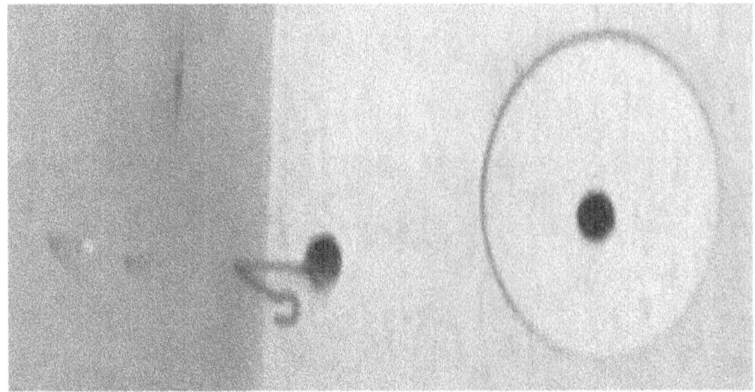

A belt from the music movement powers the water wheel.

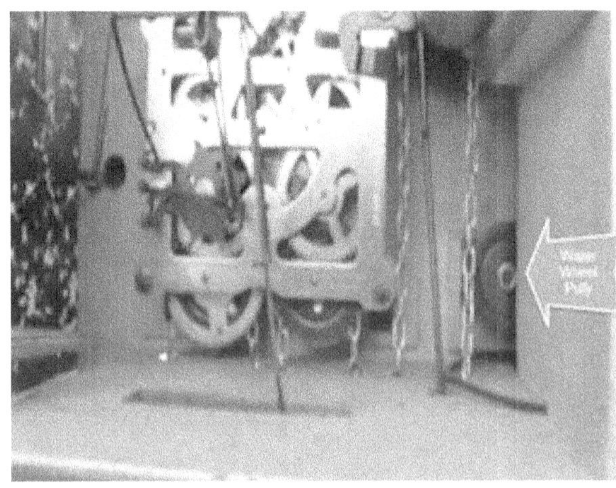

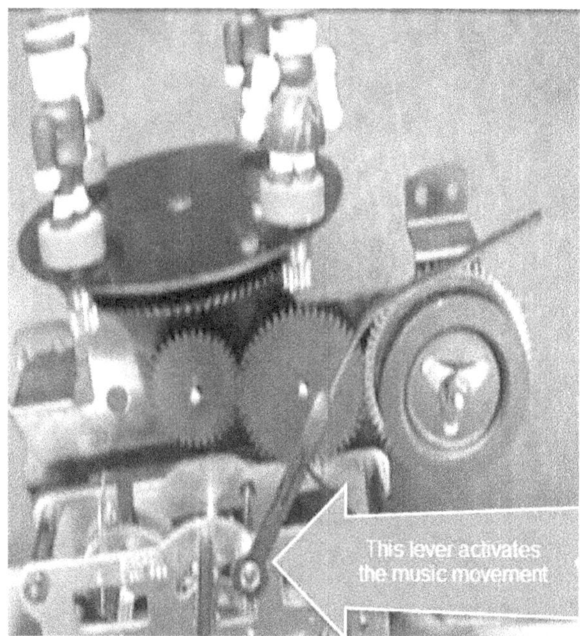

A third chain and weight power the dancing platform on top of the movement.

To remove the movement from the case, you need to remove the shutoff lever. It's disconnected by unscrewing this nut.

The lever noted activates the music movement and dancers. When removing this lever for cleaning, scribe where the setscrew is located.

Make sure you capture and record the location of the spring "thrust" washer under the lever.

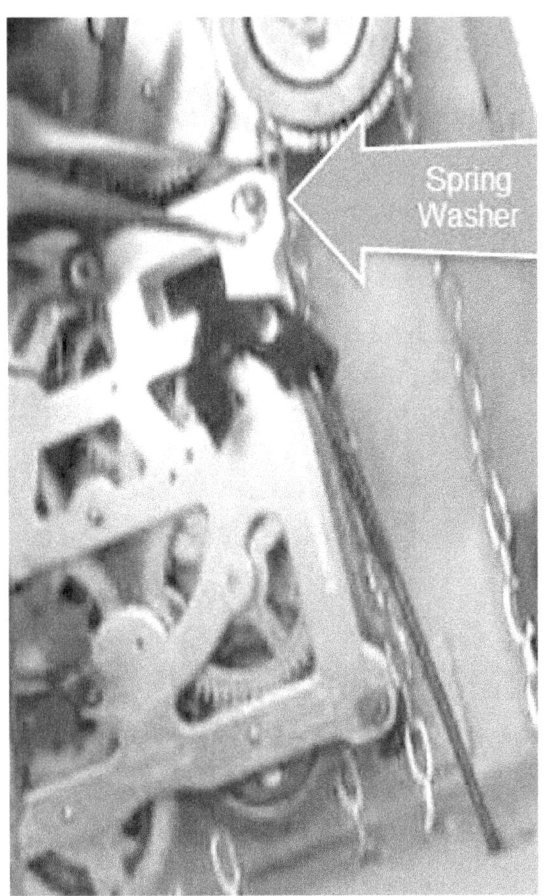

And brass spacer washer under it.

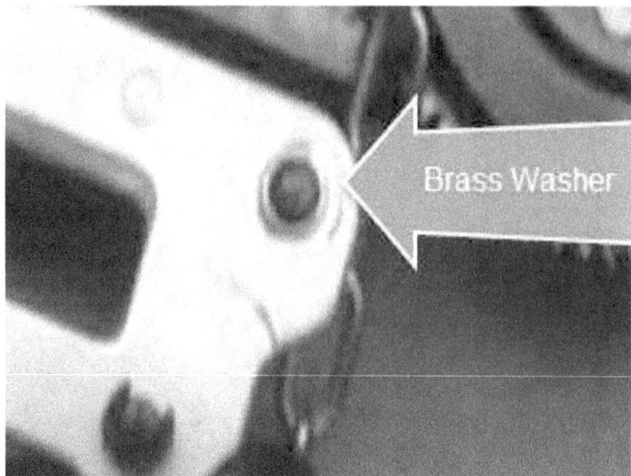

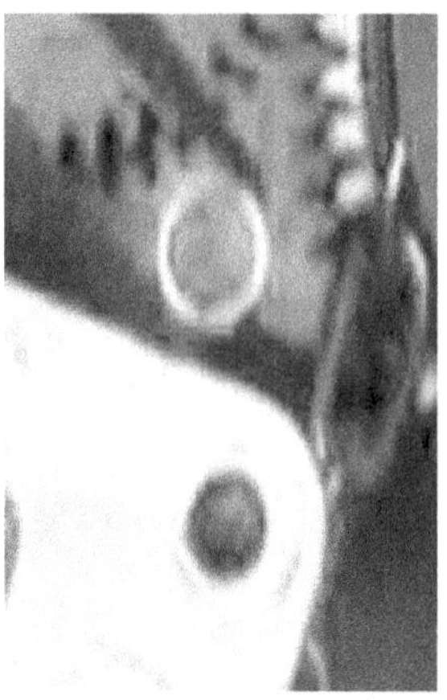

The rubber belt that drives the water wheel from the music movement often breaks. Replacement belts are available from the supply house, sold in lengths that you cut to the correct size, and joined together with super glue.

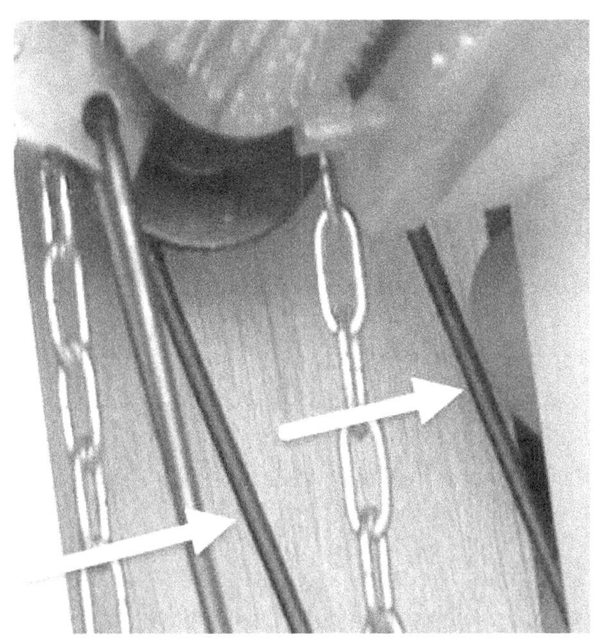

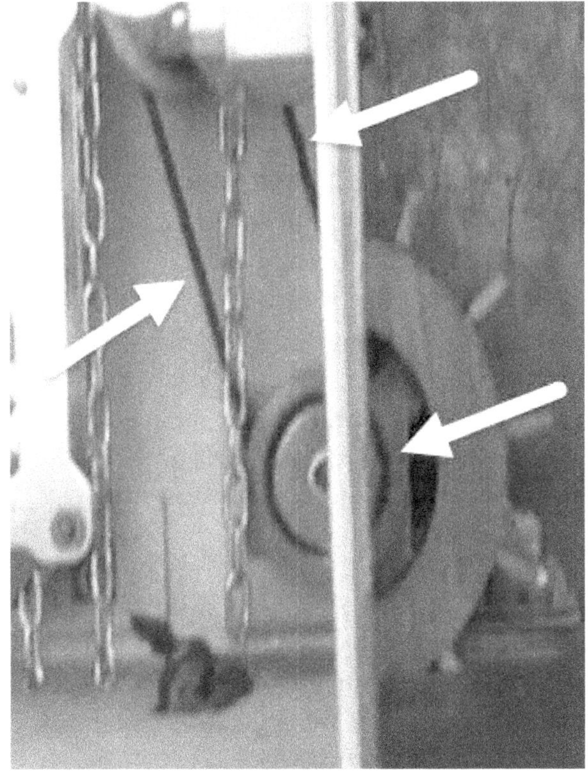

Bellows

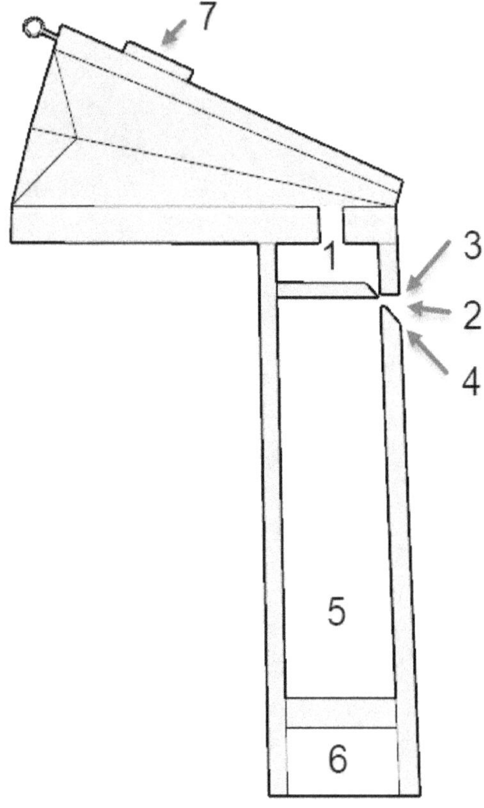

The air current from the bellows enters through opening 1, passing into a small air chamber. The air then emerges through the narrow slit 2 and escapes in puffs between lips 3 and 4. The puffs are because the air currents from 1 strike upon a beveled lip 4 and break into a flutter, the puffing sound thus produced consists of a confused mixture of many faint sounds. The air column 5 of the pipe can resound only to one of these tones, the resonance of the air column, brought about in this way, constitutes the tone of the pipe.

The notes of a cuckoo clock are a musical "one third", A and F just below middle C and should be sounded clearly and with considerable volume. Occasionally we find the bellows cracked, allowing air to escape. Repairs can be made by gluing on a very thin patch. The patch must be very pliable so as not to interfere with the action of the bellows.

Cracks in the pipe can be sealed BY gluing a small patch of ordinary paper over the cracks. Sometimes the orifice becomes clogged with dust, or the edge may become rough. By inserting a very thin file or watch mainspring, the lip may be cleaned or smoothed. If the width of the orifice is enlarged, it will change the tone. The tone can also be changed by altering the position of block No.6. By decreasing the air chamber, a higher-pitched note is the result, or by increasing the length of the air chamber, a lower-pitched note will be produced.

The lead weight 7, is to increase the air pressure when the bellows are released. If too much weight is used, the action of the bellows will be too fast, forcing the air out too quickly, causing a whistling sound. The bellows must be lifted to full capacity to get long clear notes.

The bellows, whistle, and windpipe are how the clock makes the cuckoo sound. Two notes, a high note, then a low note. The lower portion is the whistle tube or windpipe, and the upper portion is the bellows that provide the air for the whistle. Usually, the high note is located on the right and sounds first while the low note is on the left sounding second. However, there are a lot of variations to the layout.

If set up correctly, the bellows will sound 55,536 times each year. The bellows material is rather delicate and deteriorates over time, so it is common to have to recover the bellows material or replace the bellows as a unit.

Recovering Bellows

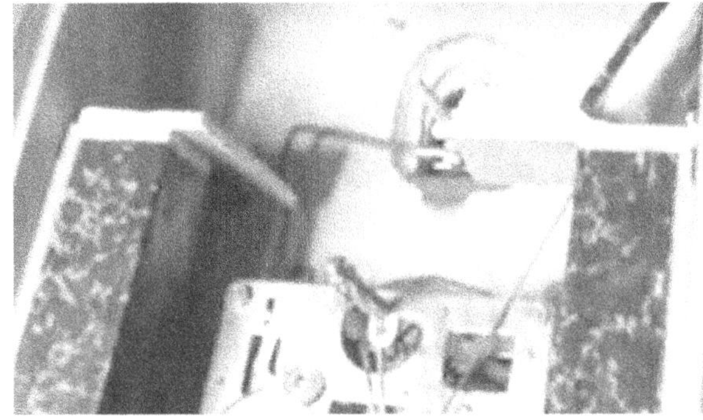

The basic steps in recovering them:

Make a tracing in pencil on paper of the bellows opening width.

Scrape away all the old covering, glue, etc.

Glue a new hinge piece on the fixed ends of the two bellow pieces-the top board, and the bottom board.

Place a business card or two between the bellows top and bottom as the hinge glue dries to allow working space once the bellows paper is applied. [Note: I use a white craft glue from Michael's art supply]

After the hinge is glued, trim off any excess from the sides.

Using the template you traced earlier, lay the bellows on its side on the tracing and open the bellows to the traced size.

Lay a piece of TYVEK* or animal skin material about 2" by 8" on the side facing up.

Position it so that it will wrap around the hinge side, the side facing up, and the bellows opening end. When you have it positioned correctly, glue it down.

Do the remaining side, and wrap the material halfway around the hinge side. You can trim the material vee-shaped to make a neat job on the hinge.

Using a popsicle stick, gently start making the creases that will eventually form the folds that will help close the bellows. Usually, I start by poking the stick on the side folds first, then do the front. Gradually close the bellows as you push the stick in deeper in the folds until the bellows close nicely. You can use new bellows to compare the folds and creases. It is best to moisten the creases with a brush and water, and then clamp the bellows [or used rubber bands] overnight. This gives a clean drop.

Open the bellows halfway and let them dry overnight. The next day, work the bellows open and closed a couple of times to ensure everything's OK.

If you are using leather, when the glue is dry, sprits the leather with plain water [not so much as to soak them or the glue may let go] then do the fold and then use a rubber band, leaving it overnight until dry. This works like a charm. The fold is crisp and correct, and a little flexing of the bellows will loosen up the hinge to proper working flexibility.

Be careful when forming the creases not to make them too crisp. The creases are the high wear points, and this is where the bellows tend to fail. If the creases are too crisp, leaks at the creases will happen sooner than later. The leather needs to be formed such that it "knows" which way to fold when the bellow is actuated.

It might take a couple of times to get it. Do a bunch at the same time. It will give you good practice.

*TYVEK is used to make Fed-Ex envelopes however it's slightly thicker and will not do as good a job.

I have heard of people using a 1$ bill to replace the paper on old bellows. It was cheaper than buying bellow paper, easy to fold, and probably the best paper to resist wear.

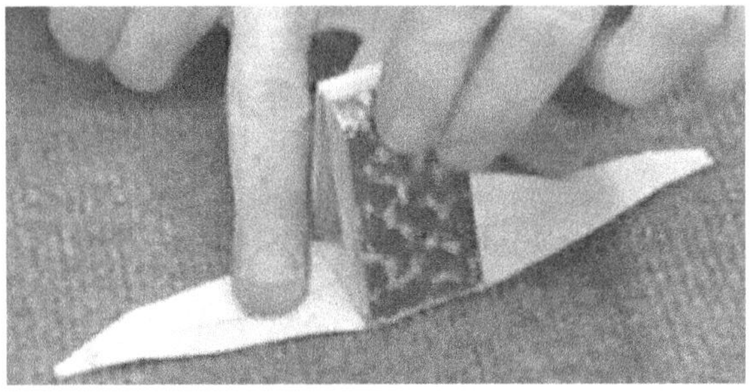

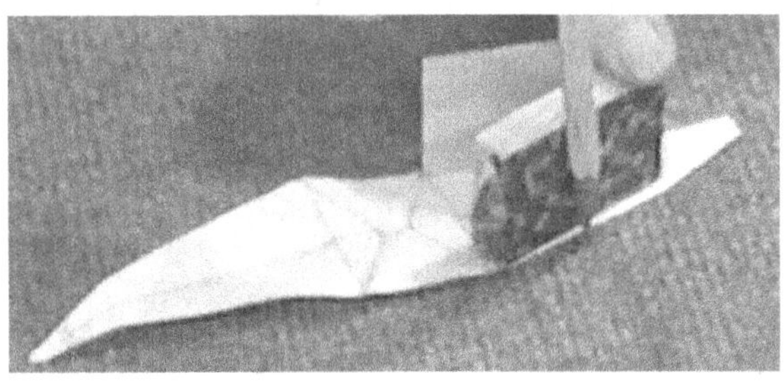

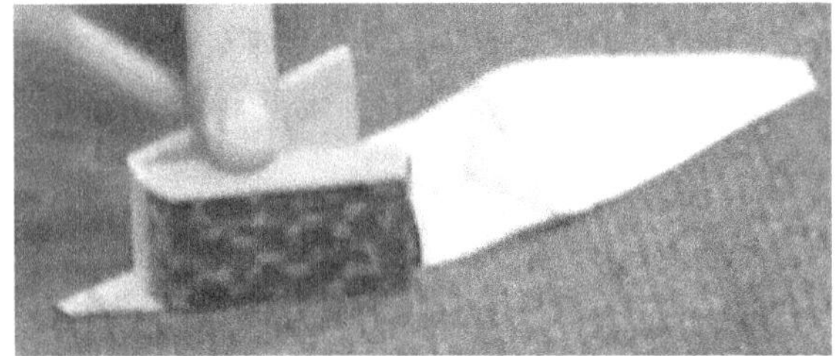

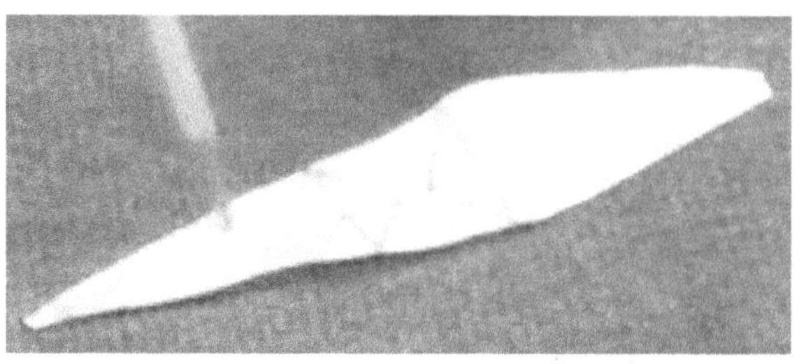

Replacing Bellows

The bellows "tops" can be easily replaced. Most suppliers have bellows tops. They come in many sizes so make sure you get the correct size, and it has the air hole in the exact location.

Remove the old [glued on] top and blow into the pipe to test it first. Remove the old glue with a knife.

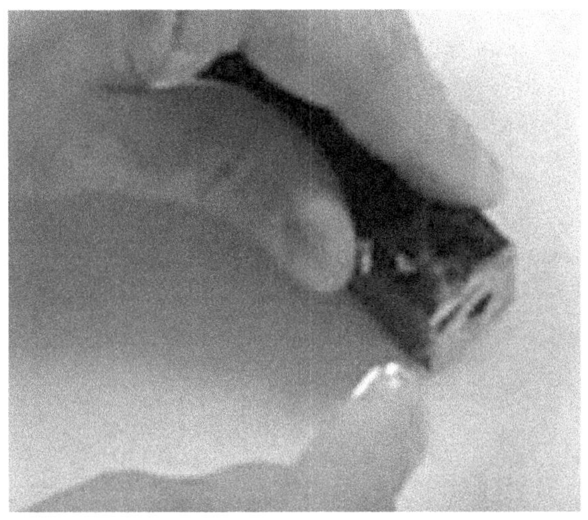

Glue the new top in place and allow the glue to set. Be sure no glue or trash gets inside the bellows. You can use a clamp or rubber bands.

Make sure you align the air hole,

and allow clearance for the bellow to rise without rubbing on the inside of the case.

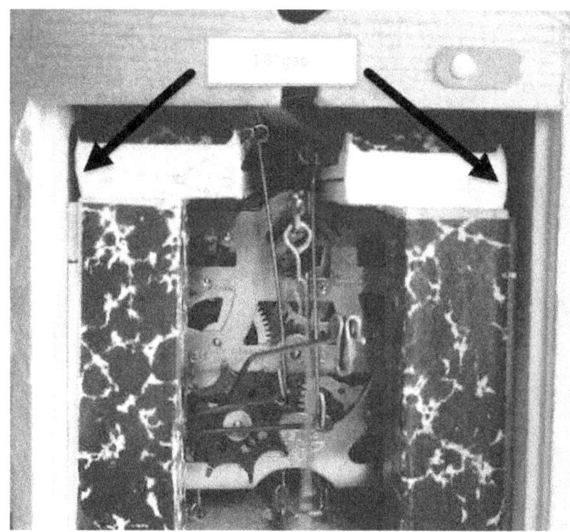

Carefully transfer all the loops and bird wire to the new bellows to the same location. This makes a nice job. The material they use today is far better than in yesteryear.

Windpipe

The body of the windpipe almost always has little holes usually made by the securing screw and or the bottom securing nail.

Sometimes these bellows' bodies have been shifted and "remounted" so many times that the body is filled with holes. These holes will dramatically change the tone and decrease the volume of sound. Once these holes are "filled" you will notice a distinct increase in volume and a clearer, more pleasing tone.

Insert wood matchstick with a point created with a knife at one end [not toothpicks as they are too hard] into the holes and cut them off flush.   These usually hold well with just friction but you could place a small dab of wood glue if you desire.

Cover the whole side of the tube adjacent to the inside of the case, with a piece of masking tape. Not only does this cover the holes more quickly, but it seems to have the added advantage that it improves the frictional stability of the tube against the case.

Notwithstanding this, it is still necessary sometimes to plug the screw hole with a glued toothpick, if the tube has been removed many times previously.

Installing Bellows in the Case

Installing the bellows and its wires is harder than it appears. It is almost impossible to connect the bellows lift wire after the bellows are installed.

The correct way to install the bellows and their wires are to first install the wire to the bellows eye and then sneak both into the case, connecting the bottom hook to the bellows arm

and securing the bellows to the case in one action.

Capture the top hook with a hemostat, so it does not come off the top bellows eye while installing in the case.

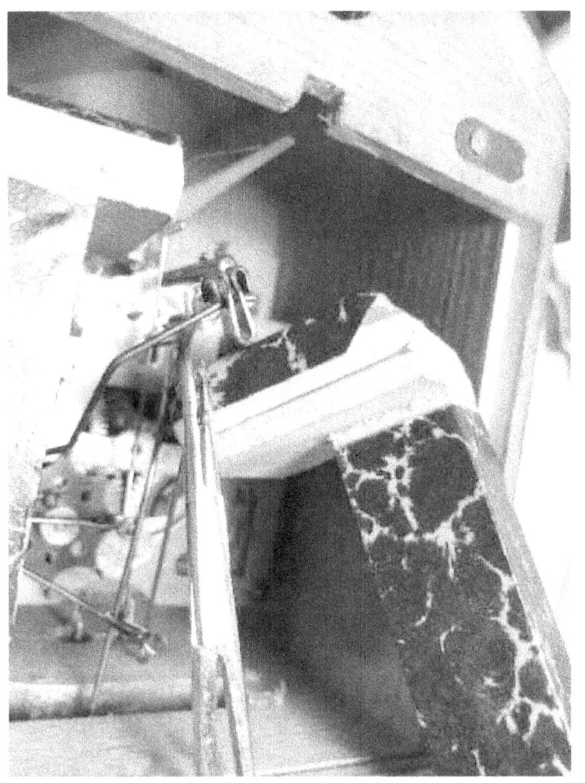

Another option is to open the bottom loop.

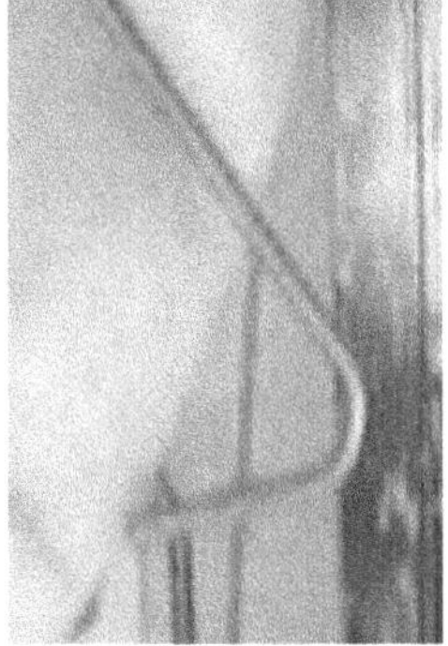

With the bellows in place, slip the top hook on the bellows eye and swing the bottom of the wire down onto the lifting eye. Then holding the back of the loop with your finger, close the bottom loop into place with pliers.

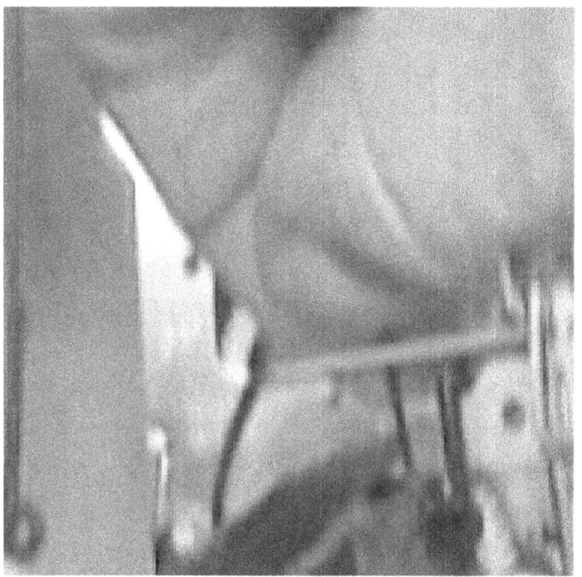

The wires are designed so they will not come off during operation and should be straight [except for the loops at the ends].

Replacement wires are available from the supply house, but if you wish to make your own, look for wire 20 gauge, #55 [0.0520"] or #60 [0.040"].

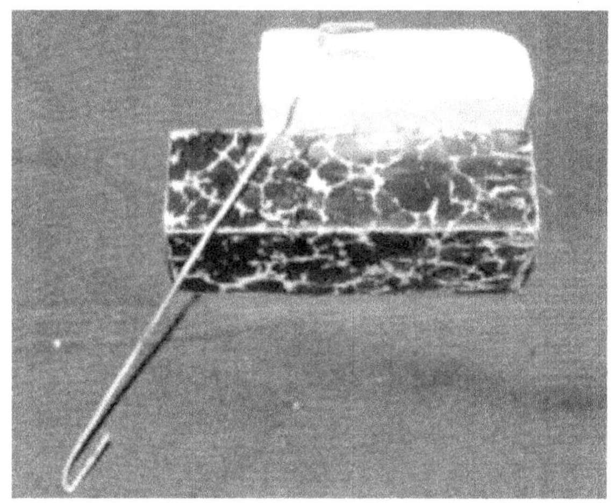

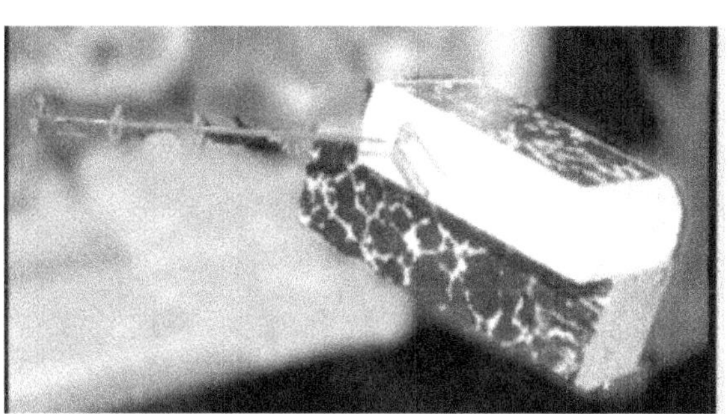

If the wire is damaged, make or purchase new wires, using the old wire as a sample. If the wires are missing, install the bellows temporally. Measure the length with dividers with the strike at the top of its action and the bellows fully open [plus the end loops]. Some adjusting may be needed. Manually turn the star wheel while watching to make sure the bellows open and close within the distance of the bellows. Make sure the bellows don't open too far or close before the tangs clear the star wheel. Too much, either way will stop the clock.

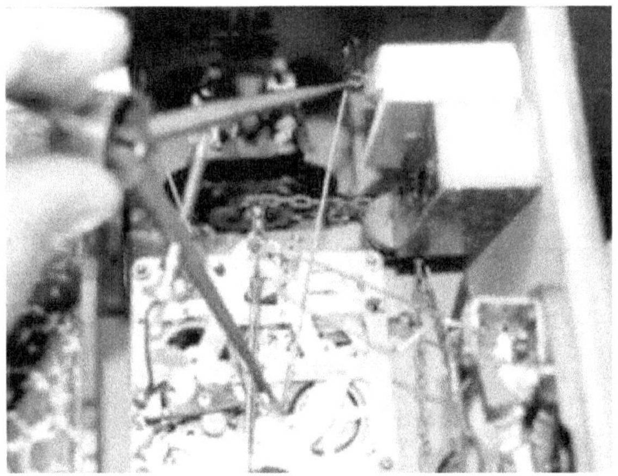

When reinstalling the bellows, you can, if you wish, discard the pin and secure them with two screws for each. I use drill #43 for the clearance hole in the case and #60 as a pilot hole in the bellows. Use 5/8 inch #4 countersunk slotted screws. Best not to use Philips head screws as they would not look like the original [unless it is a modern movement]. Don't overtighten the screw as it is only going into very thin wood.

Weights

Correct Weights

Weights made of cast iron are usually made in the shape of pinecones. There are a few rules of thumb that should work regarding weights on cuckoos. Some of the earliest cuckoos with wood plates and count wheels use odd-ball weights, try to find currently available weights that will come close to what you need.

A clean and lubricated modern 1-day [30-hour] movement - 275g;

A clean and lubricated modern 8-day movement uses 1 kg or larger weights, 1,200 grams, 1,500 grams up to about 2,200 grams.

Some modern movements, like the 1- day with quail, come with 320g weights. My definition of "modern" is the "rack strike system."

The Herrs use 320-420 gram weights.

Antique cuckoos seem to take a lot more weight. I recently inherited one [believed to be 1920's or before] that's a 30-hour but has HUGE weights - about 1,950 grams.

Probably the most important thing for you to consider is its condition. If the movement is dirty, dry, or worn, it'll need to be appropriately cleaned and repaired before you even have to worry about how much weight it needs. That's been my experience with "flea market" or "hand-me-down" cuckoos!

The best way to test the proper weight is to use a small cotton drawstring bag and fill it with buckshot [lead-shot]. Use a kitchen food scale or small fishing scale to measure the weight of the bag. Start at the low end of the scale, say around 250 grams and try the clock with the bag on the chain hook. If the clock runs, and the strike speed sounds about right, then you have the proper weight. You can add about 10-20% more weight for good measure. On some cuckoos, the music movement weight is slightly less.

Chain

The chain can be either steel or brass and can be cleaned in a regular clock cleaning solution. If in poor condition, order a new chain from the supply house by wire thickness in mm and links per foot.

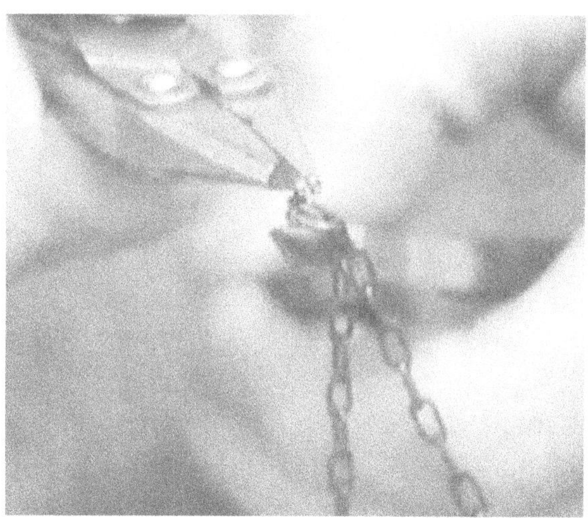

The weights should all drop the same amount over a full 12 or 24 hours. During the 1,2,3 hour strikes, it drops slower than at the 10,11,12 hour strikes...Obviously!! If the weights are unequal then you are missing strikes.

Chain Size Chart

Sprocket Size	Links/Foot	Wire diameter
8.5mm	72	.7mm
9.7mm	63	.7mm
9.7mm	63	.8mm
9.7mm	63	.9mm
11.5mm	53	1.05mm
11.7mm	52	1.2mm
12.0mm	51	.95mm
12.0mm	51	1.1mm
12.4mm	49	1.35mm
12.5mm	47	1.5mm
13.0mm	47	1.05mm
13.0mm	47	1.6mm
13.9mm	44	1.1mm
13.9mm	44	1.2mm
13.9mm	44	1.35mm
13.9mm	44	1.5mm
14.2mm	43	1.2mm
14.2mm	43	1.35mm
14.2mm	43	1.4mm
14.2mm	43	1.55mm
14.2mm	43	1.6mm
14.2mm	43	1.7mm
14.2mm	43	1.8mm
14.5mm	42	1.6mm
14.9mm	41	1.3mm
15.2mm	40	1.3mm
15.6mm	39	1.8mm
16.0mm	38	1.8mm
16.0mm	38	2.0mm
25.4mm	24	1.7mm
29.0mm	21	2.5mm

Test Stand

Cuckoo clocks and movements can be tricky to hold for testing. Luckily, homemade stands are easy to make. You can create desktop stands for short testing and adjusting, or tall floor stands for long-term testing.

They can support just the movement or the movement in the case. There must be a place for the weights and pendulum, and you can access both the front and back of the clock.

3-1/2" wide by 10" deep by 10" tall

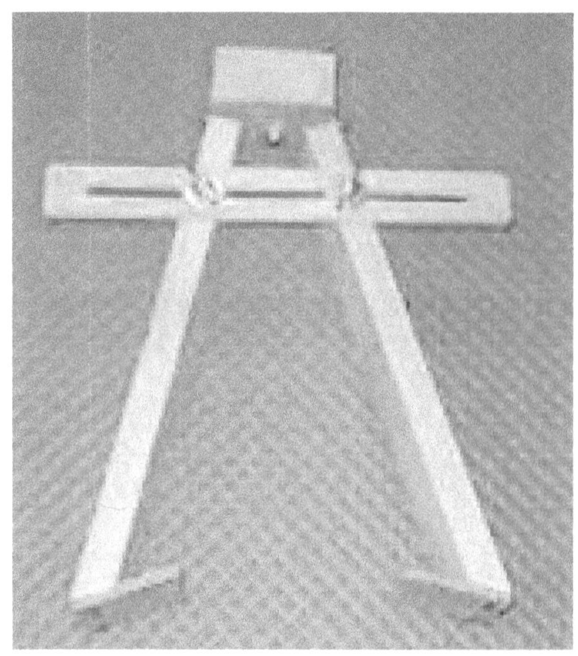

Make sure it runs for a full 24 hours before putting the movement back into its case.

The test stand below fits many movements just sitting on top. It is easy to make using ½" plywood. 12" tall, 8" wide, and 6" deep. Cut a hole in the top about 4" by 3" or to suit your movement. The pendulum [and weight chains if it has weights] fit through the hole in the top. Make a second top out of ¼" ply to fit smaller movements. An added front piece will accept movements screwed to its face. Cut a hole in it if needed.

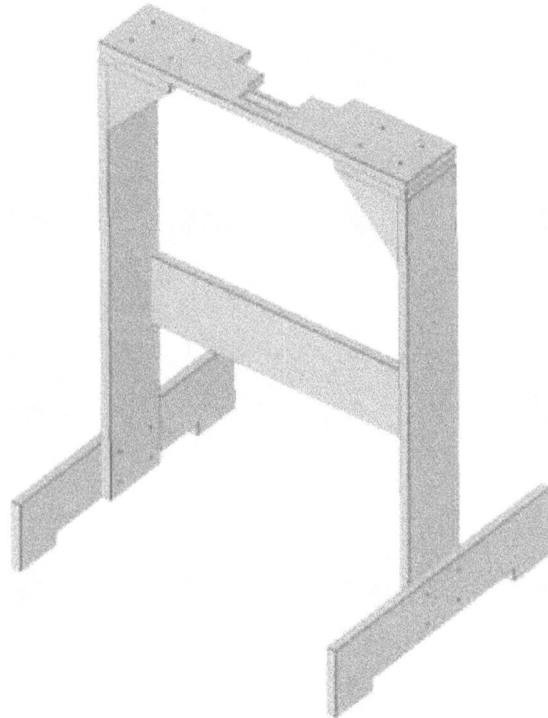

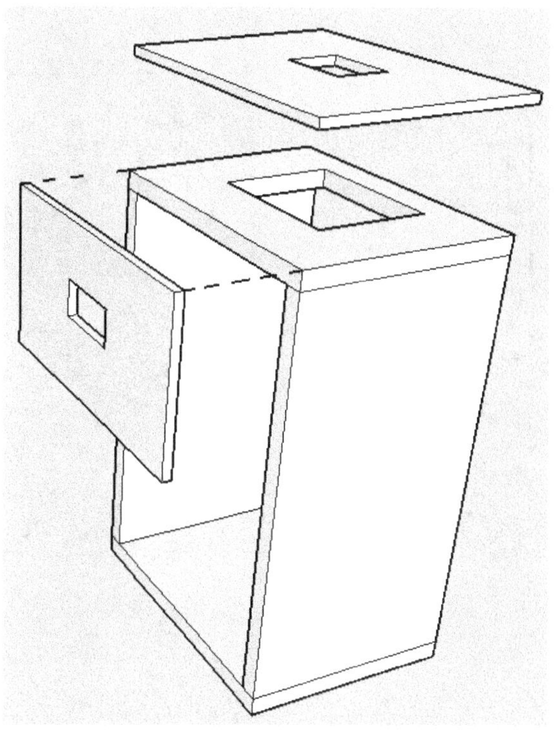

Screw the movement to a [homemade] test stand, clamped to a benchtop or table. Make sure it is level to the eye. Add the pendulum, wind it up and start the clock to make sure it runs. Closely observe the movement and listen to all sounds. The tick and tock should be even. Adjust the pendulum crutch if it is not even. Adjust its regulation until it keeps good time.

When I say level, I find my students get paranoid about 'level.' The fact is the movement needs to be placed on the stand so it is 'in beat' [see the first chapter]. There is no guarantee the movement will be set in the case perfectly level, and the place the clock sets might not be perfectly level.

If you have a table that takes leaves? Open it just a crack for the chains, hang the weights under the table, and voila! Instant workbench I did that a few times when I was first starting out.

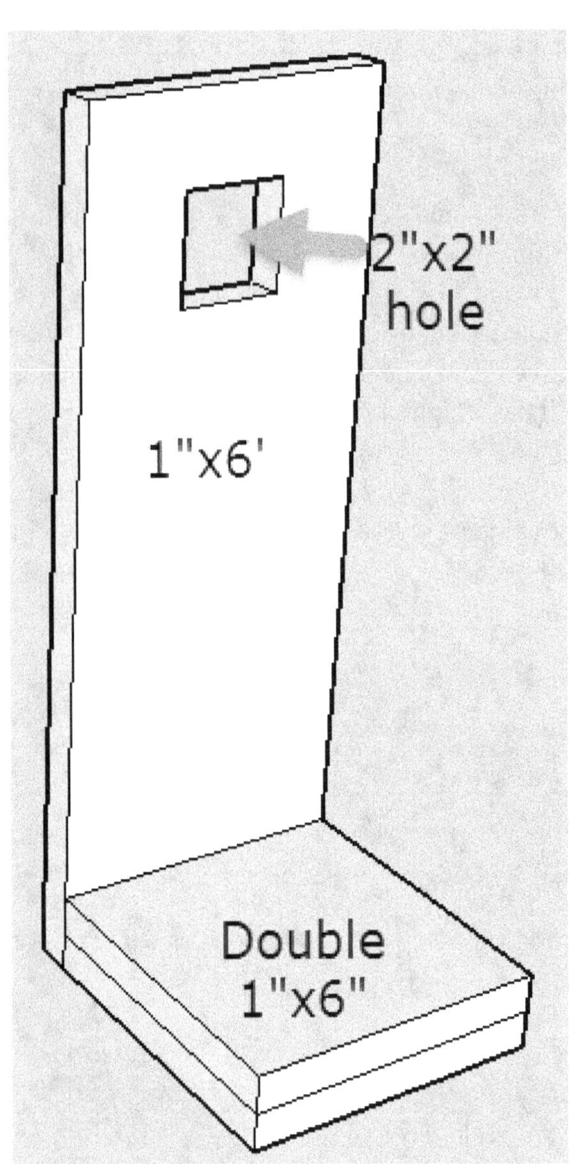

2"x2"
hole
1"x6'
Double
1"x6"

If the cuckoo action is not behaving itself, and you have a hard time figuring out what is wrong, take a video of the striking action, then study it in slow motion.

Regula

Usually says REGULA and, OR 25, 34, 35, 70, 71, and 72 have no name but have one of these numbers, it probably is a Regula. They come in one and eight-day versions.

The hammer and bellows are operated by an external Actuating Cuckoo Wheel on the lower left rear.

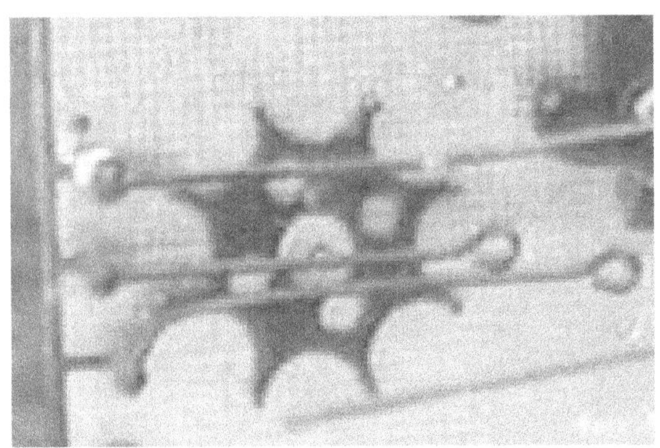

Hubert Herr

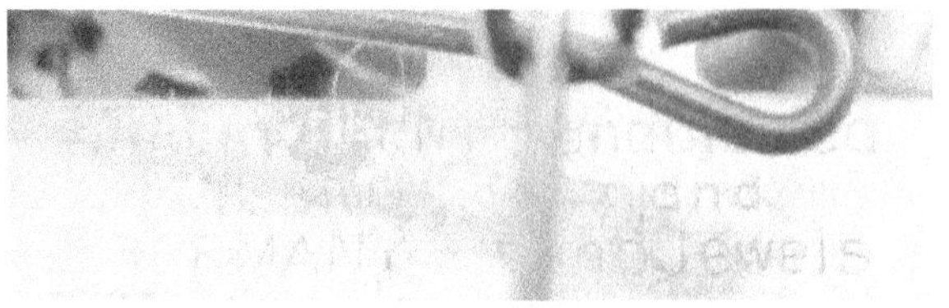

They come in one and eight-day versions.

The hammer and bellows are operated by pins located on the Striking Great Wheel.

The gong hammer is located above the bellows lifters on the lower left rear.

The stop lever has a third arm and flag in the middle.

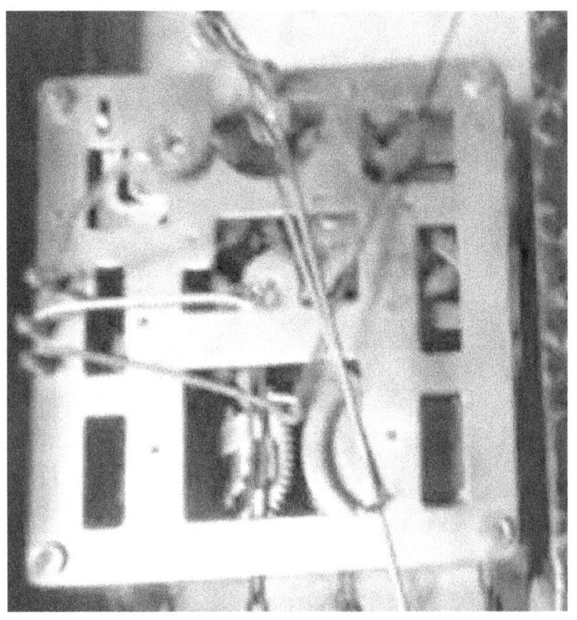

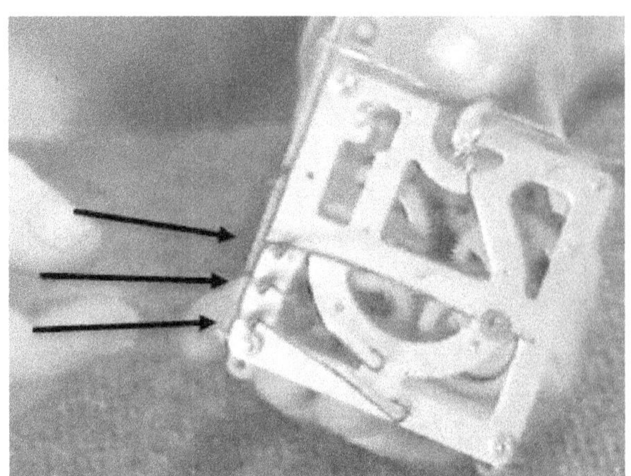

Baduf   Badische Uhrenfabrik AG.

It usually says **Cuckoo Clock MFG CO** on the rear plate.

The gong hammer and bellows are operated by pins located on the Striking Great Wheel.

Look for an L-shaped slot on the rear right-side halfway up, with a pin protruding.

The bird arm is located on the front right.

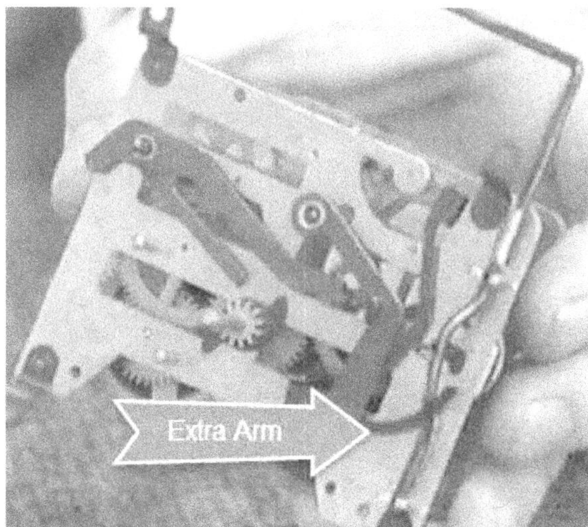

An extra curved arm is located on the lower strike lever. The bird arm is located on the front right.

Note the gong and bellows lift arms on the right of this movement.

Schatz

Often marked "Jahreshenfabrik round logo with "50" or "KU50" Germany".

The strike train is located on the right side as you look from the rear. Easily recognized by the gong hammer and bellows lifters on the upper right side of the rear.

All are 8-day run.

Look for a hoop cam on S3.

The rear plate has a bird silhouette

Other Manufacturers

Rombach and Haas
Anton Schneider
Hekas and Trenkle Uhren
GHS – Gordian Hettich & Sohn
AMS - Andreas Mayer in Schönenbach

Manufacturer   Regula 01

	High	**Wide**	**Depth** [mm]
Size	79	75	23.5
	Time	**Strike**	**Music**
Weight	420g	420g	

Manufacturer   Regula 03

	High	**Wide**	**Depth** [mm]
Size	90	92	23
	Time	**Strike**	**Music**
Weight	1500g	1500g	

Manufacturer   Regula 02

	High	**Wide**	**Depth** [mm]
Size	75	75	23
	Time	**Strike**	**Music**
Weight	420g	420g	

Manufacturer   Regula 04/05

	High	**Wide**	**Depth** [mm]
Size	47	46	17.5
	Time	**Strike**	**Music**
Weight	250g		

Manufacturer	Regula 04/05		
	High	**Wide**	**Depth** [mm]
Size	53	45	17.5
	Time	**Strike**	**Music**
Weight	250g		

Manufacturer	Regula 09		
	High	**Wide**	**Depth** [mm]
Size	66	46	17
	Time	**Strike**	**Music**
Weight	375g		

Manufacturer	Regula 10		
	High	**Wide**	**Depth** [mm]
Size	88	88	27
	Time	**Strike**	**Music**
Weight	750g	750g	

Manufacturer	Regula 18/1/2		
	High	**Wide**	**Depth** [mm]
Size	47	45	14
	Time	**Strike**	**Music**
Weight	250g		

Manufacturer	Regula 18/3/4		
	High	**Wide**	**Depth** [mm]
Size	42.5	34	14
	Time	**Strike**	**Music**
Weight	350g		

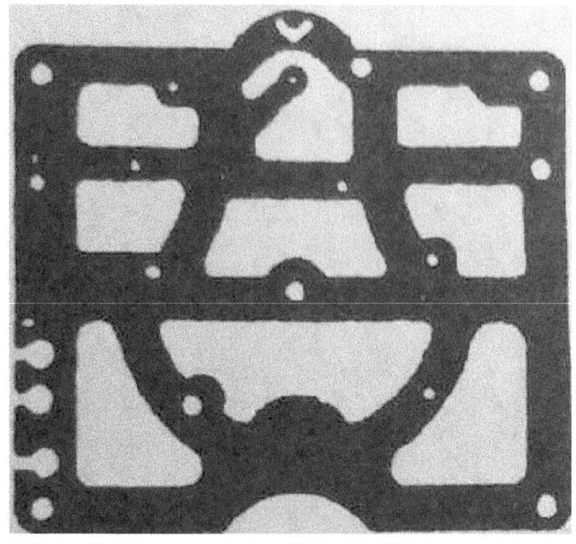

Manufacturer	Regula 21		
	High	**Wide**	**Depth** [mm]
Size	68	73	20
	Time	**Strike**	**Music**
Weight	270g	270g	

Manufacturer	Regula 20		
	High	**Wide**	**Depth** [mm]
Size	75	77	23
	Time	**Strike**	**Music**
Weight	420g	420g	

Manufacturer	Regula 21		
	High	**Wide**	**Depth** [mm]
Size	66	71	17.5
	Time	**Strike**	**Music**
Weight	250g	250g	

Manufacturer	Regula 22/1/2		
	High	**Wide**	**Depth** [mm]
Size	48	39	10
	Time	**Strike**	**Music**
Weight	150g		

Manufacturer	Regula 25		
	High	**Wide**	**Depth** [mm]
Size	68	73	20
	Time	**Strike**	**Music**
Weight	270g	270g	

Manufacturer	Regula 24		
	High	**Wide**	**Depth** [mm]
Size	73	84	20
	Time	**Strike**	**Music**
Weight	1200g	1200g	

Manufacturer	Regula 28		
	High	**Wide**	**Depth** [mm]
Size	65.5	40	16
	Time	**Strike**	**Music**
Weight	180g	180g	

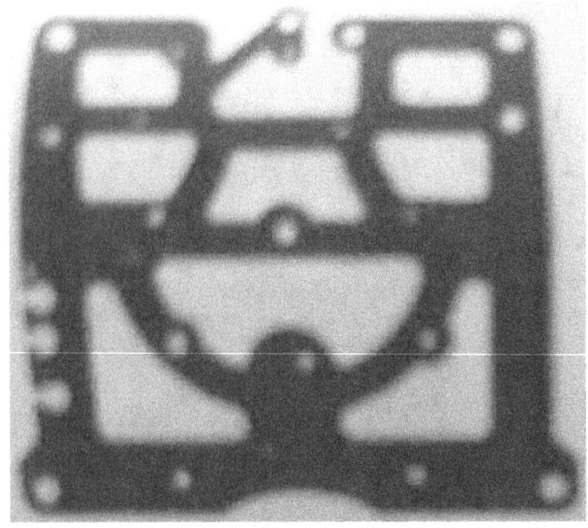

Manufacturer	Regula 34		
	High	**Wide**	**Depth** [mm]
Size	76	85	20
	Time	**Strike**	**Music**
Weight	1100g	1100g	

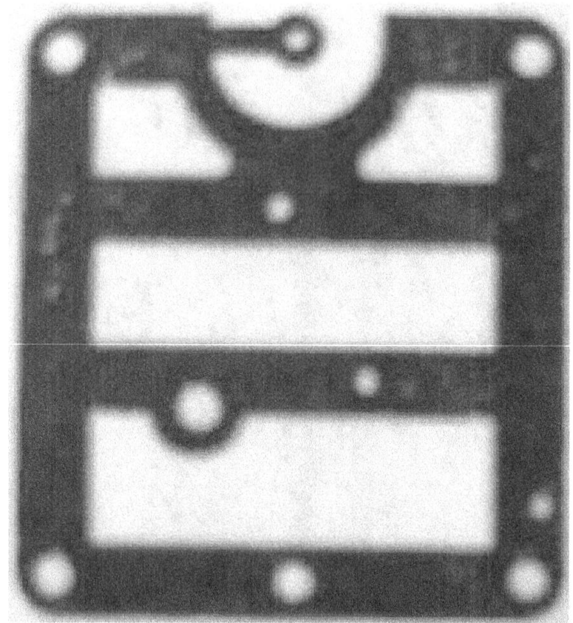

Manufacturer	Regula 44/45		
	High	**Wide**	**Depth** [mm]
Size	50.5	46	17
	Time	**Strike**	**Music**
Weight	250g		

Manufacturer	Regula 35		
	High	**Wide**	**Depth** [mm]
Size	75	77.5	20
	Time	**Strike**	**Music**
Weight	420g	420g	

Manufacturer	Herr		
	High	**Wide**	**Depth** [mm]
Size	79	75.5	23
	Time	**Strike**	**Music**
Weight	420g	420g	

Manufacturer	Herr		
	High	**Wide**	**Depth** [mm]
Size	66	68.5	21
	Time	**Strike**	**Music**
Weight	320g	320g	

Manufacturer	Herr		
	High	**Wide**	**Depth** [mm]
Size	90	85	25
	Time	**Strike**	**Music**
Weight	1500g	1500g	

Manufacturer	Herr		
	High	**Wide**	**Depth** [mm]
Size	78.5	115	23
	Time	**Strike**	**Music**
Weight	420g	420g	

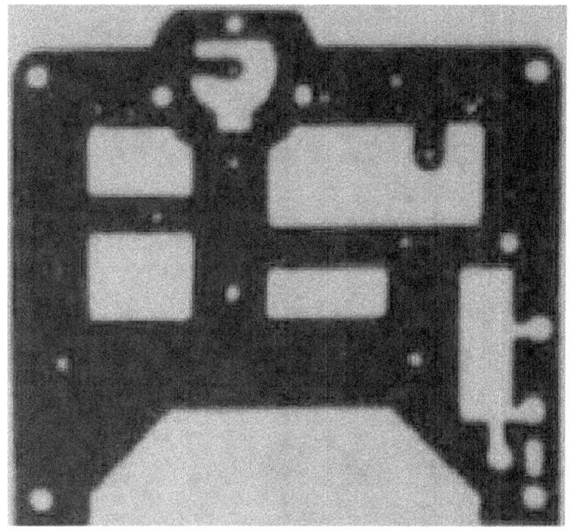

Manufacturer	Baduf 95 215mm		
	High	**Wide**	**Depth** [mm]
Size	79	90	23.5
	Time	**Strike**	**Music**
Weight	420g	420g	420g

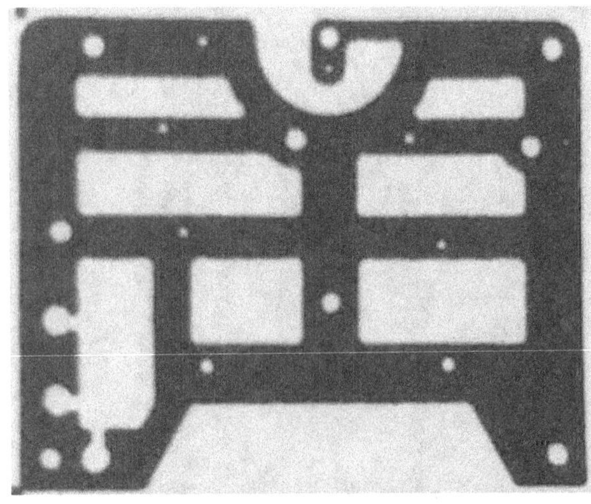

Manufacturer   Baduf 100 215mm

	High	**Wide**	**Depth** [mm]
Size	62	77	23.5
	Time	**Strike**	**Music**
Weight	325g	325g	

Manufacturer   Baduf 105

	High	**Wide**	**Depth** [mm]
Size	84	84	23
	Time	**Strike**	**Music**
Weight	1500g	1500g	

Manufacturer   Schatz 50

	High	**Wide**	**Depth** [mm]
Size	92	84.5	32
	Time	**Strike**	**Music**
Weight	1250g	1250g	

Manufacturer   Schatz 50/8

	High	**Wide**	**Depth** [mm]
Size	92	84.5	32
	Time	**Strike**	**Music**
Weight	1250g	1250g	

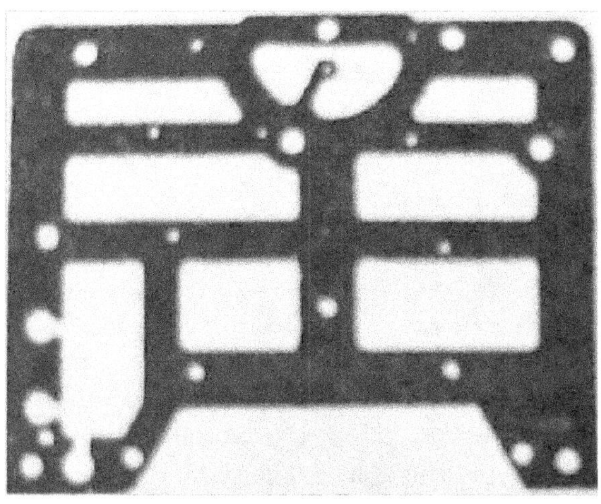

Manufacturer	AMS		
Andreas Mayer in Schönenbach			
	High	**Wide**	**Depth** [mm]
Size	63	77	23.5
	Time	**Strike**	**Music**
Weight	375g	375g	375g

Manufacturer	Imius		
	High	**Wide**	**Depth** [mm]
Size	75	77	23
	Time	**Strike**	**Music**
Weight	420g	420g	

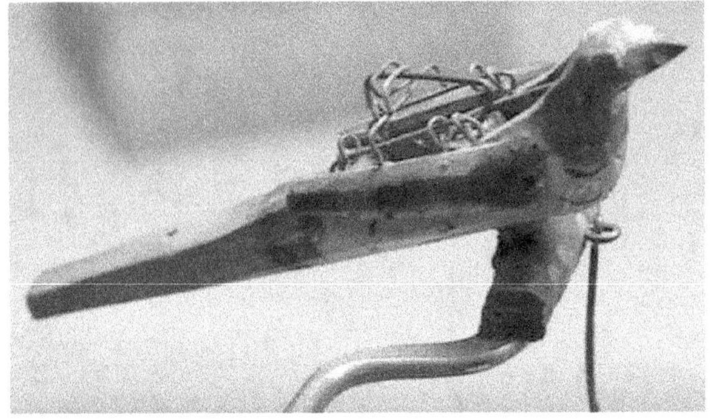

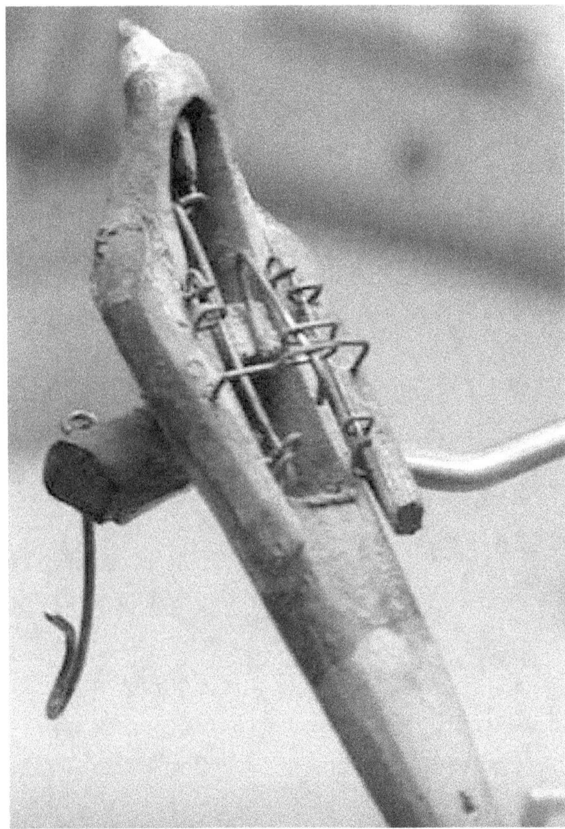

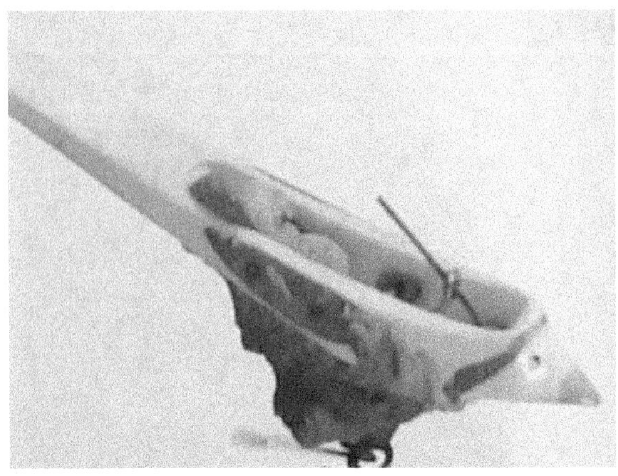

Start with plain old soap and water. If this does not work, I use a little Clorox Cleanup on a Q-tip. The smoke film comes off nice and easy from birds, hands, etc. I have never had any paint loss issues.

Wire benders

Wire benders are almost a must for working on cuckoo clocks. They are available at supply houses, or you can make your own. The longer, the better to allow for bending wires inside the case. One should have a slot cut in the end, the other a slot cut in the side. Use them as a pair.

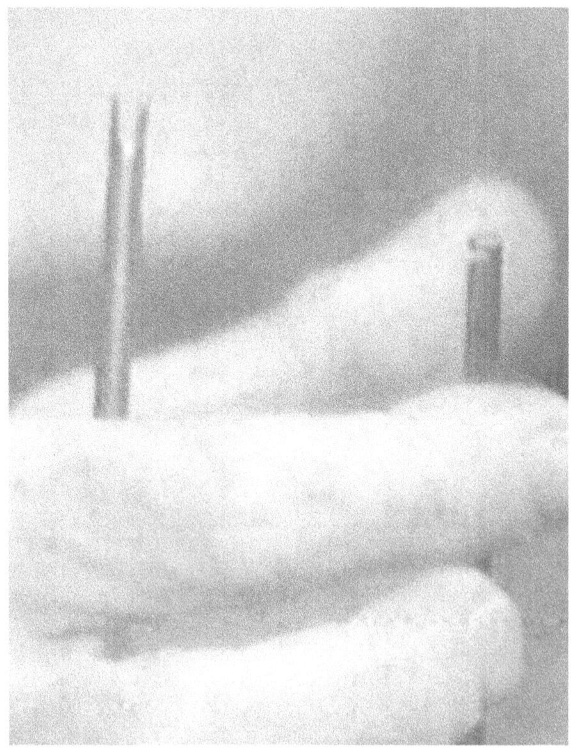

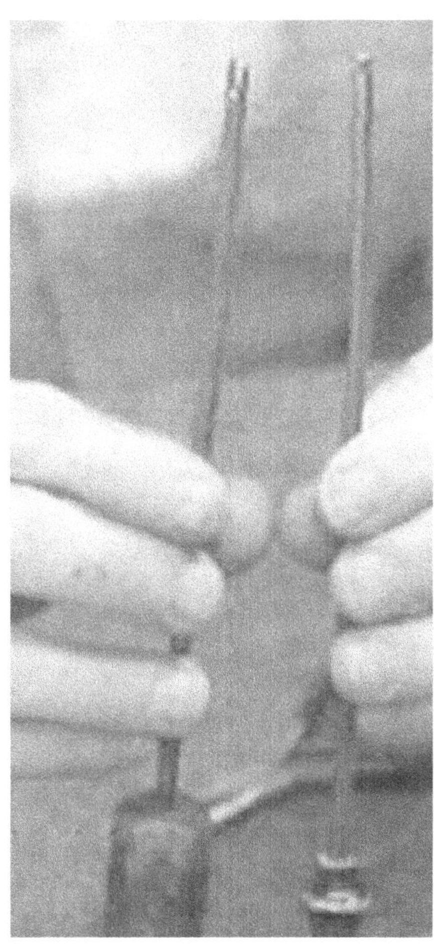

Door hinge wire, hooks, eyes, etc. are available from the supply house, or you can make your own using wire size #70 [0.027"] to #75 [0.020"]. To insert the wire into the wood, cut the end at a sharp angle, and create a pilot hole first using a small drill bit. An eye can be created by wrapping the wire tightly around a 3/32" or 1/8" drill bit shank.

Bird lift wire needs to be reasonably stiff. #70 will be satisfactory. Hammer one end to create a small flat so it will not rotate when pressed into the bellows top.

Adjusting the Gong

The gong hammer must be adjusted, so it is correctly positioned to strike the gong accurately for a pleasing sound.

First, make sure it is not rubbing on the back door.

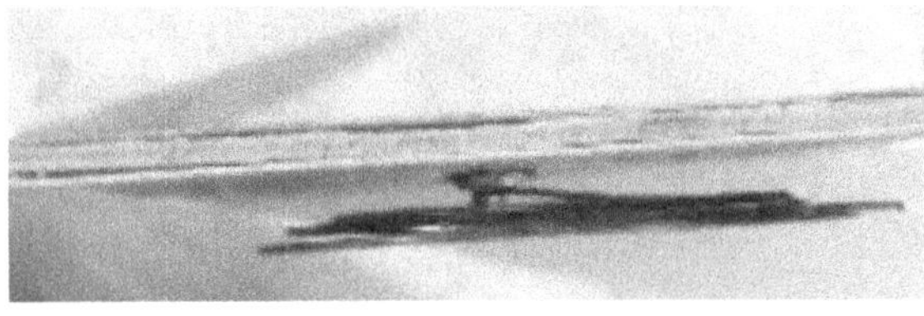

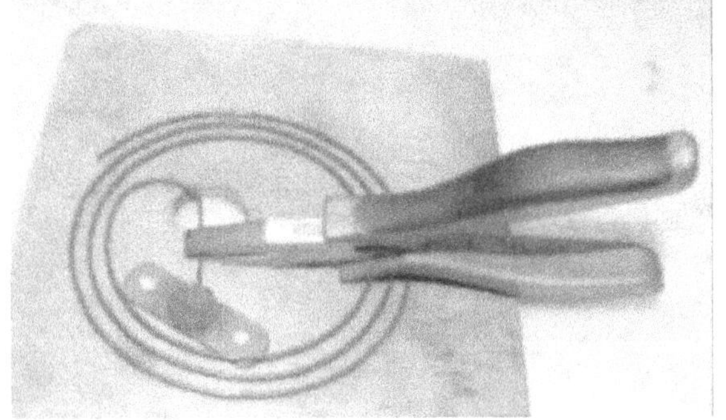

Next, fit the back door in place and observe the hammer through the hole in the back door.

It should look like the following photo at the rear door gong observation hole.

The hammer must sit about 1/64 -1/32 inch above the gong when at rest. If it sits on the gong, it will make an unpleasant, dull thud sound. When striking, it needs to hit the gong and bounce off again, allowing the sound to ring.

If it's not correct, remove the door and bend the hammer wire a little at a time using two wire benders. Keep checking and adjusting until it looks right, but more importantly, it sounds correct.

If there is no observation hole, it is recommended you create one. Drill a small hole [say 1/8"] from the inside where you think the hammer will strike the gong. Then remove the screw that holds the gong and drill a ¾" hole from the outside. Reinstall the going and make the necessary adjustments.

Transport

When transporting a cuckoo clock, especially if shipping, it is best to secure the bellow tops to protect them from damage. Note the two homemade clips connected by red yarn [red yarn will remind you to remove it again].

The clips are made by bending wire around nails in a homemade jig.

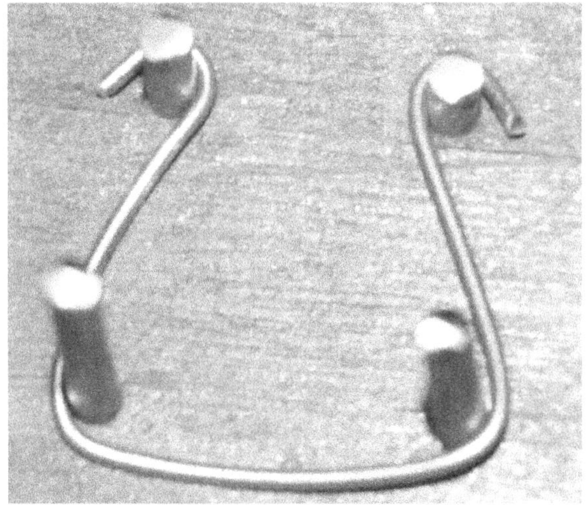

Tie the chains together very close to the bottom of the case, so the chains don't come off their sprockets. Dental floss is suitable for this, or paper clips.

You should also put some paper or something similar between the gong and the back door to stop it clanging during transport.

SECTION TWO

The following is the repair procedure for cuckoo clocks.

Pin & Collet

Look closely at the arbor of your clock on which the minute and hour hands are mounted. Use a magnifying glass to see if a metal pin is passing through the arbor, parallel to the clock dial. If you see one, your clock hands are held by a pin and collet.

Undo the hand nut by holding the minute hand as close to the nut as possible to prevent it from accidentally bending.

Unscrew the hand nut with your free hand and lift off the minute hand, followed by the hour hand. Note that some clocks have a slotted nut instead of a hand nut, which requires a special tool.

Take a pair of needle-nose pliers and pull out the pin. The pin should be tapered, so pull from the fatter end.

Lift off the minute hand, then the collet. Next, lift off the hour hand. On some clocks, the hour hand will have a small clip or screw holding it in place, which you will need to simply remove.

Threaded Hand Nut

Look for a metal nut with a serrated edge screwed onto the minute hand. If you find one, your clock's hands are held with a threaded hand nut.

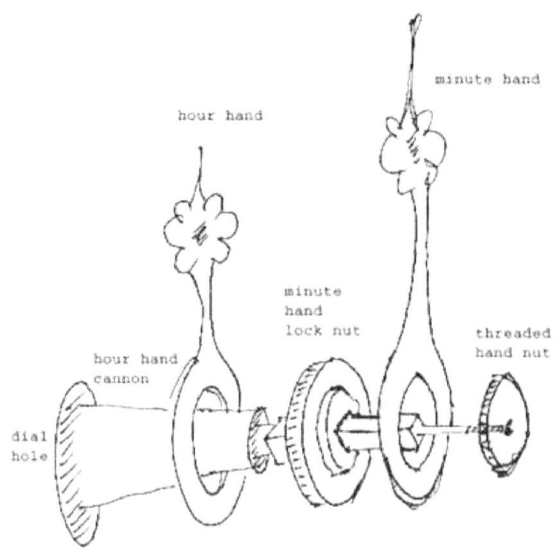

Friction Fit

Look at the arbor of the clock for a pin or hand nut. If neither is present, the clock hands are being held on by friction alone.

Grip the minute hand at the arbor and carefully pull it off.

Grip the hour hand and pull it off. Never try to pry friction fit clock hands off with a screwdriver as they may get damaged or the dial of the clock could get scratched.

Very Dirty Movement

It is possible to clean the old oil and dirt off a movement without dismantling it. It is much preferred it be dismantled, but if you do not want to go to that level, obtain a water-based clock cleaning solution from

www.merritts.com, or

www.ronellclock.com or

www.timesavers.com

Place some clock cleaning solution on a soft cloth. Do not make the fabric too wet. The movement should not be flooded with a cleaning solution. You can make a clock cleaning solution by mixing eight parts ammonia to one part of a commercial liquid cleanser, and one part oil soap. Use the soft cloth to rub off grease and grime that's stuck to easy-to-reach parts of the movement. Do not force the fabric into tight areas, as small pieces might break.

Dab some clock cleaning solution on a cotton swab or Q-tip. Insert into difficult-to-reach parts inside the clock movement. Rub gently to remove grease and grime.

Check the movement's wheels to see if they move freely, by gently manipulating the various parts with your fingers. Place a small amount of clock oil on a soft cloth. Clock oil is a unique product available from retailers. Do not use WD-40 as it may clog the movement. Lubricate only those parts that already have oil. Not all parts of the movement need to be lubricated, but those that do vary from movement to movement. Use the soft cloth to lubricate components that are easily reached. Put some clock oil on a cotton swab to lubricate smaller or hidden parts inside the movement.

Alternatively, soak the whole movement for about 20 minutes in the solution. After it has soaked, run lots of hot water over the movement to rinse off the cleaning solution and then dry the movement thoroughly using a hairdryer or in your kitchen oven. It is very important you get every drop of water dried off. Then proceed to oil the clock.

Regulation or the act of adjusting the rate or speed of a clock is a simple series of repeated steps until the desired effect is achieved. This is accomplished by governing the location of the center of gravity along the length of the pendulum.

While many factors may affect the timekeeping rate of your clock, none will make as much as changes in the ambient temperature of its environment. Any excessive friction from any source can harm the timekeeping ability of the movement. Every moving part must be in good condition and properly lubricated so the gear train can operate as freely as possible. Friction leads to wear, which is your clock's enemy number one.

Once you have observed a change in timekeeping over several days, it is time to begin the regulation procedure. Keep a pad and pen handy for recording notes. Include the starting error, and all adjustments you make as this will significantly assist the process. Remember to use a rate of error that is consistent such as minutes or seconds per 24 hours, and to use the same time source for making all of your comparisons.

Adjusting the pendulum shorter will cause your clock to run faster while lengthening it causes it to run slower or simply put "speedup, slowdown."

The oak leaf is usually held onto the pendulum rod by a friction clip. It is just a matter of sliding the leaf up to make the clock run faster, or down to make the clock run slower. You should not try or expect to correct the error in one session, but rather try to split the difference by half each session, slowly sneaking up on the error without overshooting or see-sawing back and forth.

Only make small adjustments and check the time at the same time each day.

When the clock is getting better at timekeeping, change to making tiny adjustments once per week. Before you know it, the clock will keep great time.

It will not be possible to make the movement's timekeeping perfectly accurate.

If the above information does not get your
clock running, and you want to do some actual
maintenance to your clock, strip it down for a
full cleaning, repair wear, do not despair, there
is plenty more you can do. I will walk you
through it.

 Above is a typical clock movement, and
below is the same movement dismantled.

Clock 'Fun'damentals

A crude clock needs three essential items.

1. Power – spring or weights.
2. Means of regulating the power to a calculated period – an escapement.
3. Means of viewing the results – clock dial and hands.

When you look at a clock movement, you will see a bunch of gears. We call them wheels in the clock world. What do they all do?

In a very simple clock, we have three wheels.

the escapement. We call the wheels T1, T2, and T3. [T stands for Time]

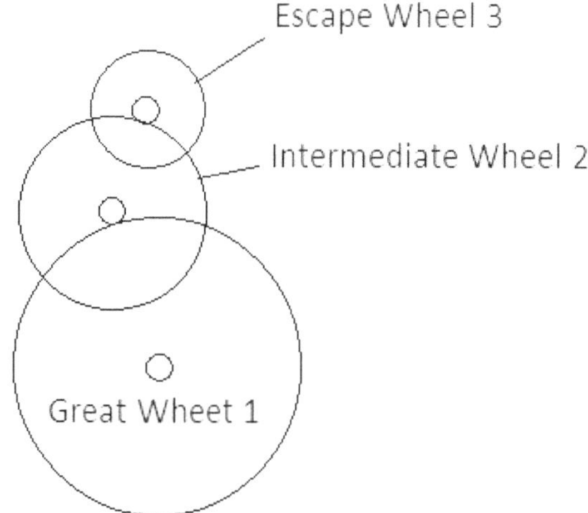

Sidebar A pinion can be cut from solid metal [cut pinion] or made up of steel rods [trundles or pins] in between brass ends caps or shrouds [lantern pinion].

driven by the weights which supply the power to the intermediate wheel which runs the hour hand and drives the escape wheel. The escape wheel has a time regulator called an escapement and pendulum. A typical three-wheel train will run for about a day [actually 30 hours]. The large wheel of the great wheel [the leader] drives the [follower] small wheel [pinion] on the next wheel [intermediate wheel] in the train and so on until you get to

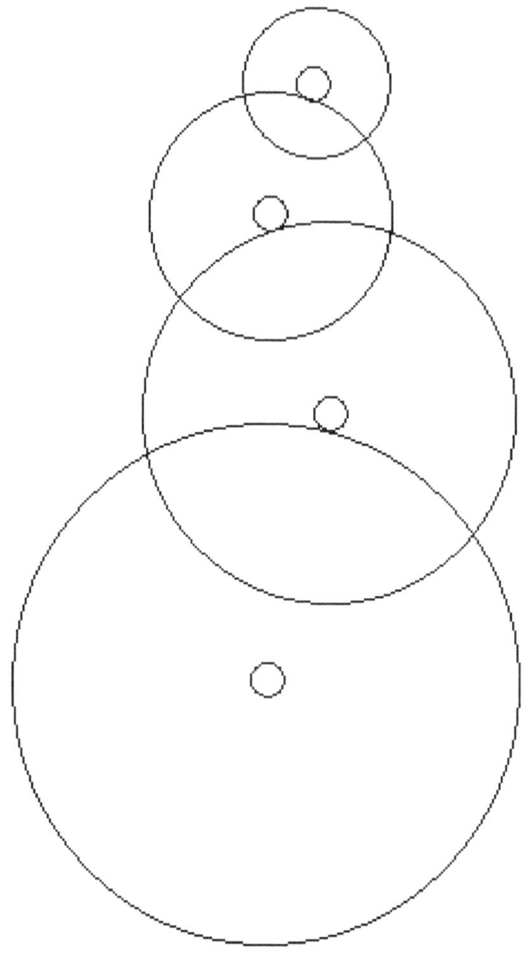

If we add a fourth wheel it will typically run for a week because of the gearing. In this case, we have T1, T2, T3, and T4.

This rule of 3 wheels and 4 wheels, is only used as an example. There are many contradictions to this rule, depending on the teeth ratios.

Clock parts tend to alternate between brass and steel.
A steel pivot goes into a brass plate
A brass wheel teeth act on steel pinions
etc. etc
Why you might ask?

In mechanics, the use of brass to steel is called an ideal combination.
- Brass-steel requires no lubrication and is still wear-resistant.
- Brass steel knows no contact corrosion.

The rule for brass-steel combination is:
The component that will wear out is made of steel. In clocks, therefore, the wheel teeth are made of brass; the pinions are made of steel.

To add striking [cuckooing], we must add a second 'train' to drive that function.

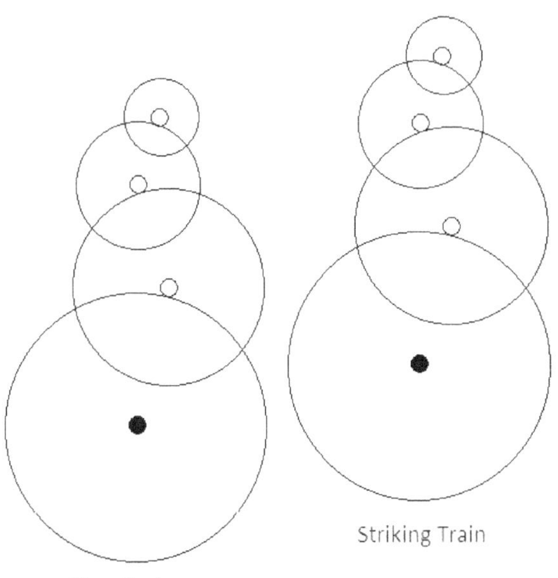

Escapement

I will keep the description of the escapement very basic.

The job of the escapement is to regulate the time. Without it, the wheels would run wildly fast until the spring wound down or the weights hit the floor. The escapement will only allow the escape wheel to 'escape' one tooth at a time with each swing of the pendulum. The design of the pendulum determines how fast each tooth advances. Using calculations of the gearing and the length of the pendulum, the clock is designed to it keep time as we know it.

Some people call the escapement 'verge'. It should be noted that a verge is a specific and very old type of escapement that you are unlikely to come across. I suggest, to be most professional, you do not use the term verge unless the escapement truly is a verge.

The most common types of escapement you will encounter are:

Anchor Escapement

Invented around 1657, the anchor quickly superseded the older and inaccurate verge to become the standard escapement used in pendulum clocks through the 19th century. The anchor is responsible for the long narrow shape of most pendulum clocks, and the development of the longcase or tall case clock [grandfather clock].

The anchor consists of an escape wheel with pointed, backward slanted teeth, and an "anchor"-shaped piece pivoted above it which rocks from side to side, linked to the pendulum. The anchor has slanted pallets on the arms which alternately catch on the teeth of the escape wheel, receiving impulses.

Deadbeat Escapement

Deadbeat escapement showing:
[a] Escape wheel
[b] Pallets
[c] Pendulum crutch.

The Graham or deadbeat escapement was an improvement of the anchor. In the anchor escapement, the swing of the pendulum pushes the escape wheel backward during part of its cycle. This 'recoil' disturbs the motion of the pendulum, causing inaccuracy, and reverses the direction of the gear train, causing a backlash and introducing high loads into the system, leading to friction and wear. The main advantage of the deadbeat is that it eliminated recoil. The teeth point forward.

Graham Dead-Beat Escapement

Recoil Escapement

Note the teeth are pointing in different directions.

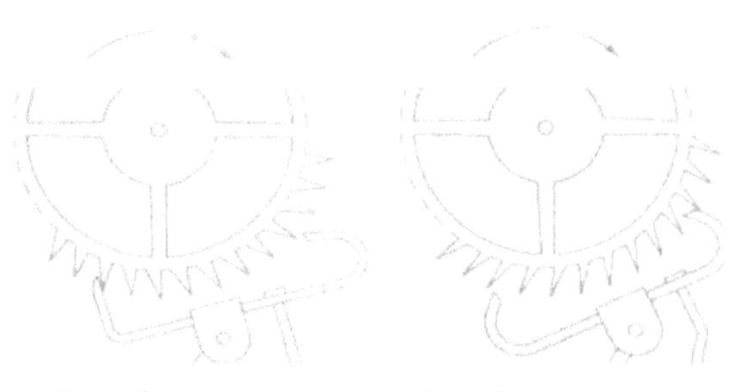

If your clock has stopped, you are sure it is fully wound up, and it is in-beat, there are two fundamental reasons it would stop.

1. Escapement Problem
2. Loss of Power

Escapement Problem

Look very closely at the escapement. If a pallet is hung up on the tip of an escape wheel tooth, mark the tooth with a marking pen and restart the clock. If the same tooth is involved repeatedly, the likelihood is that this tooth is bent, or the tooth that has just left the opposite pallet is bent. To check and correct the fault, see the next section.

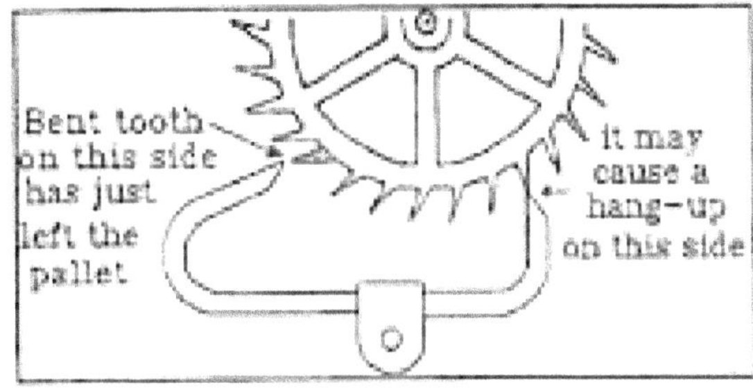

Loss of Power

If neither pallet is touching a tooth when you test its operation, that is, if the pallets are hanging freely between the escape wheel teeth, and if the pallets can be rocked without either one touching a tooth, and it is correctly adjusted as above, then the clock has stopped because there is little or no power transmitted to the escapement.

The Enemy

A clock is designed with approximately 10% additional power than is needed to run in perfect condition. This is to allow for a small amount of wear, and oils in less than perfect condition.

The enemy of a clock is friction. Clock oil gets 'gummy' or congealed because it tends to absorb the dust in the air. This gum will cause additional friction and stop the clock. The only way to remove the old gummy oil is to take the movement apart. I will explain this later.

A second problem is worse. The oil may have evaporated or run out, leaving the pivots to run dry, metal grinding on metal. The pivot connected to the wheel arbor is usually made of steel. The front and back movement plates that support the wheel/pivot are usually made of brass. You will note that brass is a softer metal than steel, so the movement plate tends to wear the most. This is by design, so the plates will wear and protect the pivot. The plates are easier to repair than replacing pivots.

This is an excellent example of why we dismantle a clock to service it. This damage was not visible without disassembly.

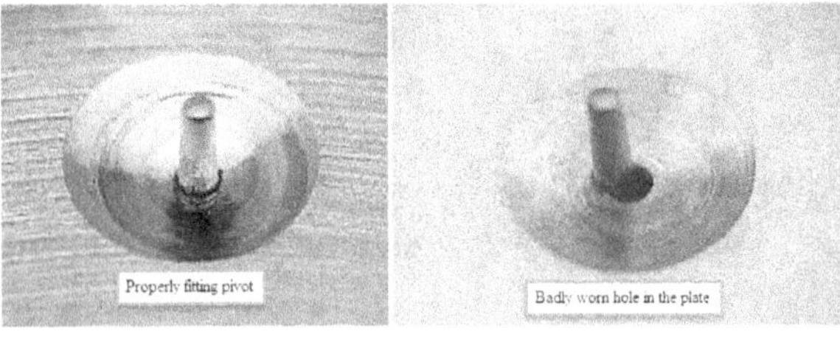

The pivot may also have some wear.

Imagine rubbing two pieces of sandpaper across each other. It will be hard due to the friction of the rough surfaces.

Now, imagine sliding two wet pieces of glass past each other. They will glide effortlessly. That is the effect we are looking for. See later for the procedure to create this.

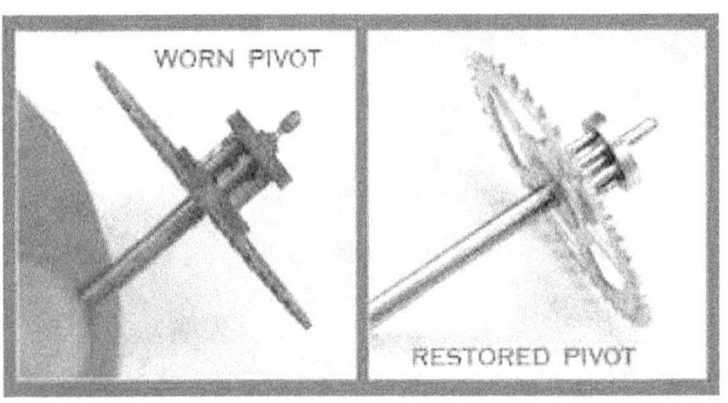

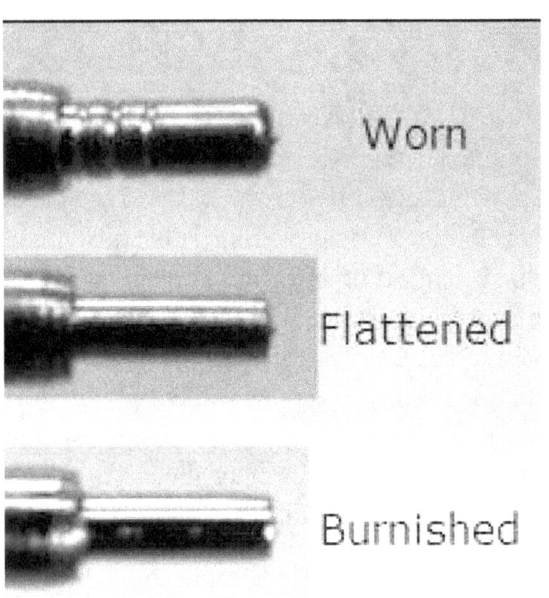

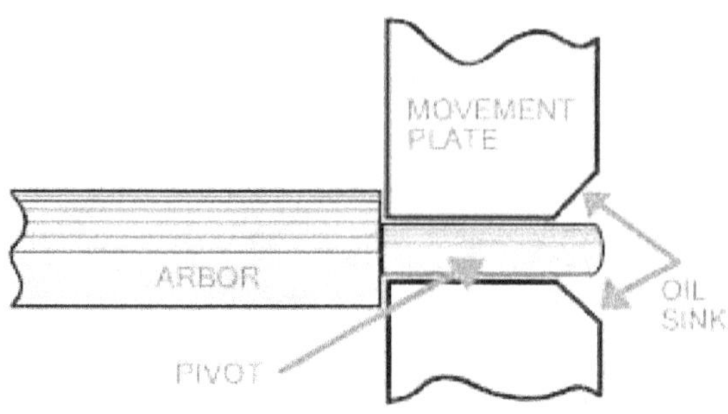

Escapement Pallet Wear

It is also essential to polish the impulse faces of the escapement. I have found, if you only do one thing to a clock, polishing the pallet faces will have the most improvement. Make sure you don't change any angles of the pallet faces.

The wear must be ground out and then polished. This is accomplished with a series of emery boards of different grits in a way that removes the least amount of metal and maintains the original angles. If too much metal is removed, or the angles are changed, the pallets must be reshaped or bent for them to be adjusted accurately once they are put back in the clock movement.

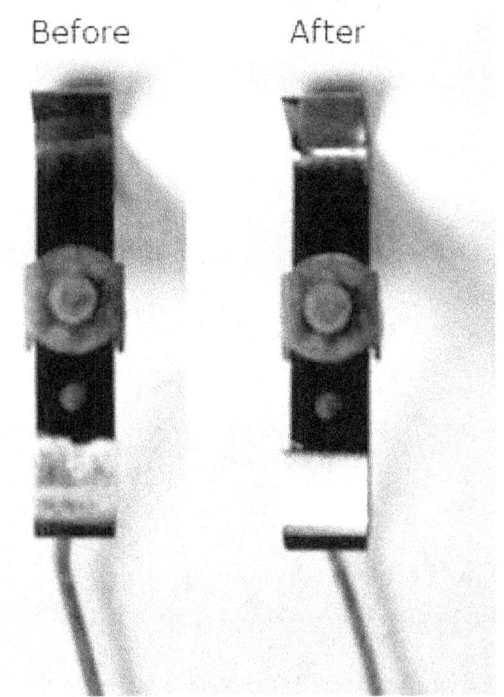

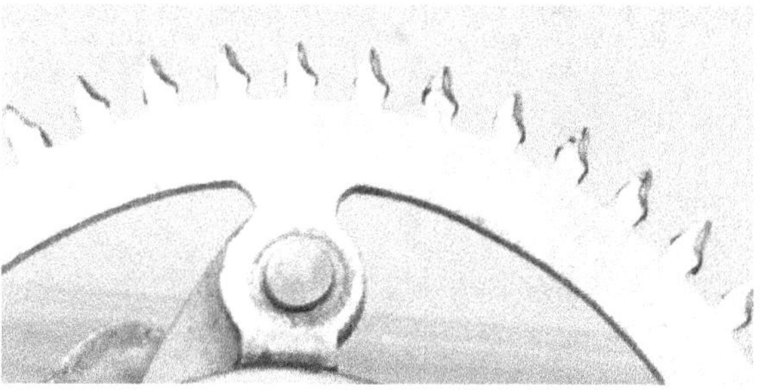

This wheel has serious wear to the teeth and will need to be sent out for a replacement wheel.

To track down problems, try a high-speed test by removing the escapement pallets and letting the movement run fast. Watch very closely. It will often reveal bent or worn pivots, warped wheels, or teeth meshing problems. Watch for it slowing down and speeding up.

Beginners Clock Repair Tool Kit for $32
[2021]

Getting started in clock repair can be intimidating, especially when you consider the tools that many clock repair people have.

I have created a list of tools that a beginner can get by with and do a lot of the work we do.

The fact is, 90% of what we do is performed with 10% of our tools. The basic idea is this list is well thought out, inexpensive, and will get someone started without breaking the bank or putting you off getting started.

The First Set of tools most people will already have [or should have] around the house:

Needle nose pliers
Small square nose pliers with wire cutters
Screwdrivers slotted medium 1/4" tip
Screwdrivers slotted small 1/8" tip
Wet & dry emery paper 500, 1000, 1500 & 2500 grit [available from auto parts store]
Cordless drill or Dremel [to act as a lathe]
Popsicle sticks or tongue depressors
Toothpicks
Tweezers fine and stout
Hammer small
Pocket knife
Empty containers and zip-lock bags for loose parts
Notebook and pencil
Small flashlight

Use a small fishing tackle box or shoebox to keep your clock tools together.

The Second Set will likely need to be purchased from a specialty house like:
Merrits www.merritts.com or
Timesavers www.timesavers.com.
Numbers are the Timesavers part number

Cleaning concentrate pint *16025*	$ 9
Clock oil *13839*	$ 2
3 Movement assembly posts *13408*	$18
Loupe 3x, 5x *15872 & 18213*	$ 3
TOTAL	**$32**

The Third Set I call a "Bushing Kit" will be needed if you want to repair worn bushings.

Bushings 2 sets [Bergeon #7 & #9] *18507 & 18509*	$11
Reamer [Bergeon #2.47] *18470*	$28
Handle for reamers *22910*	$15
Cutting Broach set .031"-.090" *17882*	$14
Smoothing Broaches .0314 & .0374 *23215 & 23217*	$ 9
TOTAL	**$77**

Note: I suggest Bergeon bushings. K&D is another brand that is just as good, but they are not interchangeable so stick to one or the other.

Then we start getting into the more advanced and specialized tools, which can be purchased one at a time as needed.

Cleaning Solution

You can buy a readymade concentrate from the parts house [which is what I recommend] or you can make your own at home using the following recipe:

4 oz. oleic acid [Use Murphy's Oil Soap]

8 oz. Acetone

12 oz. 26% Ammonium Hydroxide

1 Gallon Water

Let soak for 5 minutes then scrub the parts with an old toothbrush.

Do not use laundry or dish detergent as a substitute for oleic acid. The detergent will pit, darken the brass in a variegated form, and will generally ruin the finish on brass clock parts.

Clock Oil

I recommend Mobil 1 – 5W-30 Its formula and viscosity are perfect for clocks.

Shhhh don't tell them, they will put the price up.

Movement Assembly Posts

You need these so that you can disassemble the movement. The movement should be disassembled horizontally. There are usually several items protruding from the plate, so it will not sit flat on the table. The posts raise the movement clear of the protruding items.

You can, of course, cut some holes in a small cardboard box and set the movement on that.

A fellow NAWCC member uses a toilet roll to support his movement – clock movement that is.

Check out my homemade lathe using a Dremel. I use it for quick pivot polishing, and it is very portable and does not take up much space. Note, I have added the three-jaw chuck to my setup.

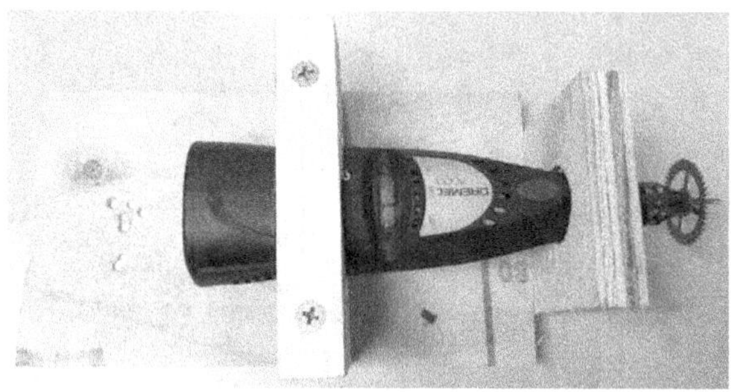

I am not suggesting you never buy clock tools. The fact is many people enjoy buying old clock tools at marts and specialty tools from the supply houses as much as collecting the clocks they are used on. I own some tools I have never used, and some I don't even know what they do!

Magnification

There are times when you need to see better than your normal vision, be it by the naked eye or with standard prescription glasses. If you use reading glasses, of course, you should use them for routine work. When you need extra help, we have several choices.

First, we need to define some terms.

Magnification – how many times bigger the object is seen.

Focal length – The distance from the lens to the object that is in focus. Typically, the stronger the magnification, the closer you need to be to your work. Some lenses have longer focal lengths than others, and the longer focal

Magnifiation for typical Reading Glasses Diopters	
Diopter	Magnification
1	1.25
1.5	1.375
2	1.5
2.5	1.625
3	1.75
4	2

length can be easier to work with, especially for extended periods. There are times when looking at an object inside a movement, you will not be able to get close enough to get it in focus if you have a short focal length.

Field of vision – How large an area is in focus at any given time.

Try stronger reading glasses. If you normally use say 1.5 diopter glasses, consider having some stronger bench glasses. Try the strongest

you can find. Lope 2 ½ x, 5 x &/or Optivisor 2 ½ x with a focal length of eight 8 inches.

I keep a strong pair of dime-store reading glasses on my bench. I usually use 1.5 diopters, but for close-up work, I find 4.0 or even 5.0 diopters work great and are easier to wear than a loupe.

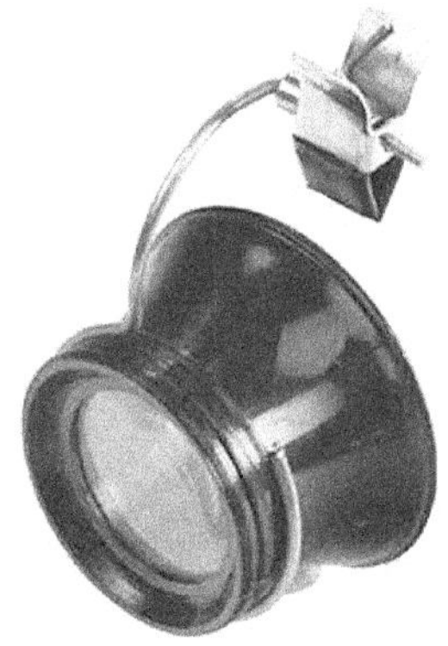

Loupes have long been favored for detail clockwork. They usually don't specify the focal length when for sale. You will likely accumulate a variety that works for various types of work, and favor one that works best for you. Ideally, buy at a mart where you can try them out before buying. Loupes can be held in the eye, clipped to glasses or on a wire around the head.

A more recent choice is the Optivisor. They come in various magnifications and often have a longer focal length. They provide magnification to both eyes, and this also helps with judging distance, especially working with tools. They are comfortable to wear and can even include a light, but the light does make it heavier.

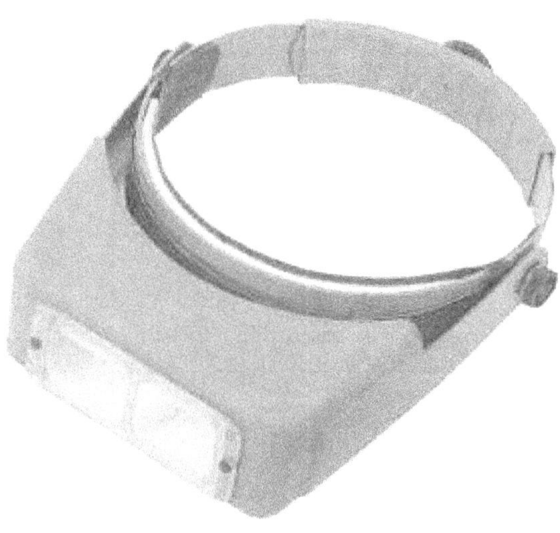

More recently, the surgeon's loupe is becoming popular, but they can be costly. They usually have a longer focal length and a good field of vision.

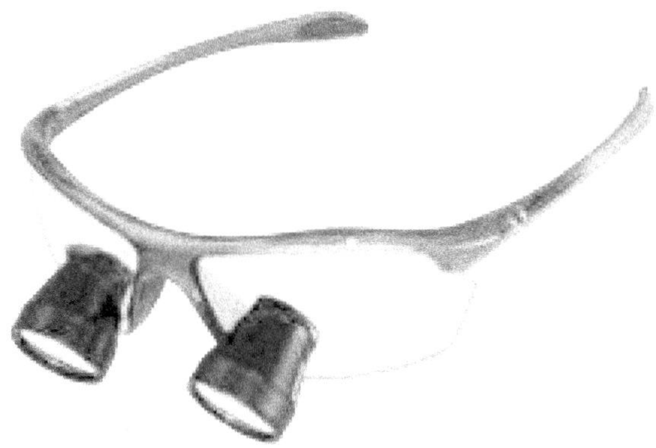

The ultimate in magnification is the microscope. This is most often used at a fixed workstation like over a lathe.

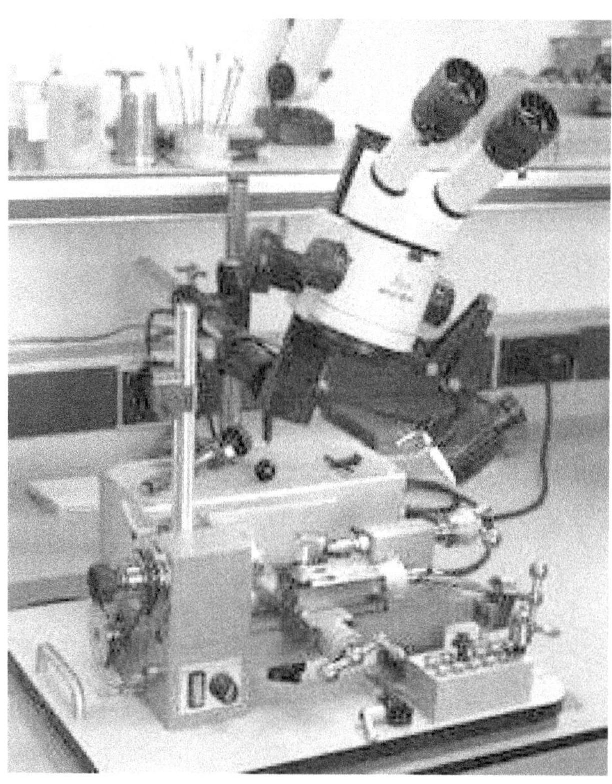

A less expensive microscope is the USB digital microscope. They are very inexpensive, under $40, and can magnify up to 1/600. You plug it into a laptop and view the image on your laptop screen.

This device will change your life and take your work to a whole new level.

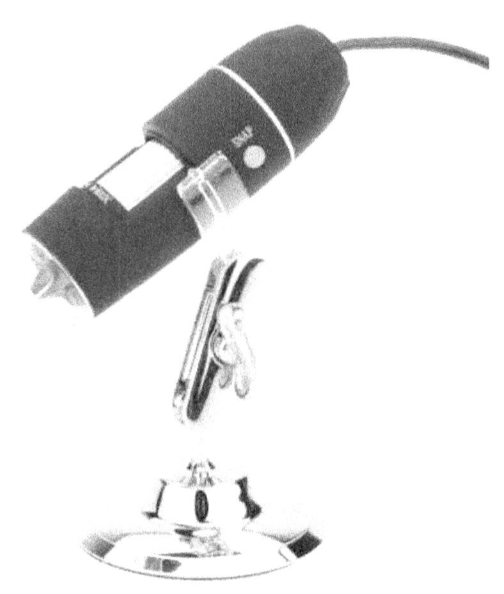

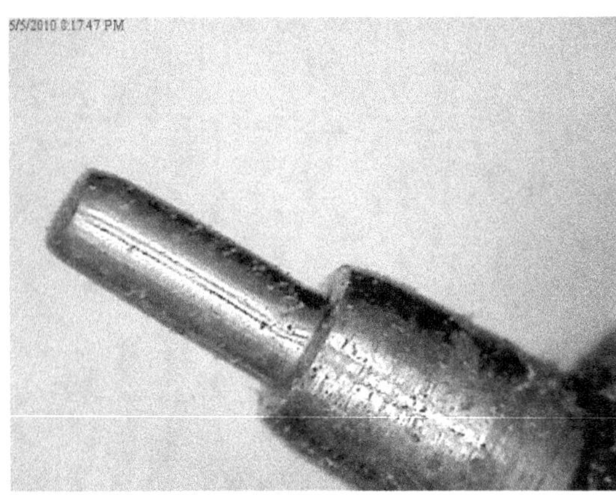

With the invention of the quartz movement, professional, full-time clock and watch repairers have almost become extinct, leaving a plethora of old and fascinating tools to harvest.

Tweezers

Tweezers come in all kinds of shapes and sizes. Long, medium, short, stout, weak, wide, fine tip, straight, dog-leg, cheap, steel, brass, and very expensive.

To start with, you can use household tweezers, but you will soon find they are not the best for our work.

For clockwork, consider Carbon Steel #3 *TimeSavers Item #: 33254*

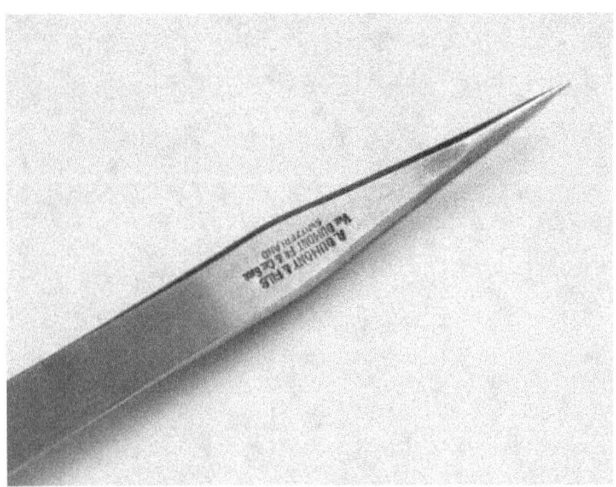

This is what I do to prepare my general-purpose tweezers. When worn, I will take 320 grit paper and with slight tension on the tweezers, pull the paper out towards the left,

then repeat pulling towards the right. Turn paper upside-down and repeat for the opposing tweezer tip. This is to give the tips "bite".

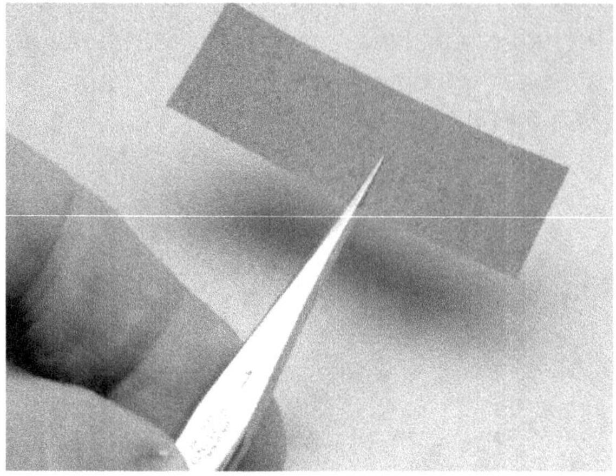

It takes a little practice to get hold of and keep hold of small parts even with good tweezers. You will often find that the part squirts out of the tweezers, across the room, never to be seen again. Consider adding a spot of Museum Wax. It will keep small items tamed.

Medical hemostats can be very handy also. They clamp onto the part. Great for inserting taper pins.

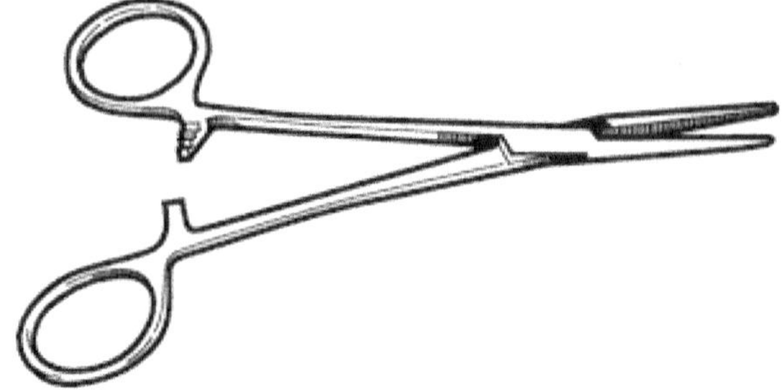

A More Comprehensive Tool Set

The following is a realistic goal to aim for

•An 8mm lathe, along with collets, a Jacobs chuck, and a 3-jaw chuck.
•A Dremel tool
•An Ollie Baker spring winder
•A bunch of mainspring clamps
•A couple of small bench vises
•A set of assembly clamps [assembly legs]
•A couple of small butane torches
•A soldering gun
•A 1" micrometer
•A dial caliper and a digital caliper
•Several homemade movement stands
•A beat amplifier
•The usual hand tools [pliers, screwdrivers, files, broaches, pin vises, saw, pivot locators, wire benders, letdown handle, drill bits, gravers, tweezers, anvil blocks, clamps, levels, and so on.]
•Various Dremel accessories.
•A small ultrasonic cleaner
•Adjustable swing-arm lights over the bench

Tools Conclusion

All I suggest is you get your feet wet first. I read a beginner book recently that contained 41 pages on tools. It is enough to put anybody off considering tinkering with clocks. I have amassed many tools over the years, some of which I have made myself and cherish. My clock shop [more of a nook] is always a fun place to show off to visiting friends and guests who are fascinated.

By joining a local clock club, you will develop friendships and contacts with experienced members that will likely work with you and allow you to use their specialized tools as needed.

Tempus Vitam Regit
Time Rules Life

Trademark of the NAWCC

The first thing we must do is inspect the movement for obvious defects. Use this checklist after you have removed the movement from the case and let down the mainspring.

- Look at the condition of the oil [gummy, dry, over oiling]
- Check the clickwork for wear
- Note any defects in the suspension spring
- Closely observe the action of the escapement with a loupe
- Make sure all the teeth of the escape wheel are correctly shaped
- Note any missing or damaged teeth
- Check for wear in the escapement pallets
- Make sure all wheels have drop [endshake]
- Check the pivot holes for wear
- Observe the mesh of all wheels to pinions
- Observe the condition of the mainspring [if visible]
- Create diagrams and photos of the movement

Dismantle the movement

- Inspect the pivots for wear

The following checklist will allow you to work efficiently without missing any steps. Perform the work n this order.

Repair Checklist

- ☐ Remove the movement from its case
- ☐ Make diagrams, notes and photos
- ☐ Contain the mainsprings with C clamps
- ☐ Dismantle the movement
- ☐ Remove the mainsprings from their arbors
- ☐ Clean all the parts in cleaning solution
- ☐ Polish ALL pivots
- ☐ Peg out ALL pivot holes
- ☐ Bush pivot holes as needed
- ☐ Test each wheel between the plates individually
- ☐ Final cleaning of the parts
- ☐ Put the movement back together
- ☐ Remove the spring C clamps
- ☐ Oil the movement
- ☐ Test the movement on the test stand
- ☐ Reinstall the movement in its case

To clean out the old gummy oil and to repair the worn pivot and pivot hole, we must take the movement apart. No whining, get it done. We need to perform our work using the surgeon's rule, "Do No Harm."

When taking off the pendulum, it is best to mark where it sits on the rating screw. Scribe a line across the top of the bob, on the pendulum rod.   Assuming it was well regulated before you started work, this will save much time in adjusting the clock when you put it back together. Alternatively, place a piece of masking tape around the rating nut so it will not get changed.

If the clock has weights, remove the weights BEFORE you remove the pendulum.

Dismantling the Movement

I strongly recommend you first take apart a junk clock that has little value and no sentimental attachment. The last thing you want to do is damage a family heirloom or an expensive Vienna Regulator. Ideally, start with a time-only movement, then move on to a typical American time and strike mantel clock.

Before you start to take anything apart, you must document the entire movement, step by step. Take good digital photos of the front, sides, and back of the movement [not the case]. Make sure the pictures are sharp, in-focus, and all parts can be seen. Also, make a diagram of the front, sides, and back.

Do not skip this step.

Take your time and make it as accurate as possible. Note each wheel and if the pinion is on top [above the wheel] as setting on the bench, or the bottom [below the wheel] of the wheel PU or PD. Note the direction of the mainsprings.

This will not only help when putting the movement back together, but it will also help you understand the various parts of the movement. The springs and any barrels may look alike but do not get them mixed up. Keep the going and striking parts separate and marked.

If the movement has a striking train, make sure the strike is in the 'lock' position [just after completing striking] and note the position of all pins located on wheels or other places, and any cams, levers, and a rack or cam wheel. When you put it back together again, these all need to be in the same position. Note the name of each wheel [Great wheel, intermediate wheel, hour wheel, escape wheel, etc] and the wheel number – time side is T1, T2, T3, etc with the largest wheel being T1. On the striking side label them S1, S2, etc. [S is for Striking]

The Diagram

Many new students taking their first movement apart, are concerned they will not be able to put it back together. Others just jump right in without any study of the movement or documentation.

The best insurance you will successfully get a clock movement back together and run is to document the movement correctly. Slow and steady is faster. Having said that, I have seen some pretty sad diagrams that have insufficient information, and others that try to be a work of art, detailing all kinds of irrelevant details.

For this reason, I will give examples of good and detailed diagrams that do not need an artist's skill and has everything you need without any unnecessary clutter.

I will use the following two train movement with a count wheel, as an example.

Sometimes the diagrams can start to get so busy it is hard to read. It is a good idea to create several diagrams, each with certain items you want to note.

Use a pencil with an eraser so you can make adjustments.

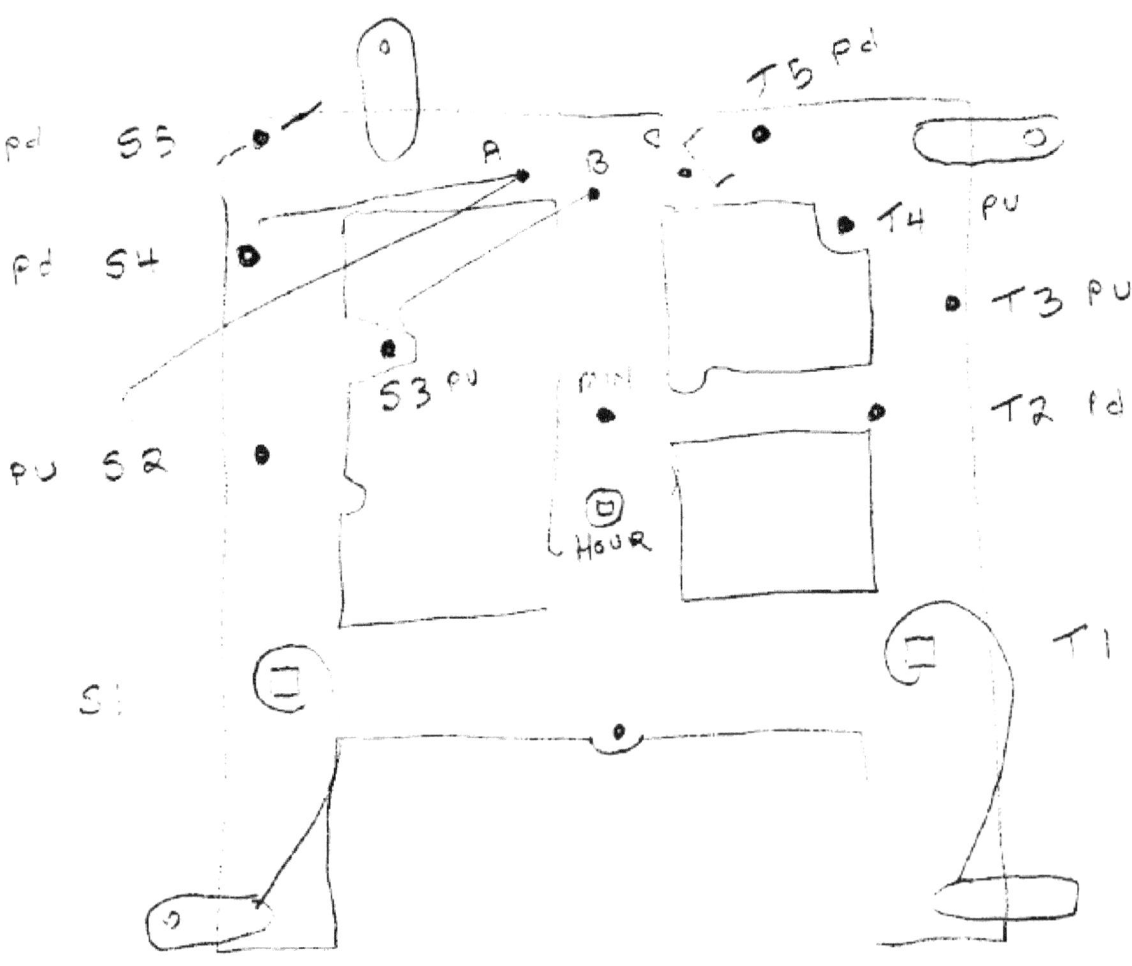

Next, make stick diagrams of each part. Orientate the parts in the position they belong. The vertical line is the arbor. The horizontal LINE is the wheel. The square is the pinion.

Use whatever symbols you like as long as it makes sense to you.

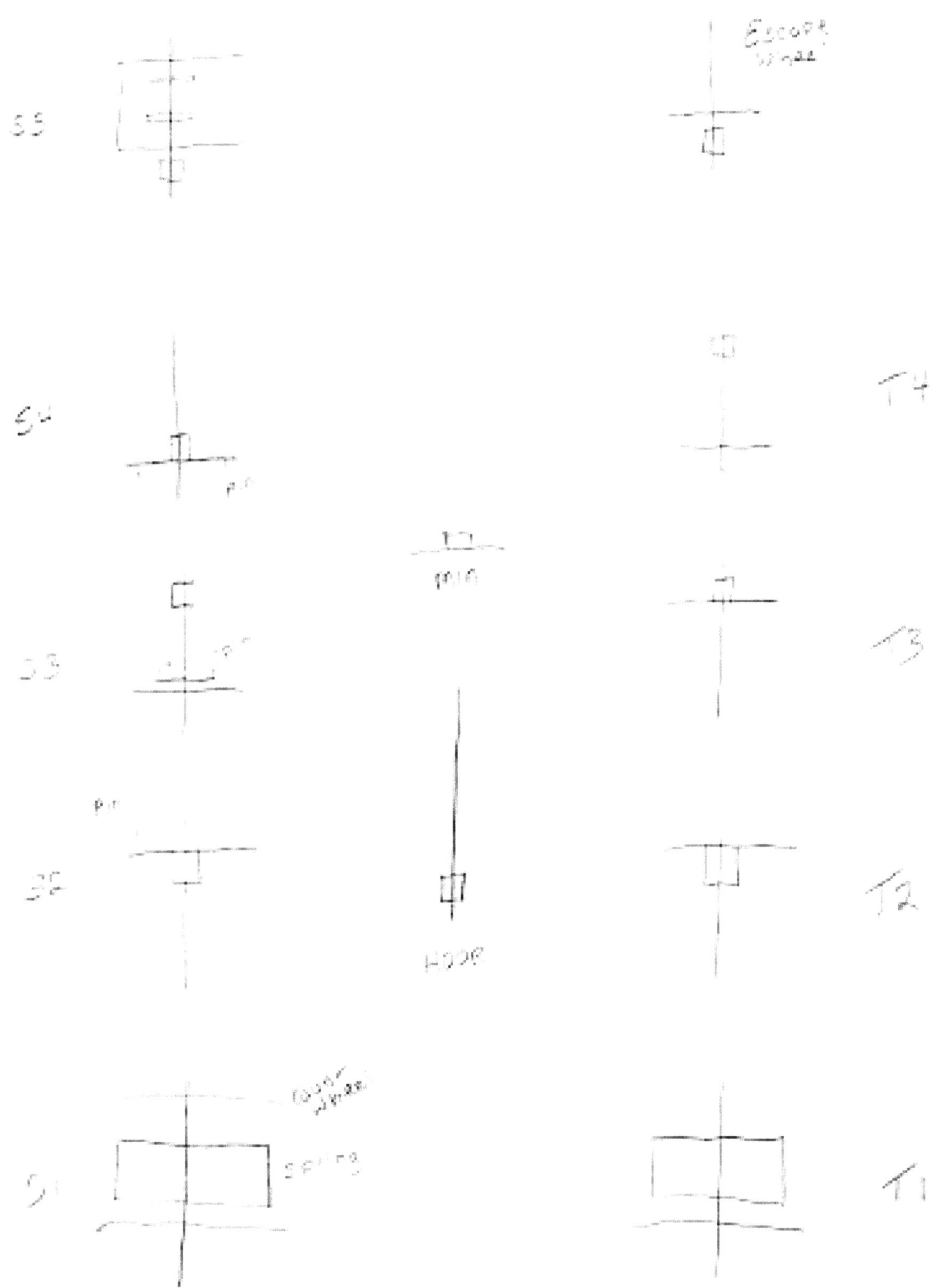

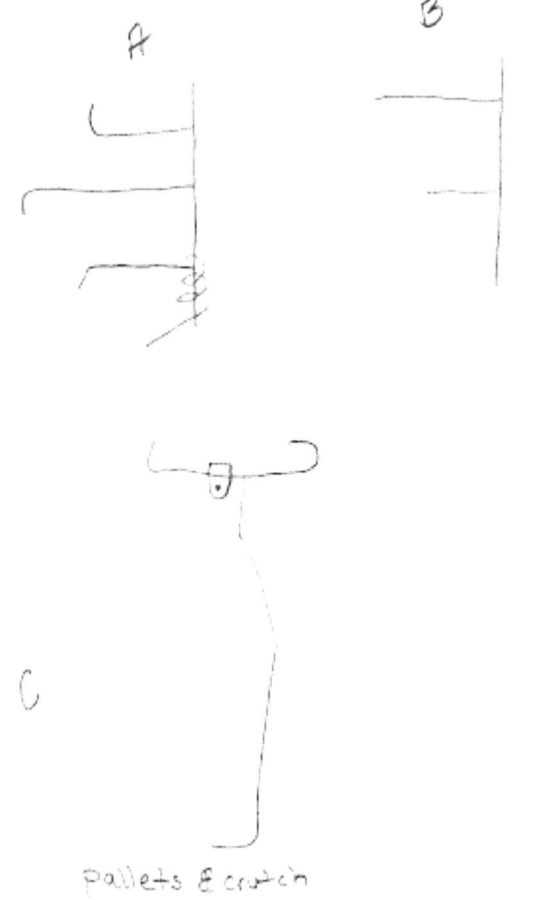

On your diagram, make notes of spring locations, pin location, and any damage you need to repair like:

- worn pivot hole needs bushing
- bent pivot
- worn pinion trundle, etc

As you get more experienced, the stick diagrams are not essential, but it is nice to always do it and keep them in a file in case you come across a similar movement later.

The stick diagrams are excellent for understanding all the parts.

Always keep records of your repairs i.e. where bushings are made, type of oil used, etc.

Descriptions

I will first describe the two trains so that you can identify each wheel.

Strike Train

I will start with the strike train because each wheel can be identified relatively easily [except the great wheel anyway].

S1 is the great wheel that contains the mainspring or the drum that houses the line or chain for the weight. It does not have a pinion but does have a winding click.

S2 [in this clock] has two pinions. One to drive S3 and one to drive the count wheel.

S3 has a cam attached to it.

S4 is the warn wheel, has the warn pin on it.

S5 is the fly that controls the speed of the strike train.

Time Train

After identifying the strike train, the remaining time train can most often be identified in size order. The largest being the great wheel, and the last wheel being the escape wheel with sharp teeth.

T1 First or Great wheel - is attached and ratcheted to the mainspring, or cable, barrel. The ratchet allows the mainspring or cable barrel to be wound without turning the wheel. The ratchet is called "the click". The first wheel turns the pinion of the Center wheel.

T2 Center or second wheel - which turns once per hour. Its pinion is powered by the teeth of the mainspring barrel in spring-driven clocks, and by the weight pulley in weight-driven clocks. Its arbor projects through a hole in the dial and drives, via a friction coupling, the cannon pinion, which carries the minute hand. It also drives the pinion of the third wheel.

T3 The third wheel - drives the pinion of the fourth wheel.

T4 Fourth wheel - This turns once per minute. The fourth wheel also turns the escape wheel pinion.

T5 Escape wheel - This wheel is released [escapes] one tooth at a time by the escapement, with each swing of the pendulum. The escape wheel keeps the pendulum swinging by giving it a small push each time it moves forward.

There are a couple more wheels for the motion works. The hour wheel has a very distinctive pipe that holds the hour hand. The hour pipe slides over the minute arbor. The minute arbor has a long arbor with a square end for the minute hand and the minute wheel, which is the only wheel with a cut pinion [not a lantern pinion].

The great wheels may well look identical, so it is best to scratch an *S* or a *T* on each wheel. On your diagram, make sure you indicate which direction the spring travels and where it attaches [usually to a post].

Levers

The most often place my students seem to neglect in the diagram and cause the most frustration on reassembly is the levers. Knowing how they fit between the wheels is invaluable. I suggest you spend more time on the levers in your diagram than anything else.

Wire Springs

There are likely several wire springs in your movement. These springs ensure the levers return to the ready position when not operating. Note the location, what it is tensioning, and how the spring is anchored to the frame.

Dismantling - Continued

Scrutinize the movement from the front and the back. Look at each pivot with a loupe or magnifying glass to see if there is any wear / elongated pivot holes. If wear is found, note them on your diagram, including the direction of the wear.

Sometimes you come across pivot holes with a double recess.

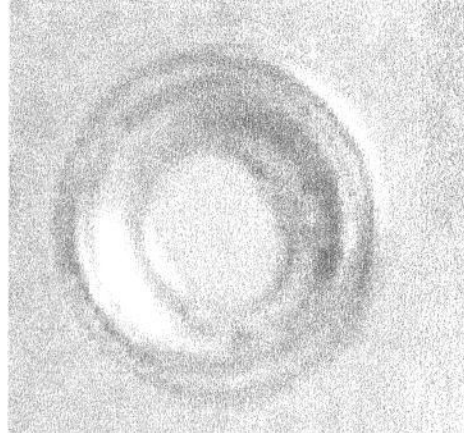

This is likely an effort by the original maker to work harden the pivot holes. This type rarely needs bushing.

Check 'endshake.' Endshake is a small amount of movement between the plates by each wheel. If a wheel were tight between the plates, it would add a lot of friction, so make sure the wheel will move up and down very slightly between the plates. Ideally, the endshake should be around 0.010inch. The fact is it can be more than this as long as the wheel does not fall out, the teeth all mesh correctly, and any striking pins still do their job.

Hold the movement horizontal, ie with the front plate up [with all the power from the mainspring clamped]. Keeping the movement horizontal, view each wheel to see if they have all dropped down onto the backplate. Then rotate the movement 180 degrees with the backplate up. Check if each wheel has dropped down to the front plate. Any that did not drop on their own have a problem. The great wheel needs very little endshake.

Take photos

If you photograph the movement from every angle, you will end up doing handstands and contortions trying to figure out where all those parts go when you get to the rebuilding stage. Photograph from the angle you will be rebuilding.

Clock movements are held together with either nuts or tapered pins, on the ends of the posts. Usually one in each corner. Remove the nuts or tapered pins and keep them safe.

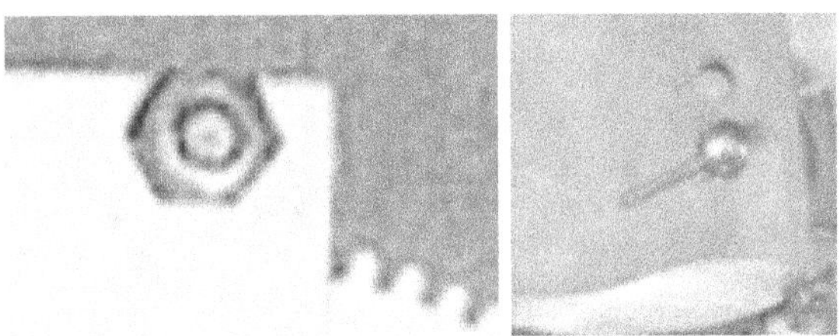

Remove the top plate

With the movement horizontal, very slowly remove the upper plate in a way that all the internal wheels and components stay in position. Take another photo inside with the top plate removed, and make another detailed diagram. Make sure you include any levers in your diagram.

Items screwed to the front or backplates don't always need to be removed. Do not remove them at this time unless it is holding the front and back plates together.

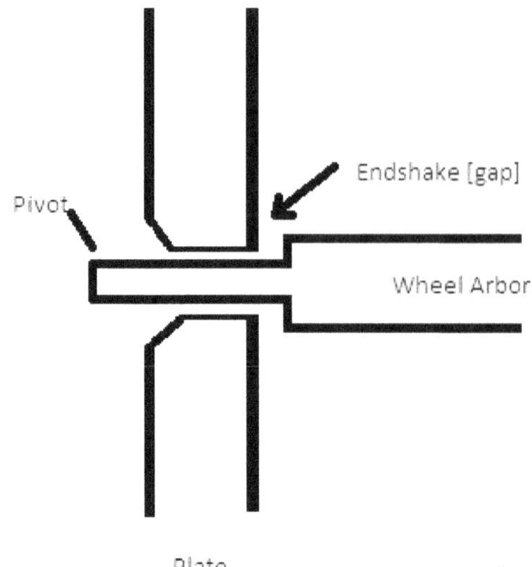

As you dismantle the parts, place them in a container, otherwise, "you may just lose track of time." String each train of wheels together in order on a wire. You can hang the wire over the edge of the cleaning container.

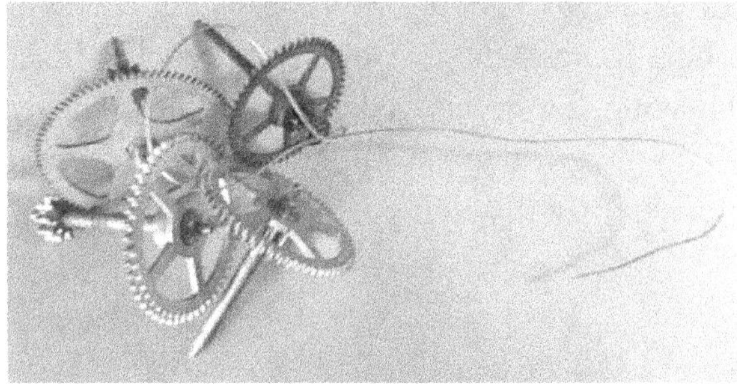

Sometimes you end up with a wheel that is press fit on the outside of the plate.

To remove them, reassemble the two plates so that the corresponding arbors aren't stressed sideways.

If you have a hand-puller, they will sometimes be helpful with removing it. If it is too close to the plate, you'll need something thin and strong to work under it. Ideally, you'll want to use two such tools or blades working 180 degrees apart from one another so that you don't bend or break the pivots. Small screwdrivers can work.

You might want to put a little masking tape on the plates or slide a business card, etc. under the pallet wheel to prevent damage or marring of the brass plate. You may not have to twist the screwdriver [or whatever] at all. You may be able to just use it as a wedge to lift the part off of the pivot/arbor. Use whatever pair of tools you have available which can fit under the part and wedge it up. Work slowly and carefully to lift the part straight up. Modified paint-can opening tools can come in handy in some cases, but if you come across a couple, save them. By grinding the tips, so they are thinner, two can be very useful in safely prying parts like this off their mounting.

If you don't need to remove the hour gear, you may wish to leave it in place. If you want to work on the pivots, and bushing pivot/hole, it will need to be safely removed. It may even come off easy.

Don't use a lot of force. Just enough to get things sliding and then ease up as the part comes loose.

The cleaning solution can be bought from specialty parts houses or made at home using the following recipe:
4 oz. oleic acid
8 oz. Acetone
12 oz. 26% Ammonium Hydroxide
1 Gallon Water

I have always been disappointed with the homemade solution and do not recommend it.

Let soak for 5 minutes then scrub the parts with an old toothbrush.

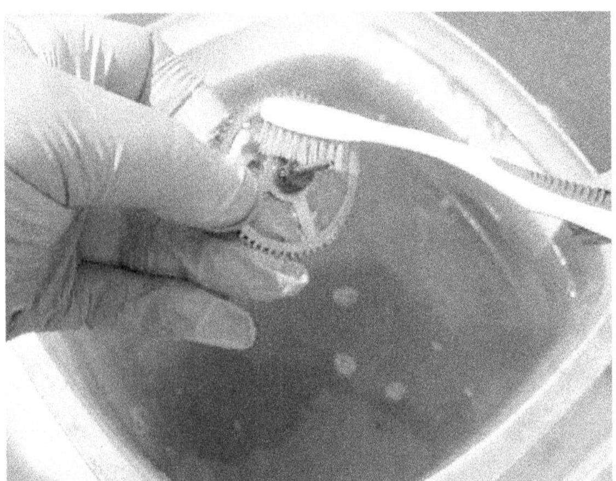

My experience is this formula does a poor job. The commercial clock cleaning solutions are designed specifically for cleaning brass, generally do not have strong ammonia smells, are safe, and will not damage brass parts when used as directed.

After diluting the product as recommended, the cost isn't much different than the kitchen product alternatives. Some "dish soap" and other household cleaners [Simple Green and the like] may remove the oil and grease and dirt but can tarnish and turn brass dark on a long exposure. Ammonia and products containing the standard form of ammonia have a strong smell and have the potential to cause or worsen "stress crack corrosion."

Dawn dish detergent IS a good grease cutter but will not brighten brass. 'La's Totally Awesome Cleaner' is also a great grease cutter and very inexpensive. I tested it on brass for a pretty long exposure and found it less likely to tarnish the brass. Still, I recommend using one of the commercial products.

My personal preference is "Polychem Deox-007 Concentrate." It has no nasty ammonia odor, and one pint makes one gallon of cleaning solution, available from TimeSavers.

- A mildly alkaline blend for the efficient removal of oils, grease, tarnish, stains, corrosion, and oxidation from brass, bronze, copper, gold, and silver.
- It can be safely used in ultrasonics, agitated tanks, or manually.
- It provides long-term protection from tarnish, corrosion, and oxidation.
- Removes tarnishes and brightens metal parts.
- Use with water in a 7:1 water/concentrate ratio.
- No strong odor.
- Nonhazardous.

The gold standard for cleaning movements and parts is in an ultrasonic cleaner.

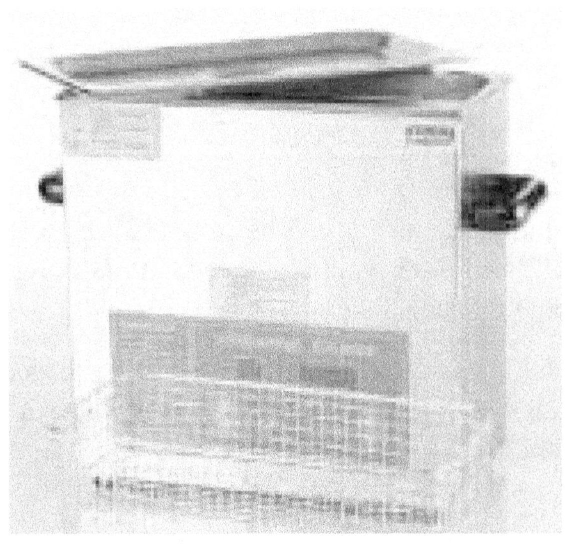

It's the same device that the health industry uses to sterilize surgical instruments. Ultrasonic cleaning is a process that uses ultrasound and an appropriate cleaning solvent. They can be spendy.

Ultrasonic cleaning uses cavitation bubbles induced by high-frequency pressure [sound] waves to agitate a liquid. The agitation produces high forces on contaminants adhering to substrates like metals, plastics, glass, rubber, and ceramics. This action also penetrates blind holes, cracks, and recesses.

You can use the same cleaning solution either in the ultrasonic cleaner or just by hand in a bowl.

You can buy a jewelry ultrasonic cleaner much cheaper, but make sure it is big enough to fit the movement plates and pillars and all the wheels.

I string the wheels together for each train on a thin wire and drape the end over the side of the tank. This saves having to fish the parts out when done. Use a teabag strainer for screws and small parts.

For extra dirty movements or parts, protect your cleaning solution by pre-cleaning. Carburetor or Brake cleaner, which is mostly acetone, works great, and the pressurized air spray helps blow away the residue. Best if you use the straw.

Some precautions should be taken during cleaning. Always wear safety glasses so fluids will not splash or flick into an eye from a brush. Wear gloves and old clothing.

Do not put two mainsprings, one on top of another while coiled in the same direction. Believe it or not, if they are coiled in the same direction, they tend to mate together and are very difficult to separate. Don't put a dial or self-adjusting anchor in the cleaning solution.

Mark all containers containing chemicals and keep the containers sealed unless currently in use.

Plan on letting the parts luxuriate in the cleaning solution as soon as you have taken the movement apart, so you can fully evaluate the parts for wear and defects.

Once the movement servicing has been completed and immediately before the final assembly, clean the parts again. Once clean, use gloves to handle the pieces, so the oils from your hands don't tarnish the bright parts.

It is a good idea to have two batches of cleaner going. Use the older cleaner to do the first wash. Use the freshest solution for the final wash. Eventually, this will become the first wash, and the new solution will become the final wash.

A word about lacquered front and backplates. The cleaning solution may harm the protective lacquered finish to some plates. I like to spray a small area of the inside of one plate with a carburetor cleaner. If the area turns white, it is best not to immerse the plates in the cleaning solution as it will likely remove the lacquer. In that case, just clean in warm soapy water.

Scratch Brush

If you have very dirty parts, in places that are hard to reach or have tarnish or minor rust, you can use a Scratch Brush. This is an inexpensive tool that contains a fiberglass cartridge that does an excellent job of cleaning the problematic areas.

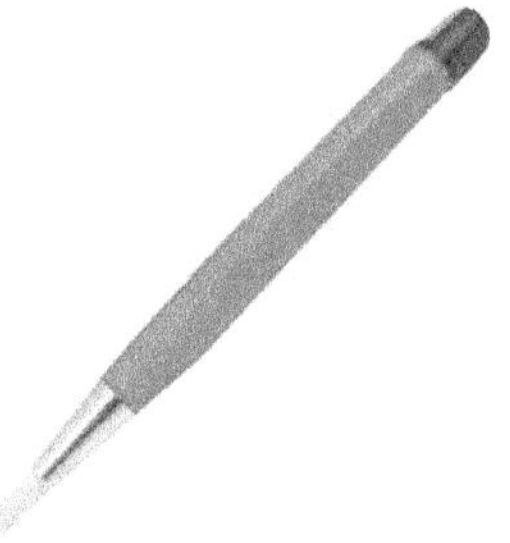

Drying after Cleaning

After immersing your parts in the cleaning solution for 10-20 minutes and scrubbing with a toothbrush, the next step is to rinse all the solution off the pieces with clean, warm water, preferably distilled water. It will not leave mineral deposits like regular tap water. Follow with canned compressed air [or air compressor] to blow most of the water off.

Use a spray bottle and a bottle of rubbing alcohol [I use 91%] and soak the movement in denatured alcohol between the rinse and dry steps. Try not to asphyxiate yourself while doing this, for the alcohol vapor is somewhat poisonous. The alcohol will absorb any water left from the cleaning. Ideally, a final rinse in acetone gives good results.

When complete, ALL moisture must be removed from the parts, or they will start to rust. This is easier said than done. The most common method is to create a simple heat box. It could be a cardboard or a plastic container with a lid. Cut a hole in the top just large enough for a hairdryer nozzle to fit. Also, make some holes near the bottom for the cooler air to escape.

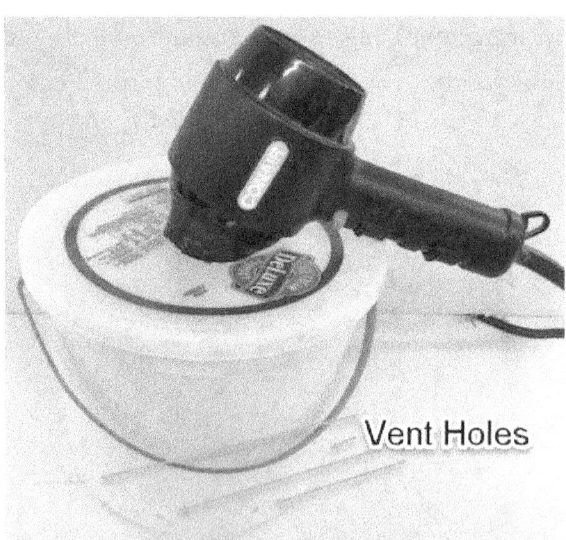

With the parts inside the container, run the hairdryer on hot for about 10 or 15 minutes. When removing the parts, they will likely be quite hot, so let them cool before handling.

The parts can also be dried in a domestic kitchen oven at 180 degrees F for 30 minutes, but don't do this for any plastic gears or parts.

Pegging

Commercially available peg wood is either orangewood or dogwood, but good quality round toothpicks or skewers will work in a pinch. Pegwood is generally used to remove any residual chemicals or oils from inside the brass pivot holes, but can also be used as a burnisher to smoothen and harden the hole.

To use peg wood as a burnisher, hold it in a lathe, cordless drill, or Dremel tool, and spin at high speed. When turned at high speed in a pivot hole, the peg wood will squeak as it burnishes the pivot hole and becomes burnished itself. Burnish from both sides of the plate, and replace or reshape the peg wood when discolored.

Using toothpicks as peg wood is faster, easier, and more cost-effective since there is no need to carve them to shape, and toothpicks are very inexpensive. When pegging, the toothpick will compress and even become dense enough to burnish the inside of the plate hole. And when the toothpick gets worn beyond use, throw it away and use another.

Use pegwood with a chisel-shaped end to clean the pinions.

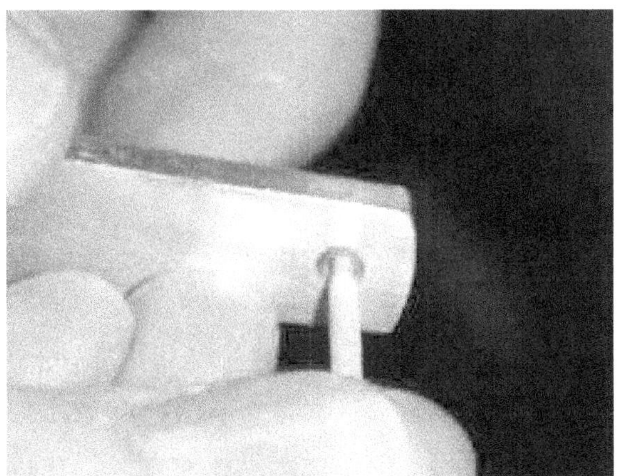

Making Repairs

The first job is to check the wheels one by one, especially noting any wear on the pivots.

The pivot should be perfectly cylindrical. After wiping and cleaning the pivot with pith wood, it should have a visibly smooth surface. Slide your fingernail over the pivot. It should slip along the surface, and there should be no grooves or roughness perceptible to the touch. Examine the pivot using a loupe [or strong magnifying glass] looking for defects. **It should have a mirror finish.** Place your fingernail up against the pivot, and you should see its reflection.

Note: the pivots must be corrected **before** pivot holes are corrected [bushed] because dressing a pivot will tend to reduce its diameter very slightly.

My homemade portable lathe consists of a cordless drill, clamped to my bench, and a second clamp to hold the trigger down while I use the drill. The keyless chuck is accurate enough for all but the most delicate clocks.

You can polish pivots without a lathe at all, by holding the arbor in a pin vice and spinning it with your fingers, while polishing the pivot at the other end with a pivot file, resting on a block of wood with grooves in it.

I made my own Emery Buff sticks by gluing wet and dry sandpaper to tongue depressors in the grades of 600, 1,500 and 2,500. Lay out 4 or 5 tongue depressors side by side, spray with contact cement on the sticks and a piece of wet and dry sandpaper, and glue them together. Use a different grit on the other side. Cut apart when dry. Don't wrap the sandpaper around one stick, or you won't get the clean square corners that you need.

Only use the very course sticks [600] for badly worn pivots and quickly move up the finer grades, ending with the 2,500 grit for a very fine and smooth pivot. Finish with a semi-chrome polishing compound.

The drawback of this system is the abrasive sticks will tend to leave particles of abrasive embedded in the surface of a pivot that can damage the metals if allowed to remain. Make sure you put the parts in the cleaning solution after polishing.

Burnishing

Burnishing is the polishing and work hardening of a metallic surface. This process will smooth and harden the surface, creating a finish that will last longer than one that hasn't been burnished.

Start by using a pivot file and a spot of lubricant. A pivot file is designed for the sole purpose of dressing hard tool steel pivots. The teeth are extremely fine cut, and the file is much thicker than any other of its size. The file will not bend when in use, and the edge is offset so you can get right to the root of the pivot.

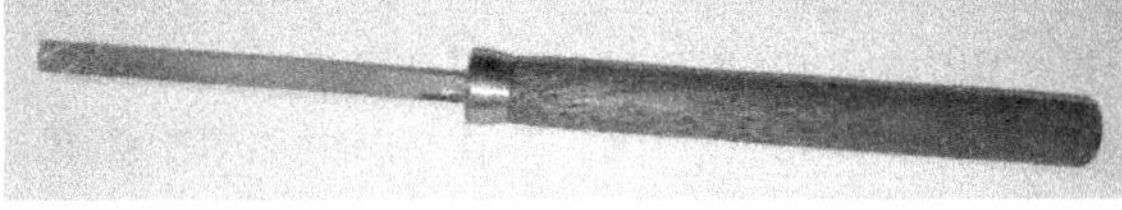

Once the pivot is flat and true, use a carbide burnisher to work harden the pivot.

Lubricate it with the same oil that will be used in the clock to avoid embedded contamination, and with the lathe [or drill], turning very slowly, begin to rub the pivot with the burnisher from underneath so you can see what you are doing. Make sure you keep it flat

on the pivot, so you don't change its shape. The accumulation of black particles forming on the surface of the burnisher will tell if you have applied the burnisher to the work flat against the length of the pivot. As with a file, run the burnisher over the pivot for the full length of the burnisher.

Apply as much pressure with the burnisher as you are comfortable. The pressure is good, but when a pivot is unsupported, it is possible to break a pivot using unreasonable force. A well-sharpened burnisher does two things. It cuts some metal away and is acting as a super-fine file. At the same time, it is compressing the surface of the metal to harden it.

As the pivot is being restored to shape using the coarse side of the burnisher, long, slow, deliberate strokes work best at between 500 and 750 rpm. Once the pivot looks acceptable, wipe the pivot and finish with the smooth side of the burnisher using more rapid, lighter-pressure strokes. Move the burnisher faster, but do not appreciably speed up the lathe. In other words, give the burnisher time to do its job.

An alternative is a 1/8" x 1/8" x 2-1/2" hard Arkansas stone with lubrication.

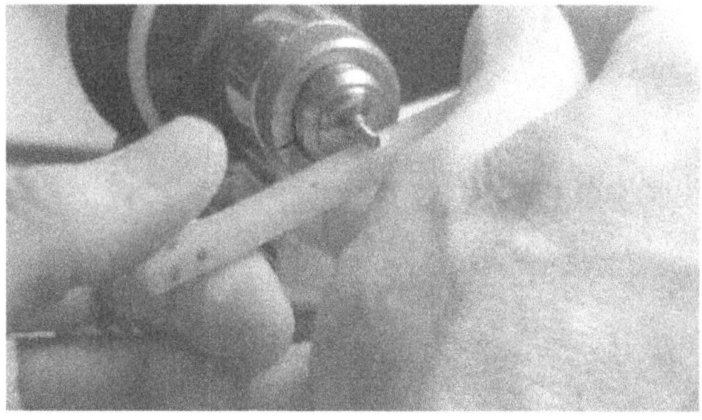

If a pivot is badly grooved, removing all the groves may remove too much material, weakening the pivot. In this case, I suggest you just soften up the groves, which will do little harm, reduce friction, and help hold the oil. However, you should focus your attention on the pivot hole to find the cause of the groves.

It is essential to polish the pivot shoulder also.

Pivot Polishing without a Lathe

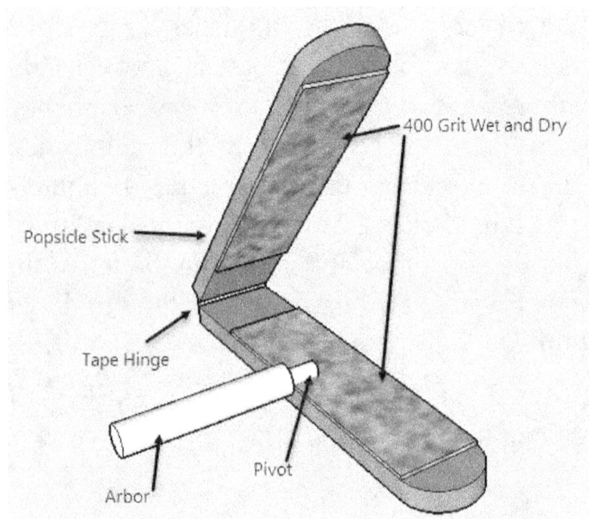

Glue 400 grit Wet and Dry abrasive paper to two popsicle sticks. Cut one end of each stick square. Create a hinge with tape so the tool stays parallel. Move the two faces of the tool together with slight pressure with your fingers over the pivot. Rotate the arbor back and forth with your other hand to smooth the pivot.

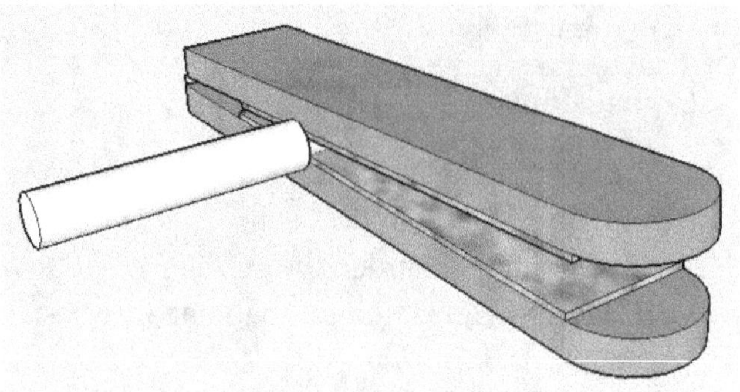

Make a second tool but use 1,500 grit. Use it, in the same way, to create a highly polished finish to the pivot.

I often get asked how to hold an arbor in a lathe when the wheel or pinion is so close to the pivot there is no way to chuck up on the arbor. First of all, never chuck up on the pivot [unless you are straightening the pivot – see below]. The simplest answer is to cut a thin strip of fine wet and dry sandpaper and run it around the pivot with your hands.

The correct answer is by using a Jacot Tool. Below are two homemade units. The wheel is fitted in a hole at the end of the Jacot Tool and the other end supported by a steady rest. The wheel is propelled by the bent metal bar that drives the wheel arm.

My Jacot tool

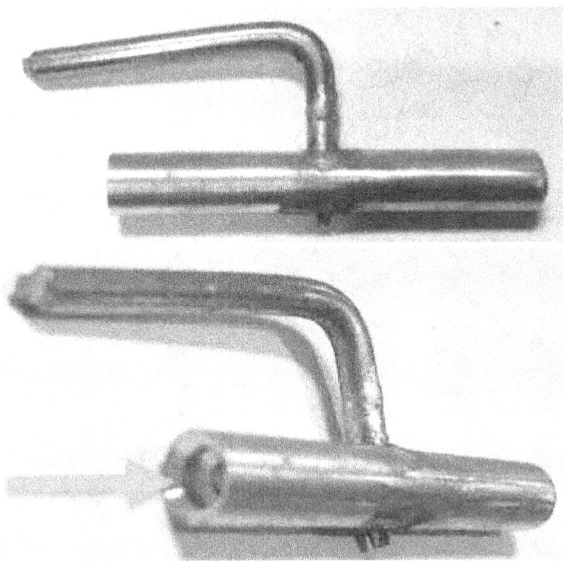

¼" brass rod that has a bent metal carrier [a nail] drilled and soldered into it, with a cone-shaped hole in the end to accept the pivot.

Homemade Polisher

I made this little polishing tool out of some scrap oak, about 4-1/2" by 2-1/2" by ¾".

The wheel sits between the centers. The left-center has a hole in the end to accept one pivot. The right center has a hole in the end then is filed ½ way down, so you can work on the pivot. The centers are made out of a 1/8" brass rod, held in place by two thumbscrews, screwed into two threaded inserts.

With the tool held in a vice, the arbor can be rotated with the finger and use a pivot file on the exposed pivot.

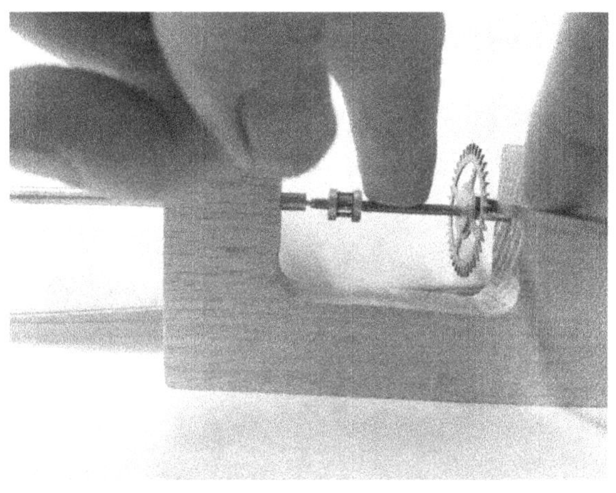

Polishing and Burnishing Pivots and Pivot Holes

Burnishing is a combination of polishing and work-hardening of the surface of the metal. The smoother and harder the bearing surfaces, the less the friction and the longer they will function well.

Polishing

Polishing can be performed by any kind of cutting or abrasive device. Polishing powders, diamond compounds, stones, sandpaper and files are common.

A pivot file is most suitable for its ability to true up defects in the pivot such as barrel, bowed, tapered or cone shape as well as pits and grooves. The pivot file should be lubricated with the same or compatible oil as will be used to lubricate the completed movement to draw away shavings. Practice is needed to develop the correct speed and pressure to obtain the finest finish. Examine your work with high magnification. Use a back-lit micrometer to reveal defects in the shape.

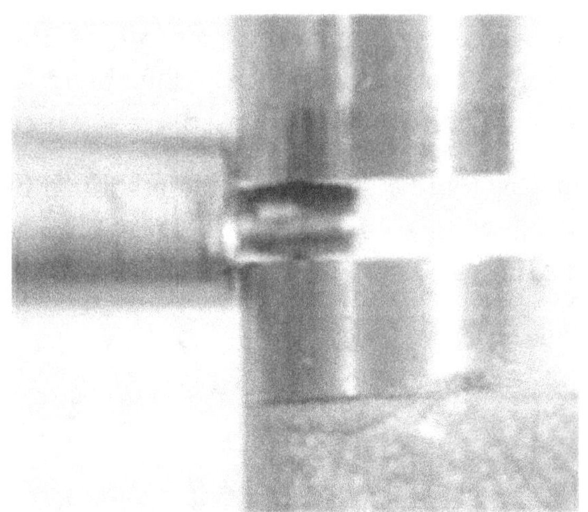

With the wheel safely mounted in the lathe, bring the pivot file to the work carefully and purposefully from underneath so you can see the pivot at all times. Watch the pattern in the lubricant to determine where the file is contacting the pivot.

Burnishing continued

A steel burnisher when new needs to be dressed to make the surface flat and free of defects and the surface scored so it will perform its function. To score the flat surface, place fine [1,500] emery paper on a small sheet of thick glass and slide the steel across and back, creating a series of fine scratches, making it into a micro file. Make one side coarse and the other side fine. Burnish the pivot using light oil at high speed about 2,000 rpm to a black shine.

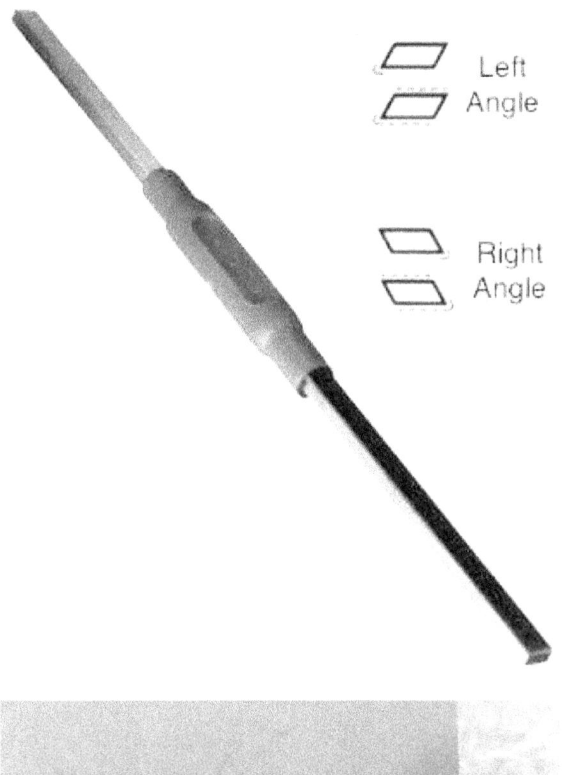

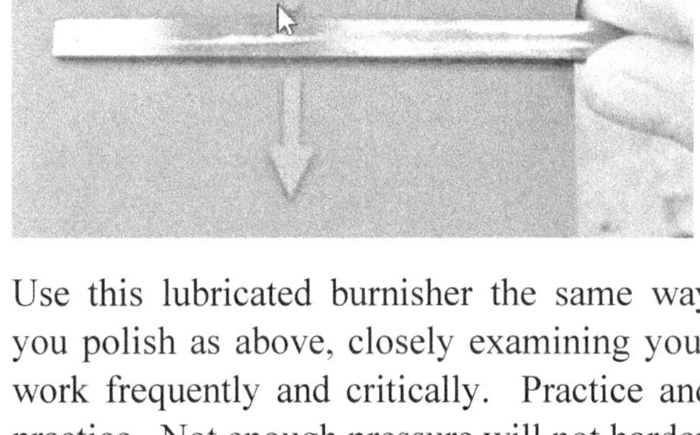

Use this lubricated burnisher the same way you polish as above, closely examining your work frequently and critically. Practice and practice. Not enough pressure will not harden the surface. Too much pressure will cause damage. Be sure to burnish the shoulder also as it will also contact the front or backplate. Be sure to remove the burnisher from the work, straight down to avoid damaging your work.

The finish you achieve will define you as a craftsman.

Burnishing the pivot hole

Burnishing the pivot hole is just as crucial as burnishing the pivot. Use a smoothing broach.

This is a tapered steel rod that needs the same prep as the flat burnisher. Fit the broach in the lathe, smooth it with 600 grit sandpaper followed by 0000 steel wool.

After pegging and installing any needed bushings, hand burnish the pivot holes with the prepped and lubricated smoothing broach from both sides of the plate using a light touch. When complete, remove any lubricant and carefully examine the back-lit pivot hole to be sure 100% of the bearing surface is shiny and bright.

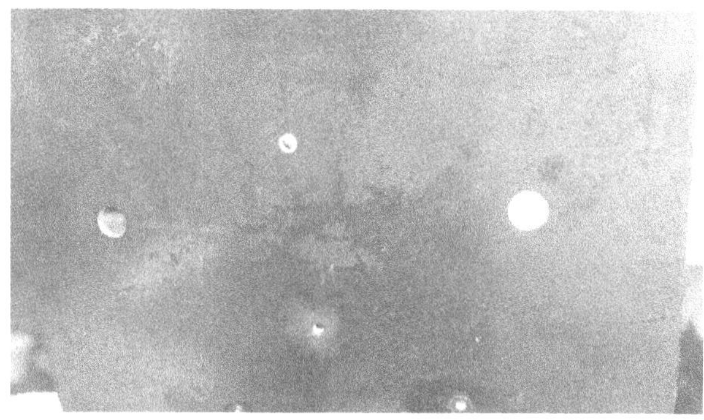

This is a good time to examine the pinions and clean them using pegwood to make them shine. If any rods need repair, see the later chapter.

My son Jon age twelve, came home from Boy Scouts one day with a block of wood and some parts to create a race car for the upcoming Pinewood Derby. This was intended to be a father-son project. I was not familiar with this project but did a little research.

The next weekend we sat down to work out our strategy. I told my son the secret of making a winner was the shape of the car; streamline with 2/3rds of the weight at the back, making sure it had the maximum weight allowed. The plan was he would make the car shape in the wood, and I would help with the wheels.

An hour later, he came back with a design and explained how he arrived at it. He had taken to heart the 2/3rd rule and streamline, so we traced the shape onto the car, and I cut out the rough shape on the bandsaw. From there, he whittled away and sanded the final shape.

While he was busy doing that, I disappeared into my clock shop and polished up and burnished the axles that held the wheels. I also did my best to burnish the holes in the plastic wheels.

When the car shape was finished, I fitted the axles onto the car and mounted the wheels. My son painted the finished car, and we added some lead to bring the weight to the maximum limit.

On the day of the races, the car was inspected by the judge and approved for racing. I added a tiny amount of my best clock oil to each wheel. He won every heat and became the champion in the final.

My son was so proud of the shape he had created and 20 years later he still has that car proudly displayed.

I think he suspects that I had something to do with its success based on my clock talents.

The morel is of course - polishing and burnishing the axles and wheels made a big difference, and it will help your clockwork just the same.

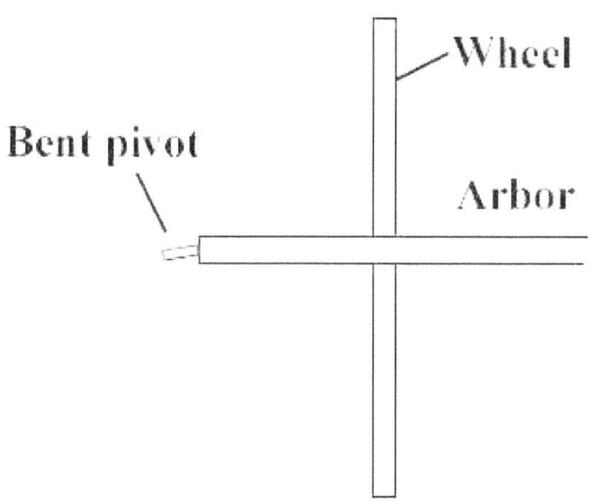

When you come across a bent pivot, you need to straighten it, hopefully without breaking it off.

First, you need to determine if the pivot has been hardened. Use a file to see if that arbor is hardened. Take a fine-toothed file and see if it will remove any metal from the arbor. If the arbor has been hardened, you'll find that the file just scoots over the arbor instead of digging in and cutting. If so, you can anneal it by heating it red-hot in a gas flame for a few seconds, and then let it cool down in the air. Retest with a file to confirm it is now workable.

Place the pivot in a collet in a lathe. Manually, [By Hand] turn head headstock. You will be able to observe the wobble. The high point and the low point.

With a peening end of a light hammer, gently tap the arbor to true it. Rotate it, so the high spot is on top, and gently tap in a very gentle downstroke. This method will work with hard or soft pivots. This task can also be performed vertically on a drill press.

Be forewarned, it takes a learned touch and

very gentle taps. There is no need to reharden the part after the repair.

Another way, but this takes some skill, is to run the lathe at a very high speed and tap downward. You will be hitting the high spot. A series of gentle taps, and suddenly you will see the arbor/pivot running dead true.

For a bent arbor, again test for hardness. Place the arbor on a bench block or open vice and rotate it until the high spot is at the top and lightly tap it down with a punch until straight.

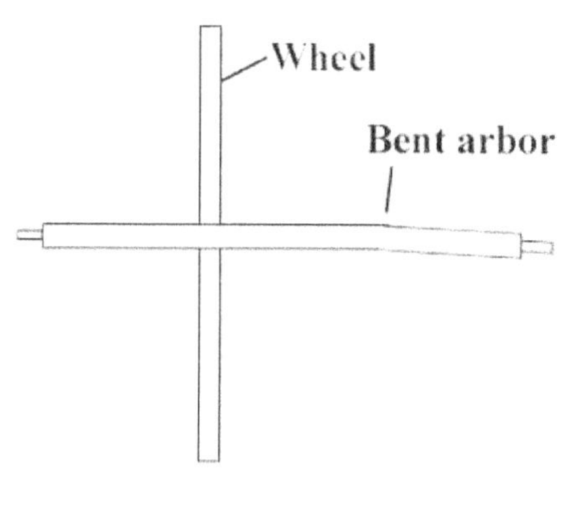

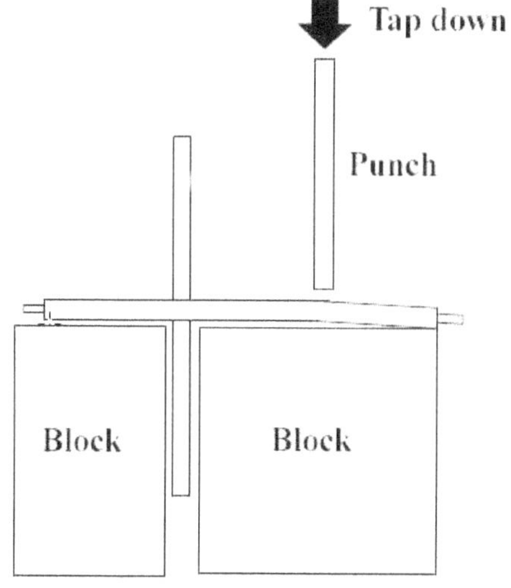

From time to time, you will come across a badly worn or broken pivot.

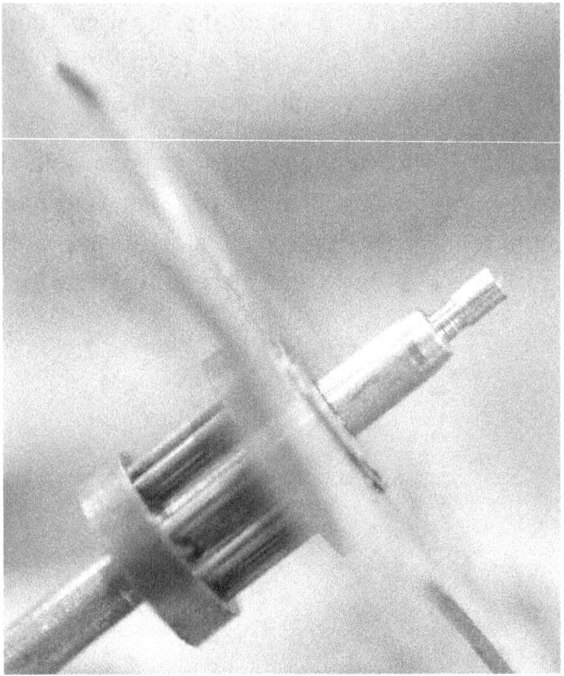

The only solution is to replace the pivot [or replace the whole arbor]. This is surprisingly a straightforward process, one that I enjoy, but it does require the use of a lathe [or a good drill/Dremel setup], a set of small drills, and an assortment of pivot wire. Most likely, the original pivot was formed by reducing the arbor diameter from a solid piece of material.

Use a file to see if that arbor is hardened. Take a fine-toothed file and see if it will remove any metal from the arbor. If the arbor has been hardened, you'll find that the file just scoots over the arbor instead of digging in and cutting. If so, you can anneal it by heating it red-hot, which shouldn't take more than a few seconds in a gas flame, and then let it cool down slowly.

Typically, the broken pivot leaves a bump that must be removed "dressed," so the end of the arbor is flat. Chuck a Dremel cutoff wheel in the lathe and hold the end of the arbor to the wheel until flat.

Chuck the wheel arbor in the lathe and chuck a drill bit in the tailstock. Use a drill one size smaller than the replacement pivot wire. Drill the end of the arbor to a depth of about three times the pivot diameter. Make sure it is drilled in the dead center of the arbor. I recommend using tungsten carbide bits. Frequently remove the drill to clear the swarf.

Insert the pivot wire with Loctite 638 retaining compound to hold it in place. Cut to length when set, dress up the end and polish the newly exposed pivot.

The new pivot should ideally be tapered a little to ensure a tight fit. Wait overnight before working on the new pivot.

Timesavers sells this Staff and Pivot Wire set for $7.50 and they work well for lantern pinions also.

Staff & Pivot Wire 37-Piece Assortment

37 piece assortment of 6" long hardened staff and pivot wire. Diameter ranges from .027" through .152". Made in India.

Base Pricing $7.50

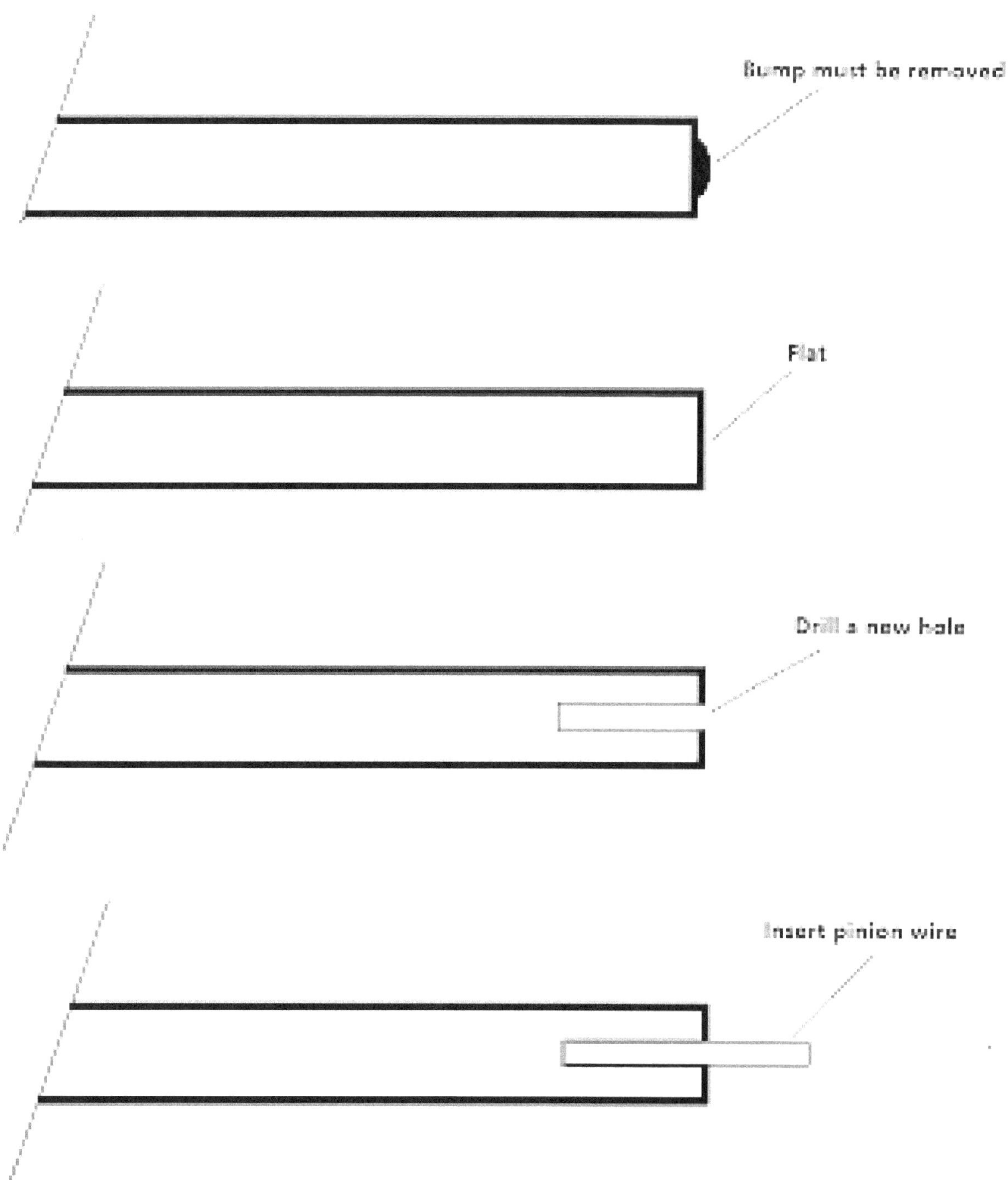

Bump must be removed
Flat
Drill a new hole
Insert pinion wire

If pivot wire is not available, it is acceptable to use a portion of the back end of a drill bit, one size smaller.

With a Dremel cutoff wheel in the lathe chuck, take any remaining bump off the old pivot.

Stone the end very flat

You must drill the new pivot hole dead center of the arbor. You can use a centering bit [slocombe],

Or better still make your own centering tool.

Use a piece of ¼" brass stock. I prefer to use an octagon shape, but a round profile is just fine. Cut it about ¾" long. Drill a hole down the center using a 1/16" drill bit, then countersink one end. Now you can slide the countersunk end over the arbor. It will automatically find the center of the arbor. Use the same 1/16" drill bit to create a small divot in the end of the arbor, which will be dead center. Once you have a divot, you can use the correct size drill bit in a pin vice [or your lathe tail stock] to create the pivot hole.

Keep this drill bit with the tool. They are now one toolset. Only use this drill bit for making a center divot with the tool, nothing else.

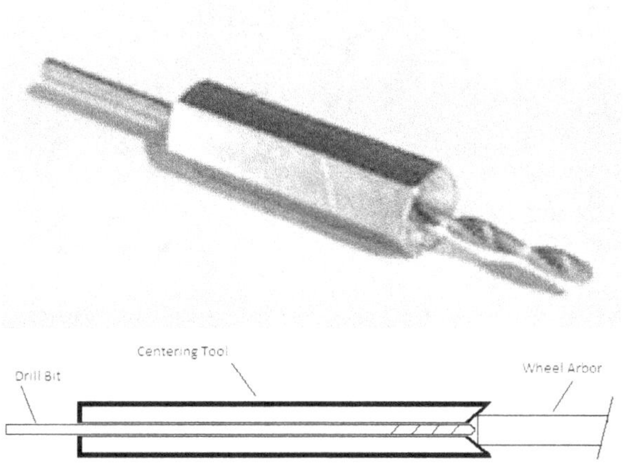

With the wheel in the headstock and a drill bit in the tailstock [or pin-vice], slowly bring the drill to the arbor and bore a new hole for the replacement pivot. Don't add any oil to the drill bit as it will interfere with the adhesive when we install the pivot wire.

You can use any of these Loctite products to hold the pivot. Clean the hole with alcohol before inserting the pivot.

Another method of re-pivoting a problem arbor is to install a replacement machined pivot end. The arbor will need to be shortened to allow for the new pivot.

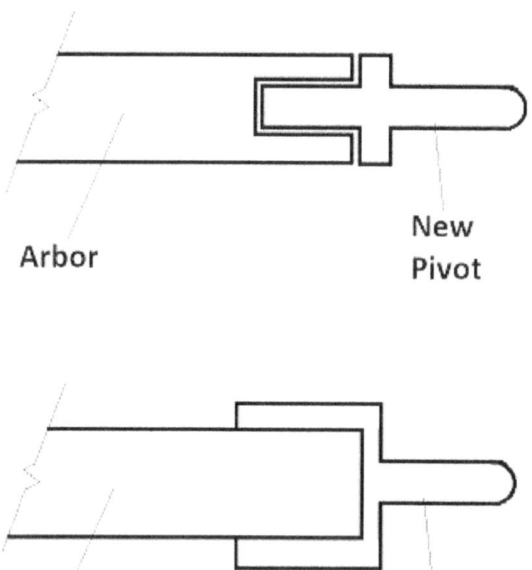

Product Lists by Feature or Application	Top Products by Feature or Application
Fast Cure	LOCTITE® 638™ Retaining Compound
High Temperature	LOCTITE® 640™ Retaining Compound
High Strength	LOCTITE® 648™ Retaining Compound
Close-Fitting Parts	LOCTITE® 603™ Retaining Compound
Loose-Fitting Parts	LOCTITE® 680™ Retaining Compound
Machinery Repair	LOCTITE® 660™ Retaining Compound

Pivoting a Practice Nail

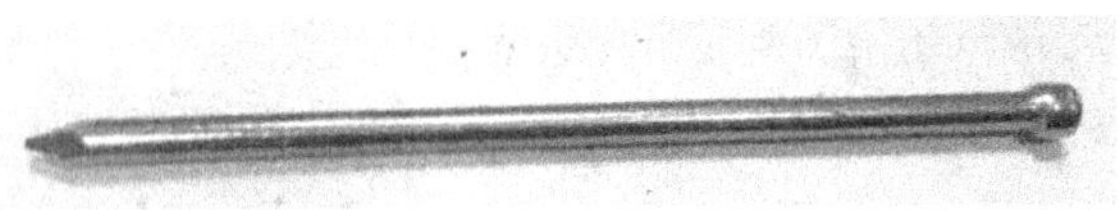

This is a 2 ½" finish nail. I used this because it is soft, cheap, easy to find and easy to work with.

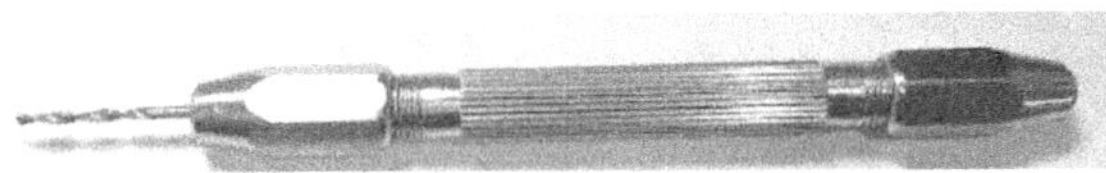

A drill bit in a pin vice.

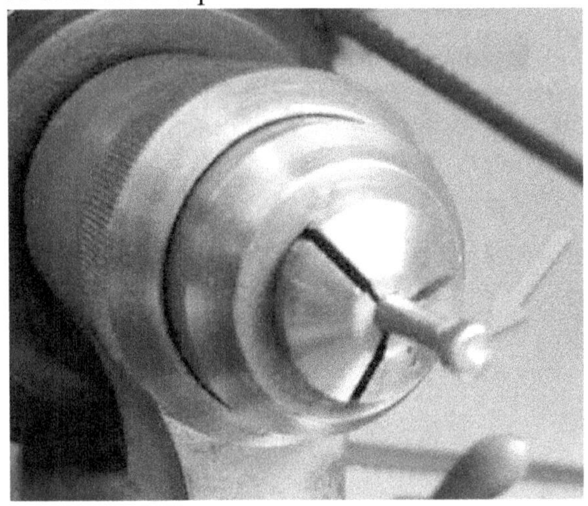

I chucked it up in a lathe [or you could use a dremel] and used my centering tool, just with hand pressure to find the dead center of the end of the nail head.

I put a drill bit in the tailstock, but it could be in a handheld pin vise.

After drilling the hole, I inserted a taper pin. I probably would not use a taper pin for a real repair, but it uses parts you will likely have to hand for practice.

When you need to bush a clock, it can be done either by hand or with a bushing machine. A bushing machine will cost about $900, and if you have access to one, feel free to use it, but I can bush a clock just as quickly and just as well by hand without the machine.

The following explains the procedure by hand.

What starts as a round hole becomes oval or pear-shaped. As a pinion drives the next wheel, it presses that wheel's pivot against the opposite side of its pivot hole. That's where the wear takes place.

You can see where the wear is, just by looking at the pivot hole. The rule is- *If it's round, run it, if oblong, bush it*. It's a good idea to use a marker to indicate where the wear points are before disassembling the movement. A good rule is if the pivot moves more than the thickness of the suspension spring, it needs repair.

When a gear train is turning in its normal direction, each of its pivots will be pressed against the wear point of its pivot hole.

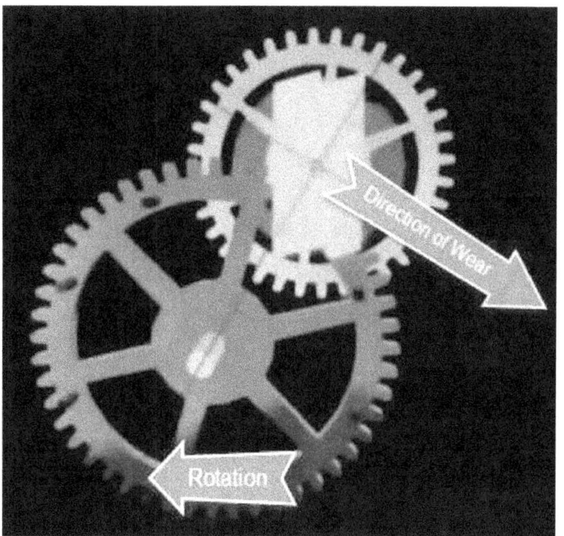

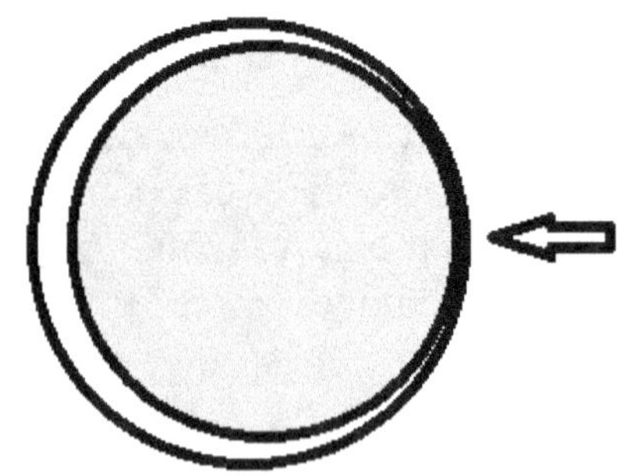

A well made pivot only makes a
small contact with its pivot hole

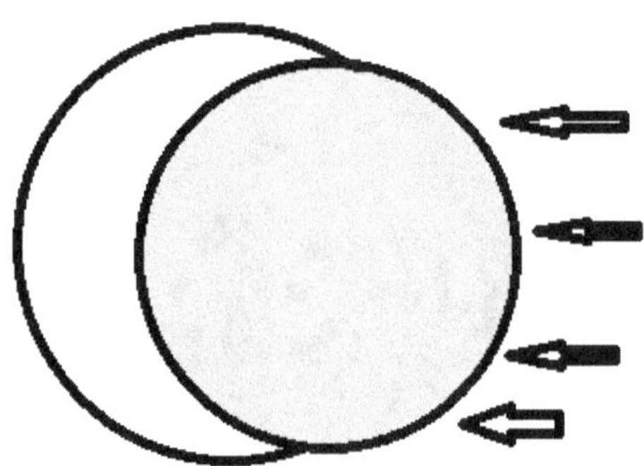

A worn piot hole makes much
more contact with its pivot

We call this oval wearing 'tunneling.'
If one pivot hole is worn, the other pivot will
be out of alignment and will bind on its pivot
hole.

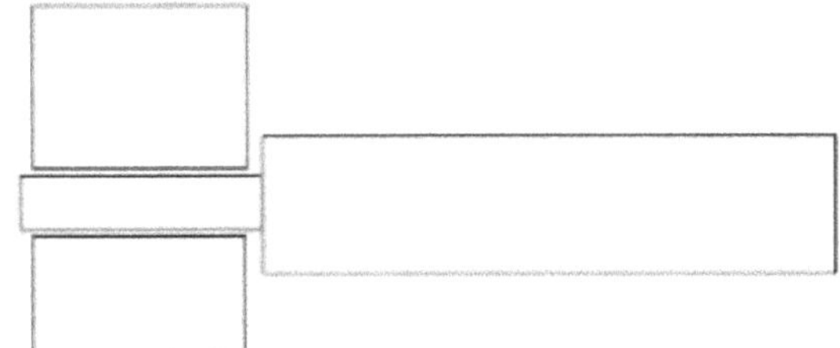

Well Fitting Pivot

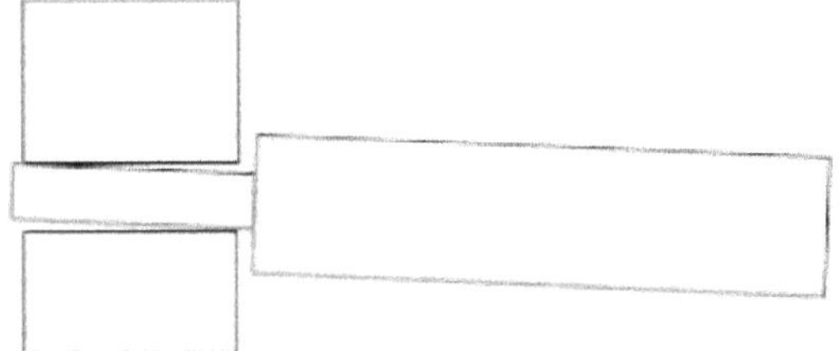

Worn pivot at the other plate causing binding

A worn pivot will also change the mesh
[depthing] of the wheel teeth to the pinion.

Correct mesh

Mesh too shallow

Another way to check for bushing wear is to
let down the springs till they are almost all the
way down. Just a little power left. Then watch
each bushing on each side of the movement as
you rock the train back and forth using the
great wheel. If a pivot moves back and forth
very much [oblong hole] while doing this, it
needs a bushing. Mark the direction of the
wear.

The challenge is to install a new bushing with the same center as the **original hole**. The first step is to change the pear-shaped hole into a symmetrical oval.

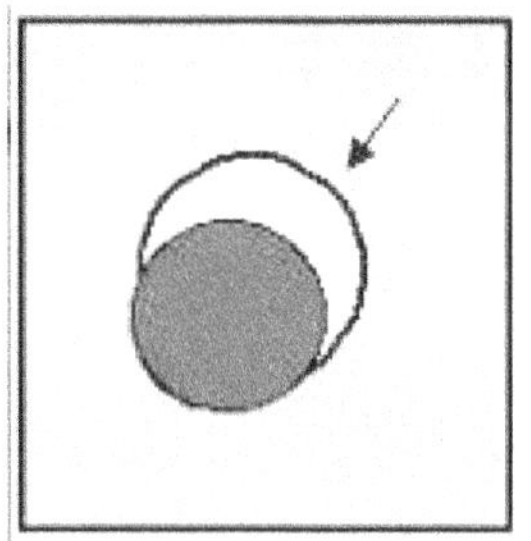
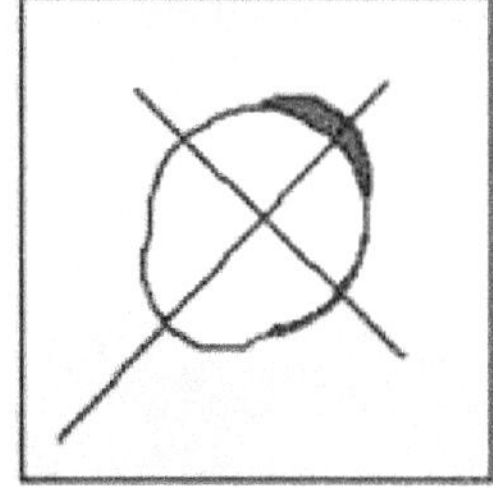

AMOUNT TO REMOVE WITH FILE

Determine [by eyeball] where the center of the original circle was.

To do this, let the mainsprings down into C clamps. Then wind the spring one half turn to give a little power to the trains. Now put reverse power on the second wheel back with your finger. The pivot will go back to the original side of the hole. By rocking that wheel with your finger, you can see the ware.

Mark the unworn side of the pivot hole with scribed lines and make notes of the ware.

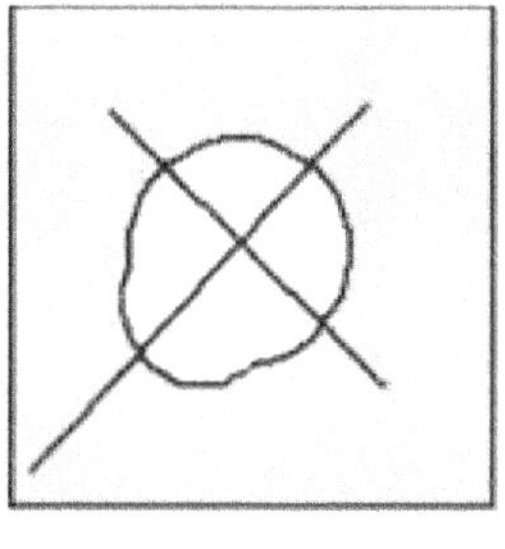
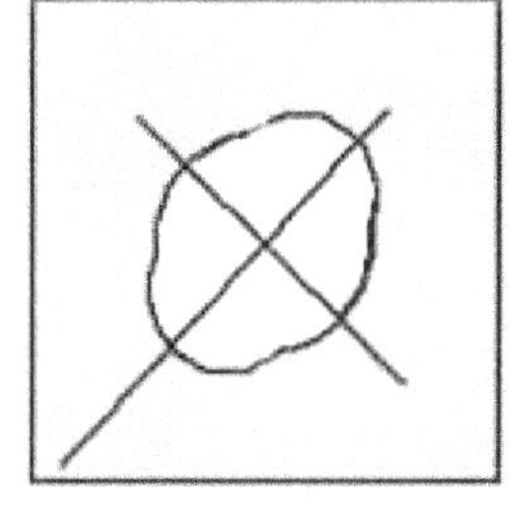

WORN PIVOT HOLE　　　**AFTER FILING**

With a small round needle file or Dremel, create an opposite oval identical to and exactly opposite the original oval, until you have an oval hole centered on the original round hole.

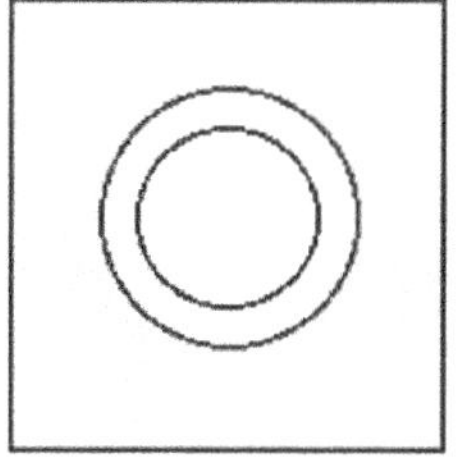

BROACH TO FIT PIVOT

With a cutting broach, enlarge the hole from the inside of the plate until it is round. A broach automatically centers itself in the middle of an oval. Since that is where the center of the original hole was, the broached hole is still centered on that point.

Continue broaching until the hole is not quite big enough to accept a bushing as a tight force fit. Make sure to keep the broach at a right angle to the plate in both dimensions, so the hole is straight through.

Select a new bushing that is the same thickness as the plate and has an internal hole just **smaller** than the pivot.

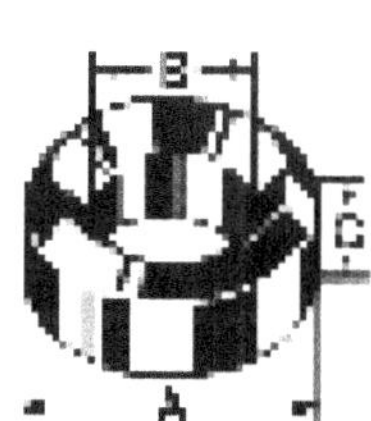

Use a reamer oiled with the same clock oil you will use when the clock is complete, that is made to fit that bushing, and cut the hole to final size.

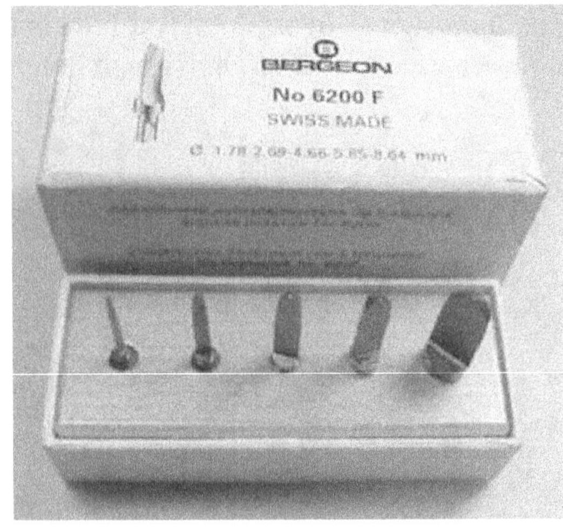

The reamer is a half-circle cutter, sharp on both edges. It gets gradually larger as you cut and press on the tool until you get to the parallel portion, which is the correct size for a friction fit for the corresponding bushing [3/1000th smaller than the pivot].

When you are just learning, you can use cutting broaches instead of a reamer. Test the size often and stop when the bushing almost enters the hole for a tight press fit.

Lightly remove any burs with a countersink bit then install the bushing into the hole, from the inside of the plate with the oil sink on the outside, until it is flush with the inside of the plate. Use a small hammer and punch on an anvil block and tap it into place.

Use a 5-sided cutting broach to the inside hole of the bush, so the pivot perfectly fits the hole in the bushing. Then use a round smoothing broach to remove any roughness in the hole and work-harden the inside surface. Allow five degrees of play. Slightly chamfer the inside edge of the new bushing.

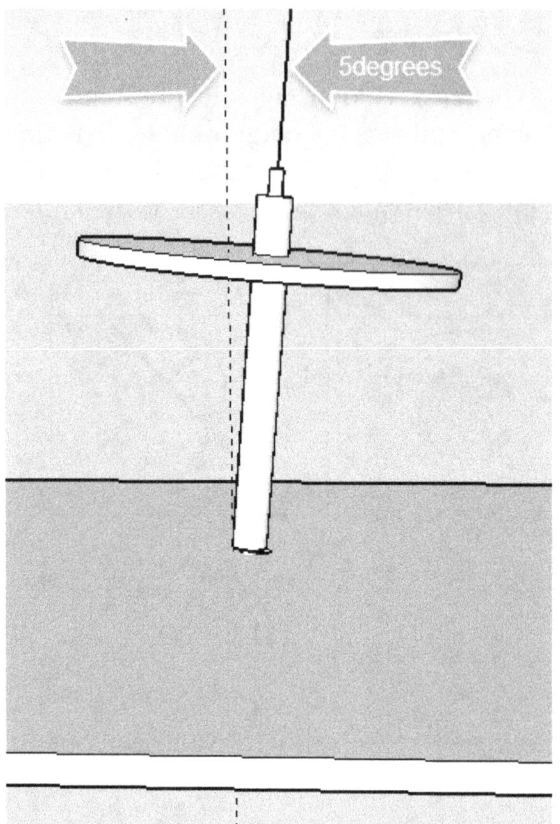

Alternatively, if you just use a reamer instead of a file, make sure you ream out the hole centered on the original hole instead of the new oval. Insert the reamer with the round edge facing the side that is worn. Rotate the cutter ¼ turn left and back to the starting position, then ¼ turn right and back to the starting position. Repeat until the cut area is equal to the worn area, then continue cutting by making full rotations until you reach the parallel portion of the reamer. This is called nibbling.

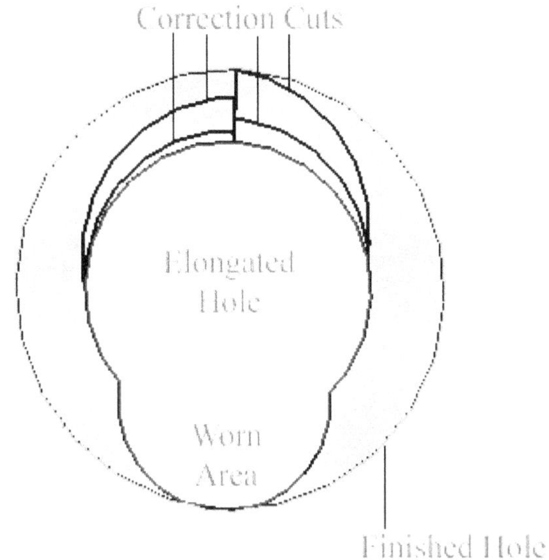

use a drill that just fits the hole in the strap to drill the initial hole and get it in the correct position.

Then, follow-up with the reamer you usually use for that bushing.

Reaming out the hole will likely leave a burr on the plate. Remove this burr by gently rotating the chamfer tool, two rotations.

With the plate supported from the back, lay the new bushing on the hole from the inside of the plate and drive it into place using a punch or brass hammer. Smooth the bushing with emery paper, so it is flush with the plate.

Use a Dremel bit #100 in a pin vise to recess the oil sink correctly if needed.

When the bushing is complete, insert the wheel in between the plates by itself and test it spins freely, and gradually slows to a stop. Then add the wheel on either side to examine the mesh of the teeth to ensure the bushing is installed in the correct location.

One way that you can be sure of a good outcome for oval holes is to double drill the holes.

This is done by making a drilling guide out of an old hacksaw blade [or another appropriate steel strap] and clamping it to the plate in the correct, original position over the hole. Then

Despite its name, the bushing machine is powered by a hand crank. Probably a better name for it would be a bushing jig.

Some say you must use a bushing machine to make sure the bushing is fitted perfectly vertical. I am not convinced of this. The final broaching is what must be perfectly vertical, and that is always done by hand.

The main advantage of the bushing machine is you can lock the plate to be precisely in line with the correct location of the pivot hole, not the worn location. Start by loosely fitting the plate in the clamps with the oil sink facing down and the inside of the plate facing up. Insert a centering point in the chuck, bring down the point and adjust the plate, so it lines up precisely with the original pivot hole with the centering point.

Now lock in the clamps.

If the pivot hole is worn oval, align the centering point with the center of the original pivot hole [not the oval], and lock everything down tight.

Next, insert the reamer in the chuck of the tool, add some oil to assist the cutting, and rotate it slowly by hand. Bring it down to cut a hole for the new bushing.

Start with a small reamer and work up to the correct size.

Next, lightly use the chamfering cutter to take off any sharp edge. Place the correct bush in line with the hole, insert the pusher in the chuck, and tap the bushing into place with light taps of the clockmaker's hammer.

Steel Plates

Occasionally you will come across a movement with steel front and backplates. Steel plates are very hard on reamers. I suggest you predrill the holes just undersize and finish with the correct reamer. Use some cutting oil on the reamer, this saves wear on reamers. Use them only for the final 'few thou.' if at all.

Reamers can be redressed [sharpened] with a fine Arkansas stone. Put the flat of the reamer down on the stone and use a light machine oil on the stone. Hold the reamer down firmly and work it back and forth a few strokes. That way the cutting edge is honed without reducing the OD. This can be done many times without any degradation in performance.

Finally, the hole in the new bushing must be hand opened using a 5-sided cutting broach to suit the polished pivot and burnished with a round oiled smoothing broach.

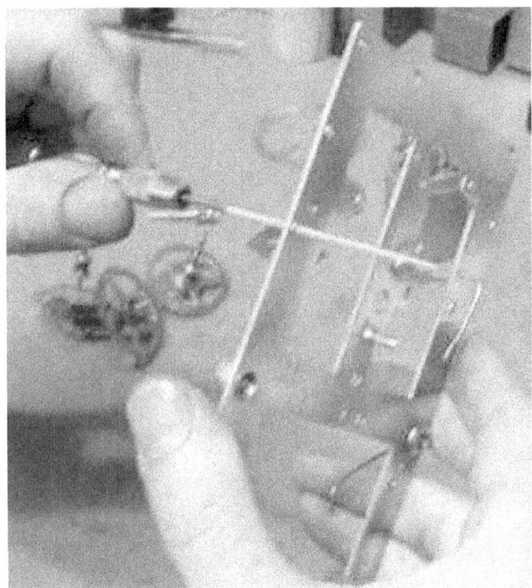

Finish up with pegwood to remove any dirt and debris.

Benchtop Drill Press

An interesting alternative to a bushing machine is a small bench drill press and vice. You can do just about everything a bushing machine will do and a lot more with this setup for under $100. *Timesavers 10305* This one is only 12" tall with variable speed.

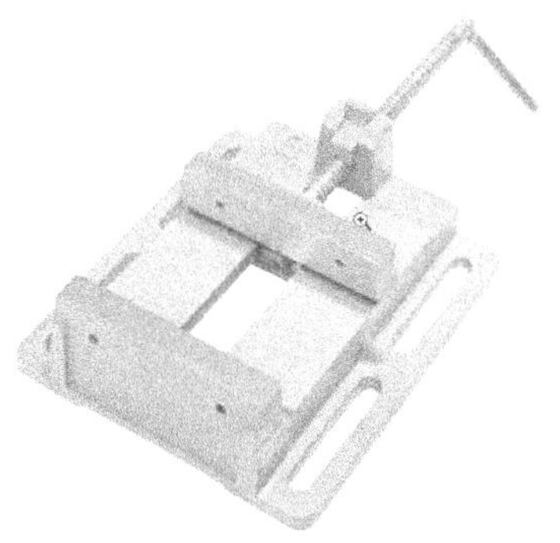

There is a Drill Press Bushing Tool Adapter available at Timesavers. A bit spendy.

Capture the clock plate with a 6-Inch Drill Press Vise, which can bolt to the base of the drill press or clamp it down to a piece of backing wood.

With the drill press method, I prefer to open up the pivot hole with a drill bit just smaller than the reamer, then finish up the hole with the reamer. This saves wear on the reamers.

This setup has many other uses, including pivot polishing. Lay it on its side, and you have a lathe.

Making Bushings

It is quite easy to make bushings in the lathe from a standard 1/8" brass rod, available from many good hardware stores.

Chuck up the rod in a collet with about ½" protruding. Face off the end, find the center of the end of the rod with your centering bit or homemade tool.

Drill the center hole just a little smaller than the finished pivot, about ¼" deep, with the drill bit held loosely in a pin vise. If the bit grabs, let the pin vise spin freely in your fingers until you can shut off the lathe. This technique will save many broken small drill bits.

Brass Rod   *New Bushing*

Part [cut] the new bushing to length, just a fraction long. Do not part it all the way off just yet. Remove the rod and bushing from the collet and turn it around, so the newly formed bushing is held in the collet. Snap off the extra rod, face up the raw end, and chamfer the hole very slightly.

Slip a toothpick into the hole and release the bushing from the collet.

Drill a hole in the plate one drill size smaller than 1/8", dead center on the location of the original pivot center. Broach the hole until the new bushing just starts to enter the hole.

Slip the new bushing into the hole. Lay the plate, outside face up, on a heavy bench block, and using a round face punch, give it a sharp hammer stroke. This will lock the bushing to the plate and create an oil sink all in one process.

Merritt's also sells bushing wire. Long tubes in various diameters can be more economical than buying individual bushings.

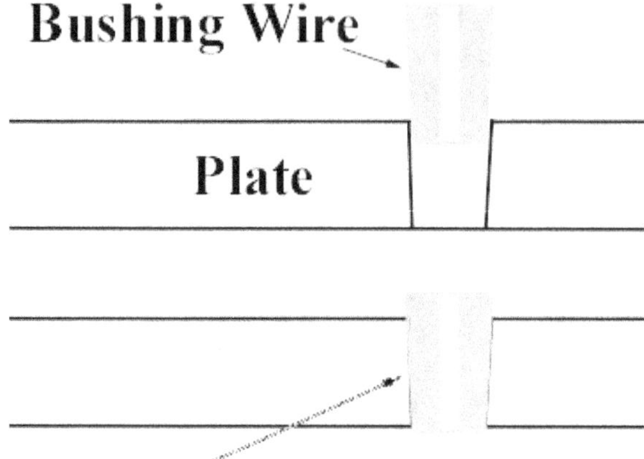

Bushing driven home

For the record, pre-made bushings are available in two grades, Bronze and Brass. Bronze bushings are more durable than brass, however, try to match the same material to the existing plates for fine clocks.

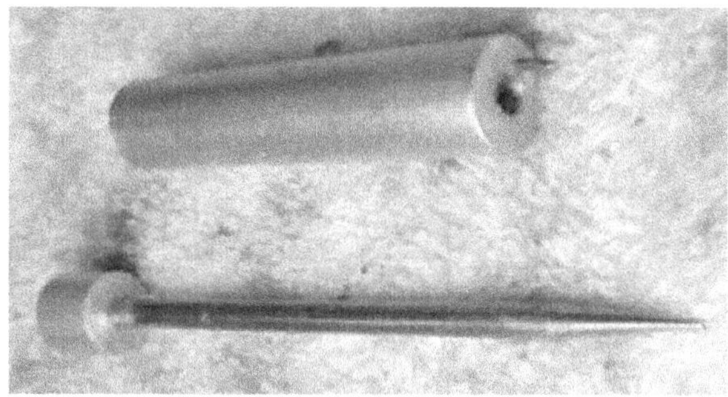

This little shop-made tool is excellent to permanently scribe a concentric circle around a worn hole. It also helps you make judgment on how good you are doing your bushing placement.

It is a brass pipe with a small hardened pin inserted in the end. The longer pin is inserted in the pipe to locate the tool at the location of the original pivot hole.

From time to time, you will come across [or create] a broken tooth.

To repair a broken tooth, use a sharp scribe to score a line from the center of the base of the old tooth on the radial line to the center of the wheel, no deeper than half the depth of the rim.

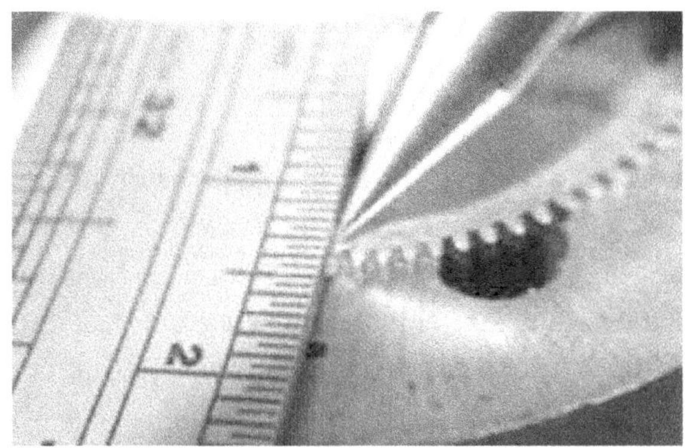

Use a jeweler's saw with a very fine blade, set to cut on the pull stroke. Use only ¼ of the blade in your saw to give you better control.

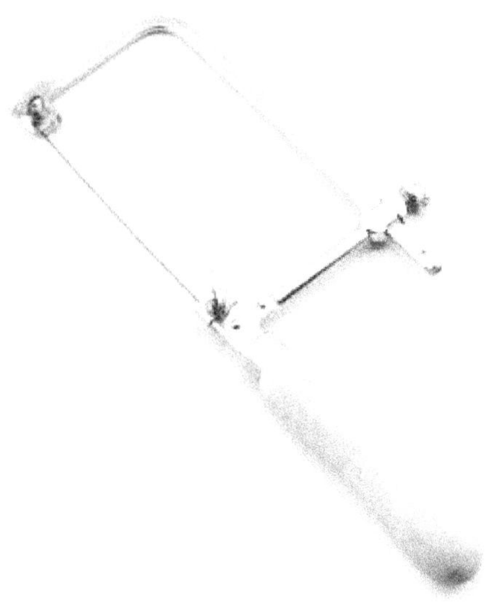

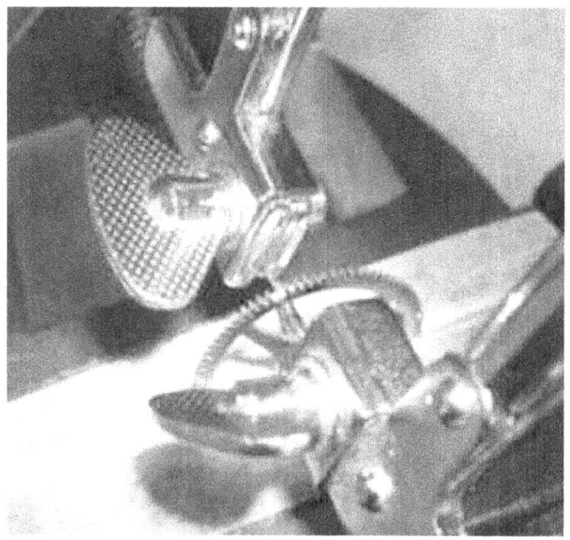

Cut into the wheel along the scribed radial line to the desired depth.

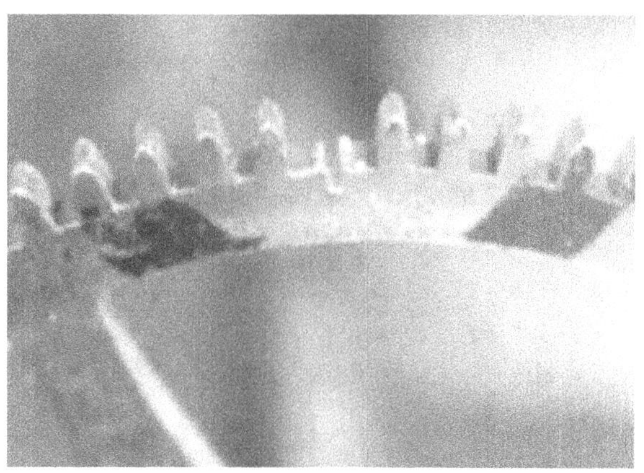

Cut out a dovetail-shaped key halfway into the rim.

Using a very thin cut of 600 grit wet and dry cloth in a 'to and fro' motion with both hands will effectively smooth the base of the dovetail. Wet and dry paper will break doing this. The fiber-backed type is ideal for this.

Finishing or widening the dovetail side is tricky in such a tiny space. My preference here is to use the cheap suspension springs with wet and dry paper glued to one side. This technique creates a tool that can work effectively in this small space and will not abrade other areas of the working space.

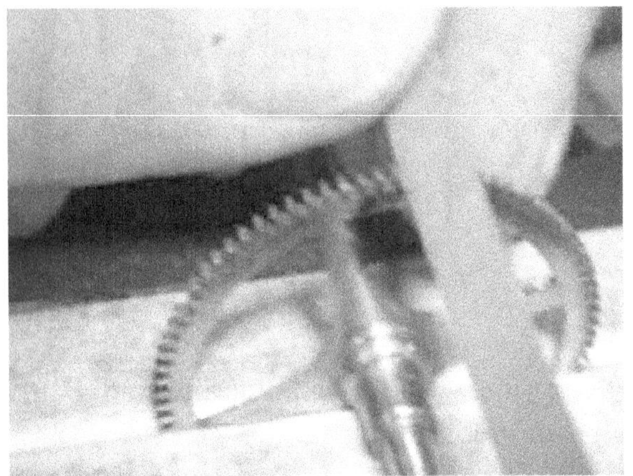

Once you're happy with your dovetail hole, cut a piece of donor brass, "clock making brass "C-353", place it under the dovetail hole, mask the wheel up with tape, holding the donor piece tight to the wheel with the tape. Other types of brass might work, but they will be harder to cut and fit to the exact shape. Spray the dovetail very lightly with aerosol paint and leave it to dry.

Any paint on the wheel will dissolve in acetone. You will have the impression of the dovetail left on the donor brass, which will be a great help when sawing the new tooth. Leave plenty of brass at the large end of the donor piece for handling and holding in a vice.

The donor piece needs to be a tight fit. It is a good idea, with a very fine paintbrush, to apply a little solder flux in the joint before fitting. I use Tix flux [not anti-flux] and solder. This solder is very hard when set and will withstand the forces acting on the new tooth.

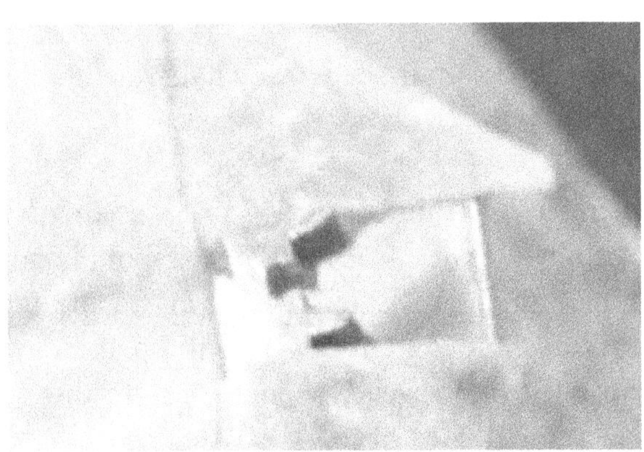

When you are happy that it will go in with a little gentle persuasion, a little tap with a brass-ended flat punch will fit the piece squarely. Ensure there is excess donor brass on either side of the wheel, and using a flat steel punch, 'peen' the donor brass to fit/fill the dovetail hole well. Do not hammer so much that the wheel is deformed, making it out of round. The flux has already been applied to the joint.

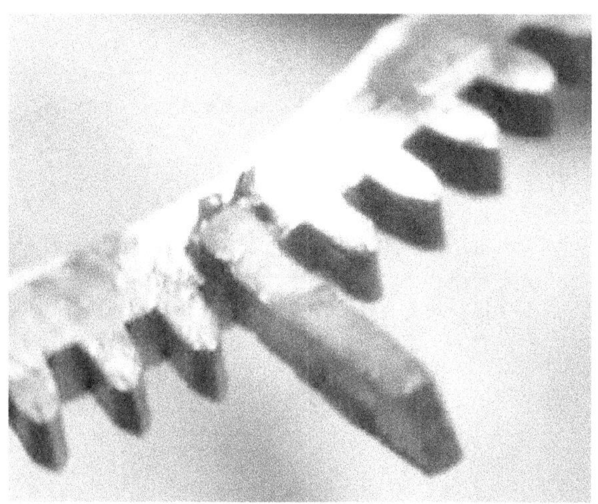

Place <u>small</u> chips of Tix solder on top of the joint. A mini butane soldering torch with a fine hot air nozzle from underneath does a great job. After it has cooled, clean off any flux thoroughly.

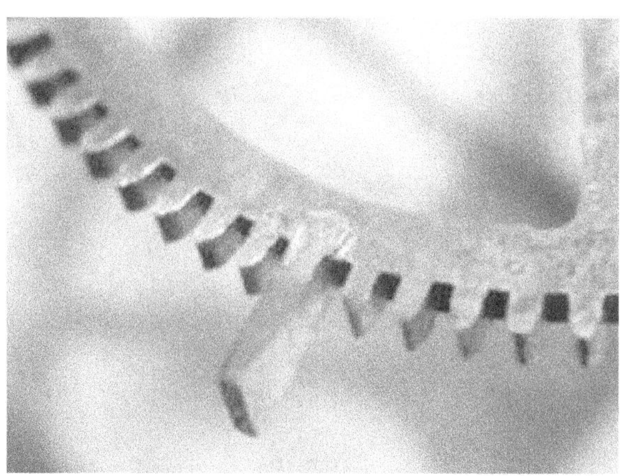

Cut the tooth to length

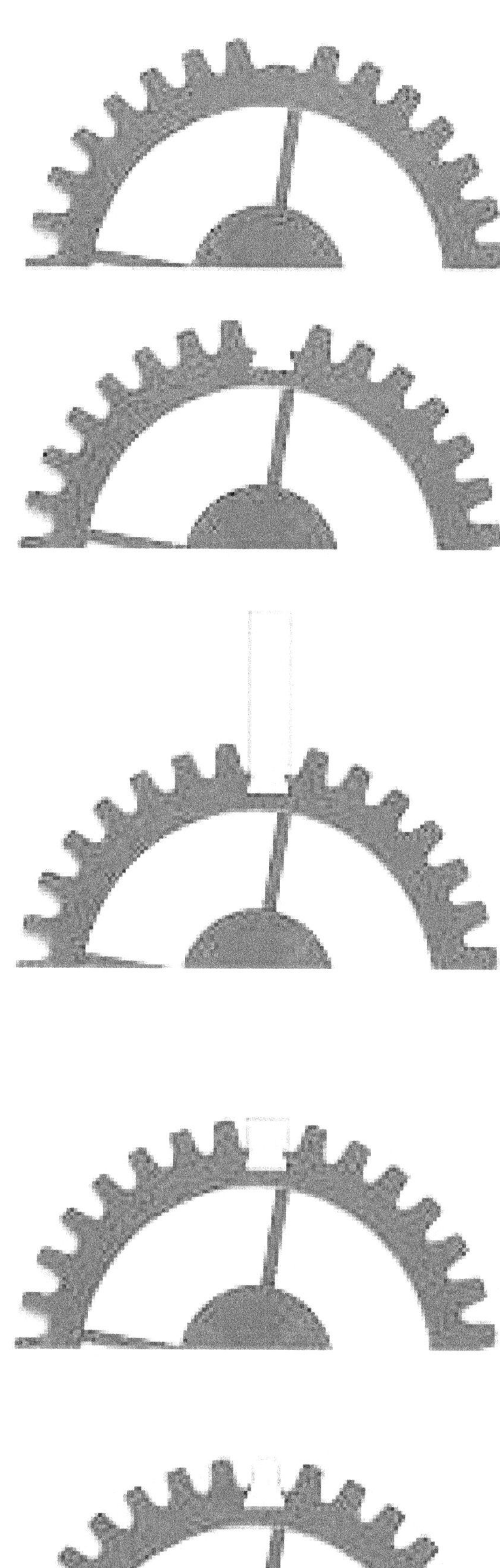

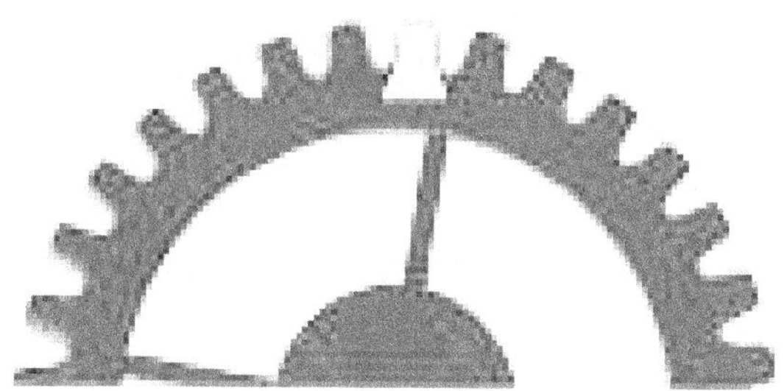

Slowly file the tooth to the correct profile, frequently testing its mesh with the matching pinion between the plates. Use a barrette file with a "safe edge" [an edge without a file profile] so you don't file unintended areas.

The dovetail can be carefully finished/ polished with very fine wet and dry paper, to a point where it is virtually invisible to the naked eye.

When using files to shape the tooth, it is best to use as fine a file as you can, cut grade 4 and above. 'Escapement' files are smaller than other needle files. For shaping the top of the tooth, a Barette/safety escapement file is ideal. Good ones are not cheap and should be saved for delicate jobs.

An alternative approach is to find an old scrap wheel of similar diameter and tooth count. Cut out 3 or 5 teeth and its rim, and solder it to the side of the damaged wheel, matching the teeth even or slightly proud. File down the teeth as needed. This method can only be used if the mating pinion will allow the extra width.

This approach can also be used to solder a solid piece of brass alongside the missing tooth and hand filing it to the correct shape.

For mainspring barrel teeth repair, you will need to cut out more material, as shown.

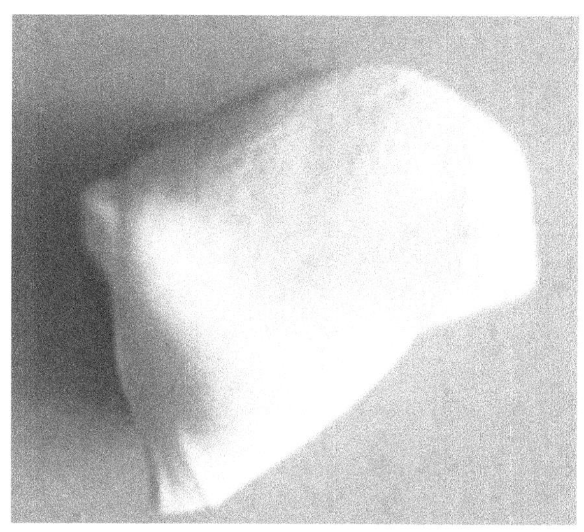

Rodico is available from TimeSavers for $5.00

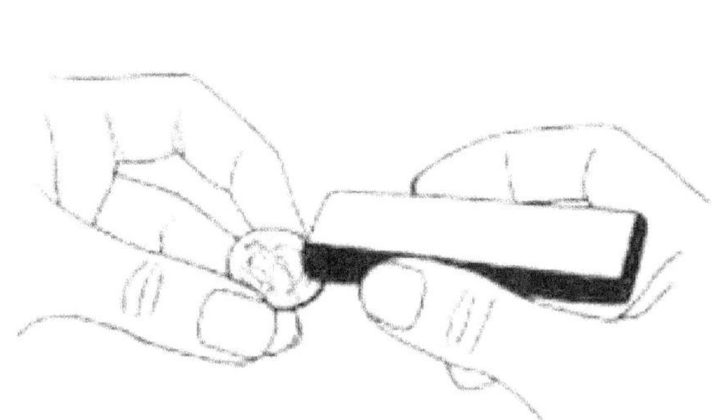

Rodico has many uses in clock repair, including picking up very small parts safely. In this case, I pressed some Rodico into the wheel that needs a tooth replaced, then used the imprint to make sure the repaired tooth is perfectly profiled.

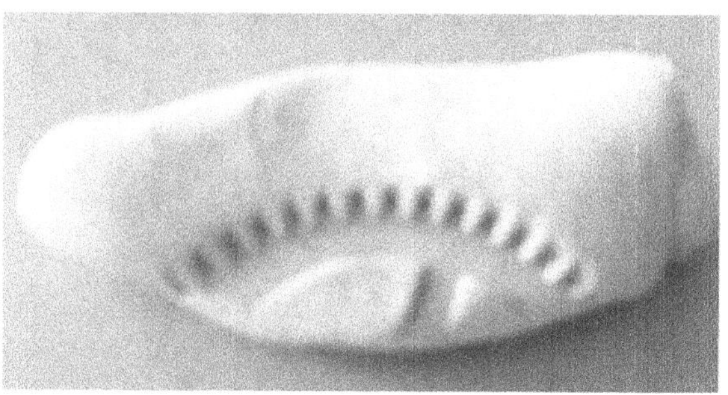

You can add a small amount to the end of a screwdriver to hold the screw while reaching inside the case to secure the movement.

I have not tried this myself, but dental 'burrs' have been used to create the dovetail shape for a replacement tooth.   Search for "Dental Carbide Straight Handpiece Inverted Cone" Bur number 34 or 35.

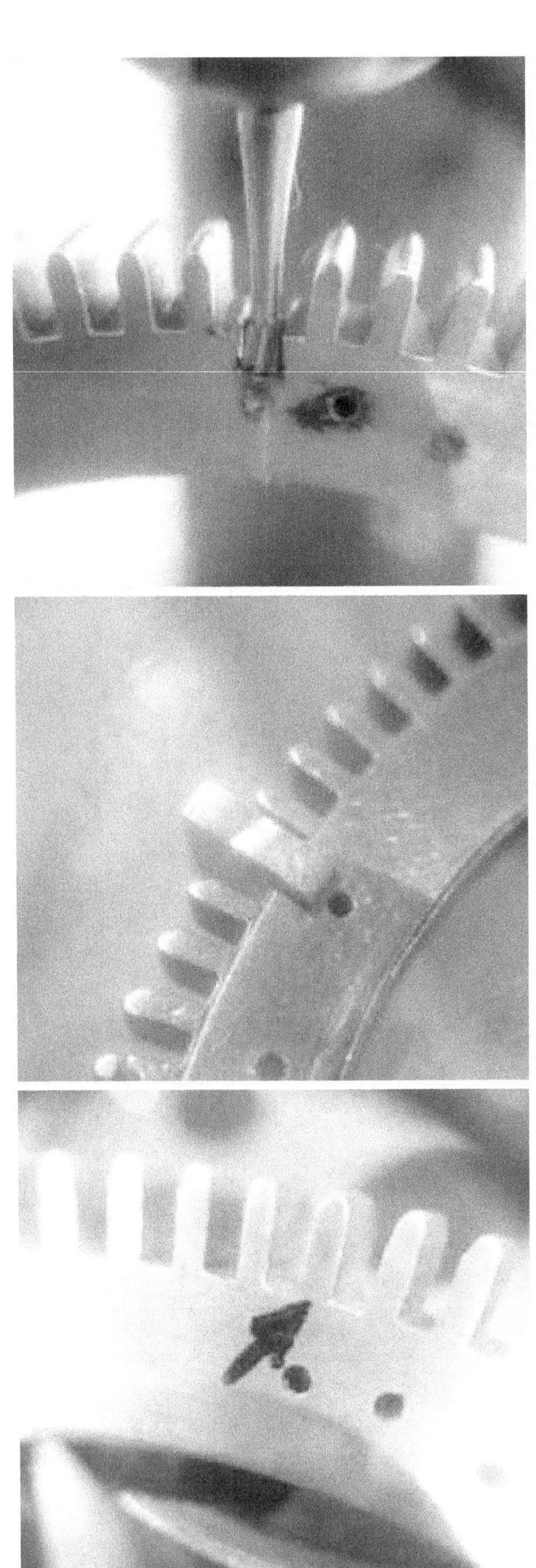

Barrette files

Barrette files are machinist's files that are easily identified by the fact they are only cut on one face. There is a large, safe surface that is referred to as the 'back.' This means only one part of the file will cut a workpiece, leading to a high degree of security against mistakes.

Barrette files usually have trapezoid cross-sections, but sometimes they may be triangular, and taper in both width and thickness, which allows them to access small spaces.

They are double-cut, but only on the flat face. The uncut face is referred to as the 'back.' This means that they can be used for filing keyways, internal angles in slots, and general finishing and deburring, without fear of accidental wear to another surface during the filing process.

When combined with their taper, the fact that only one of their faces is cut makes them perfect for precision filing.

The coarseness rating ranges from #00 the coarsest, to #6 the finest.

To clean any file, rub a piece of copper over it. An offcut of copper pipe is just fine.   Copper is soft enough to form grooves in it the shape of the file grooves, which then clean out the file grooves.

A lantern pinion consists of two end caps called shrouds, with hard metal rods or pins called trundles fitted around in a circle creating a very efficient and cost-effective pinion.

It can often be found that these rods are worn, bent, broken, or missing.

The rods should be loosely fitted, so the first step is to rotate the rod to a new position.

It is not hard to replace the rods, but I recommend you do not take the whole thing apart at one time. It can be challenging to get back together again. Instead, replace each trundle one at a time as needed, and the job is quite easy.

To replace one trundle, take a small drill bit, about #55 [0.052"] fitted in a pin vice, and turn it by hand in the end hole to release the brass that is riveting it in place. It only takes a few turns to remove the soft brass.

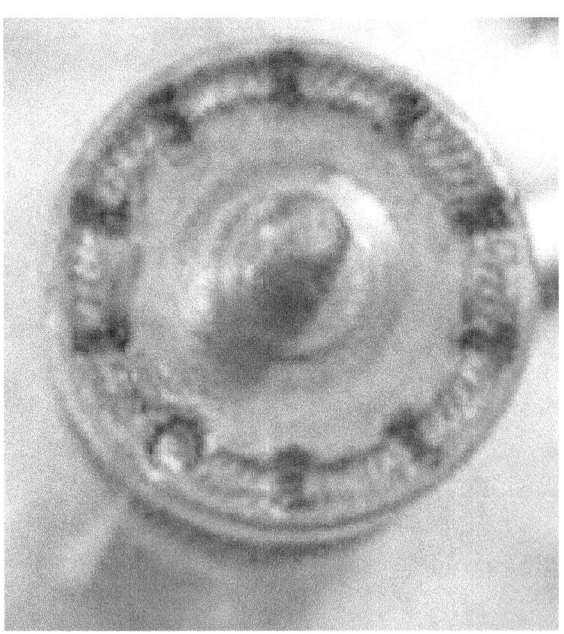

Once it is released, you can slide the trundle out using needle-nose pliers.

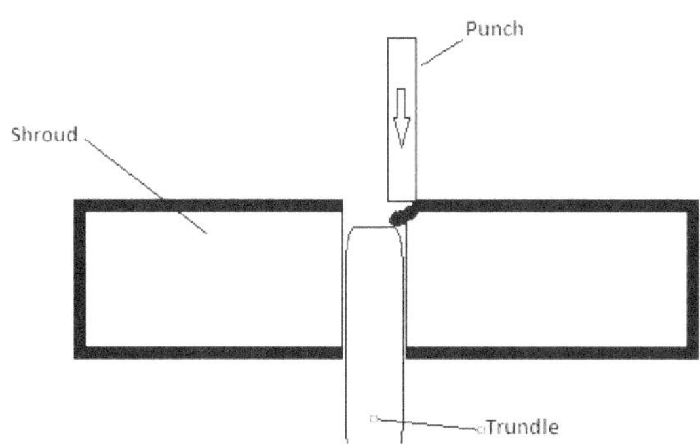

Find a pivot wire that is the correct size, cut it to length using a Dremel cutoff wheel, leaving room to rivet [swage] it back in and close the hole a little with a small punch.

It is important to support the upper shroud, or it might slide down when riveting.

This pair of needle nose pliers have been modified. The bottom jaw was slotted with a Dremel tool and a cutoff blade. The top was heated, bent, and ground to shape as shown. It will support the shroud and close the hole in one motion.

An alternative is to hold it in place using Loctite. The disadvantage of this method is it does not allow the trundle to roll when in operation.

Timesavers sells this drill bit set for $6.50, and they work well for many repair projects, including re-pivoting. *#17531*

polish the tops of the leaves. If rusted, use a scratch brush or soft wire wheel in a Dremel tool.

Another option is to secure a washer to the top of the shroud, to hold all the trundles in place.

You might come across a clock with 'rolling pinions.' In this case, the trundles have a pivot formed on the ends, and they rotate between the shrouds as the clock wheel teeth pass by, allowing less friction and wear.

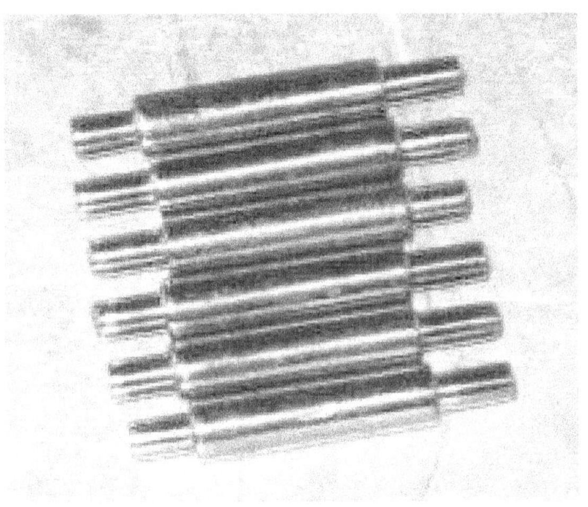

If you have solid leaf pinions that are badly worn, it is best to move the wheel down the arbor a little way, so the wheel falls on a sound part of the pinion. There is usually plenty of room to do this. If this is not possible, a new pinion will need to be made by a specialist company.

Very dirty or rusted pinions can be cleaned using pegwood with a chisel end formed with a knife to clean the bottom of the leaves. If needed, use a polishing compound. Cut a second piece of pegwood with a slot in it to

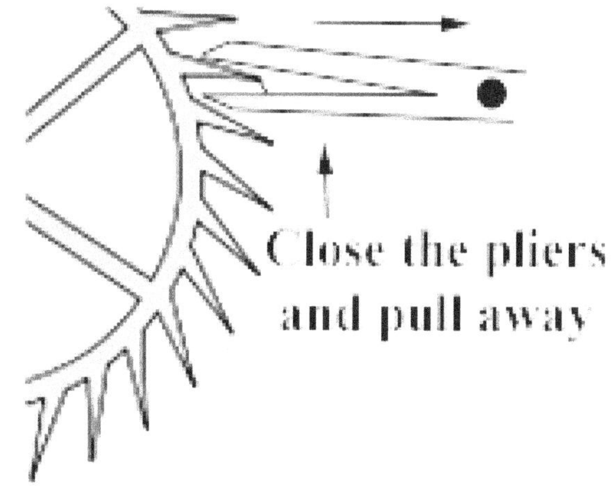

Using a good pair of pliers with smooth jaws [no serrations on the inside face], carefully grasp each tooth at its root and gently squeeze, 'draw' the pliers out at the correct angle to straighten and stretch the tooth. This needs to be done with great care while the wheel is out of the movement. It will correct any bends and smooth out any imperfections. Every tooth on the escape wheel must be in 'perfect condition.

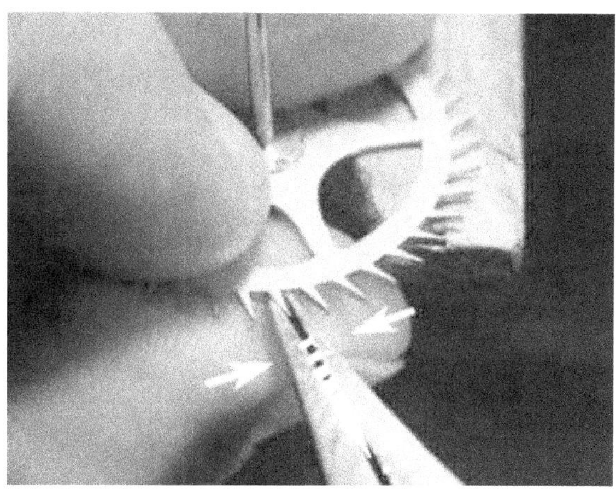

After straightening teeth, the wheel will likely need topping to make sure all teeth are the same length and perfectly round. Use a lathe [or drill] and very light strokes of a fine buffing stick.

After topping, the backs of the fat teeth will need filing down to between 0.1mm and 0.2mm and make all the spaces between the teeth equal. Create a simple gauge to test the gaps. Press several known good teeth into Rodico to make an impression, then compare this impression to suspect teeth.

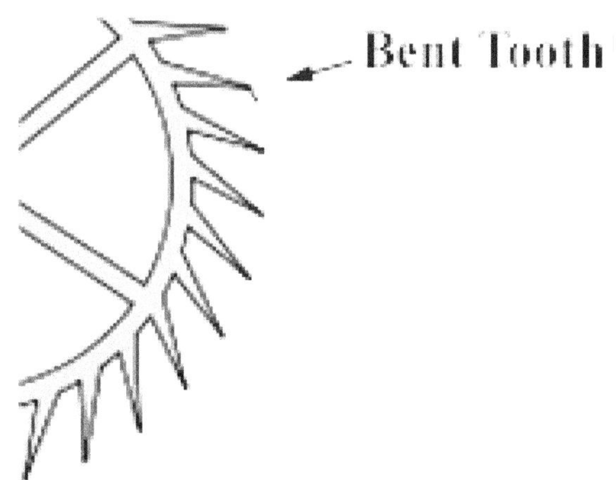

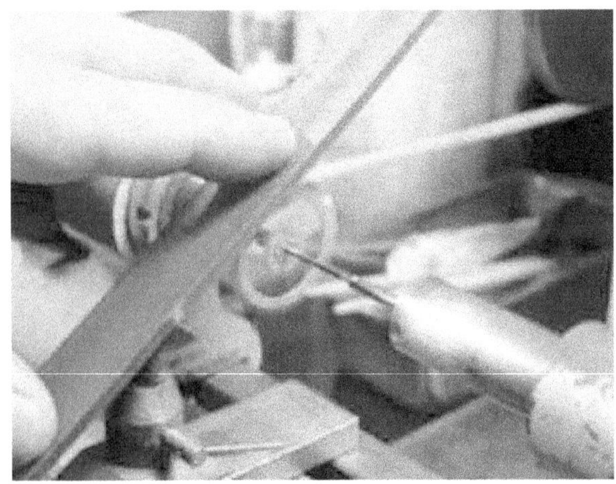

Make sure the escapement is properly adjusted. Each tooth should only just clear the pallet. The drop should not exceed 1/6th of the distance between teeth. Check with a feeler gauge. A loud tick or a large drop indicates it is adjusted too far away. Adjust it closer until it catches the tooth, then back it off a fraction until it just clears.

Look closely at the escapement pivots. They should not move from side to side when operating. If it does, the offending pivot hole needs repair.

For the escapement to work correctly, everything about it must be in good working order. If there is any play in the saddle pivot, it will give inconsistent and thus poor performance. For this reason, we should pay close attention to the condition of the saddle pivot and its pivot hole.

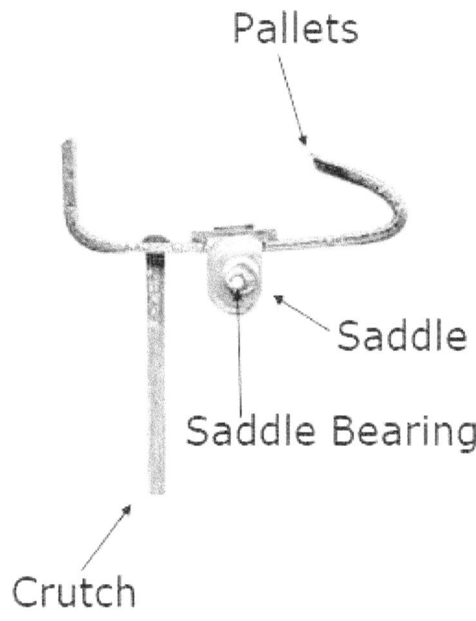

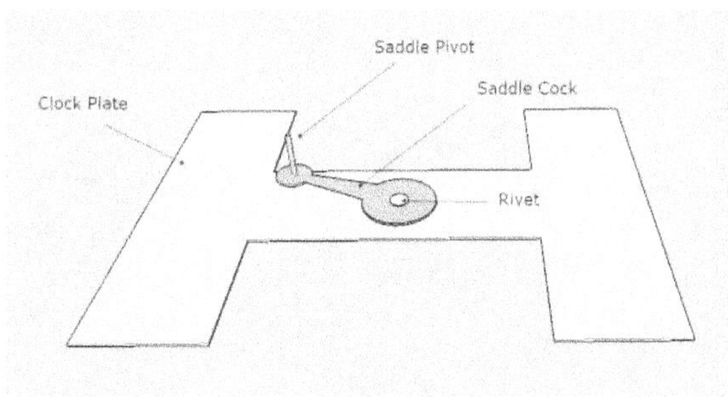

The saddle is not suited to be bushed. If there is excessive wear, the saddle pin must be replaced.

To begin, the saddle pivot is removed from the saddle cock.

This can be done by securely grasping the pivot with pliers and pulling it out while rotating it alternately clockwise and counterclockwise.

Another method is to use a pair of diagonal cutters [wire cutters]. Grip the pivot with the cutter close to the saddle cock and push downward on the handle. This will cause the pivot to move up and out of the cock.

If more leverage is needed, place the blade of a small screwdriver under the pivot point of the pliers, between the cutter blade and the cock. This will effectively provide a greater lever arm.

Next, measure the diameter of the pivot. For discussion, let's say it measures 0.042" diameter. Choose a piece of pinion wire several thousandths larger – about 0.045" diameter.

Test fit this larger wire in the saddle bearing. This wire should not be able to fit into the saddle bearing. Cut the selected wire to the same length as the original pivot. Now insert this new pivot into the hole in the saddle cock. It may be necessary to broach out the hole in the saddle cock to drive the new pivot tight into the hole. Be careful so as not to end up with too large of a hole in the saddle cock. It needs to be friction-tight.

It may be necessary to swivel the saddle cock about its rivet to achieve working clearance to drive in the new pivot. If this is needed, make a small scribe on the plate to mark its position before swiveling.

After installing the new saddle pivot, the saddle bearing needs to be realigned back to its correct position on the scribe. Do this carefully. Check to ensure there is no burr at the end of the new pivot. If there is, file it smooth.

Broach the outboard saddle bearing first to achieve a good pivot fit. Then flip the saddle unit over and broach the inboard bearing. DO NOT attempt broaching through the outboard bearing to broach the inboard bearing, the taper of the broach will cause the outboard bearing to be too large when a good fit is achieved for the inboard bearing.

Once a good fit is achieved, place the saddle on the saddle pivot and secure it with the retainer. Lubricate both the inboard and outboard saddle bearing. Hold the clock plate in a plum position and give the crutch a swing to test for a good fit. Ensure there is no binding in the escapement swing. If necessary, re-broach the appropriate bearing.

This completes the worn saddle pivot repair.

As you dismantle a movement, you might find a broken or even missing spring that keeps a striking wire in its correct location. It is easy to make a new spring. Purchase Wire-Brass Spring #28 [*timesavers #23908*].

Cut off about 8". Starting 1" from the end, coil the wire carefully around a screwdriver acting as a mandrel, making sure not to overlap the coils. Stop one inch from the other end, then shape a hook at each end around the tip of needle-nose pliers, and there you have a custom-made spring.

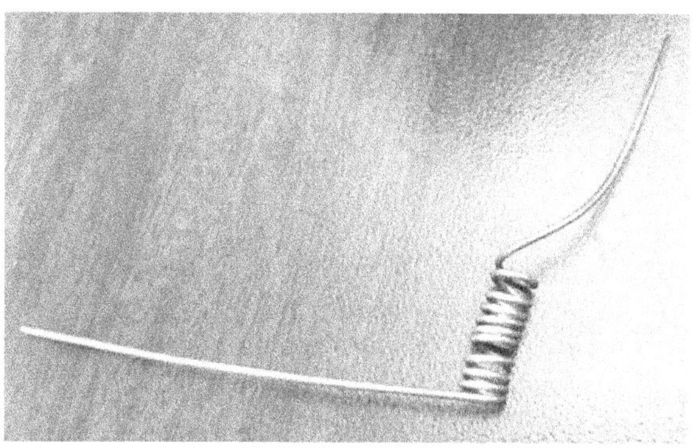

If you want to get fancier, this is a homemade spring-making machine.

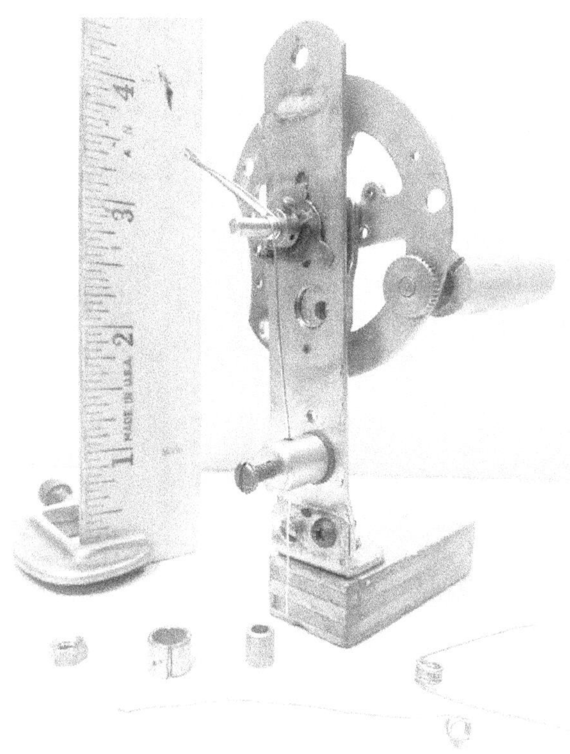

Here are a couple homemade tools using parts that were laying around the shop [or use your lathe]. Keep tension as you wind and make springs that look "factory"

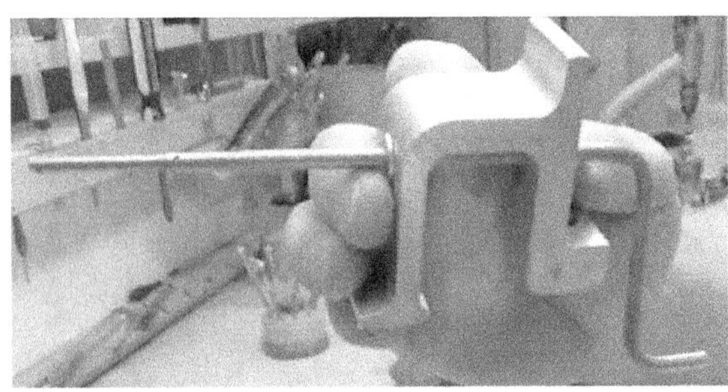

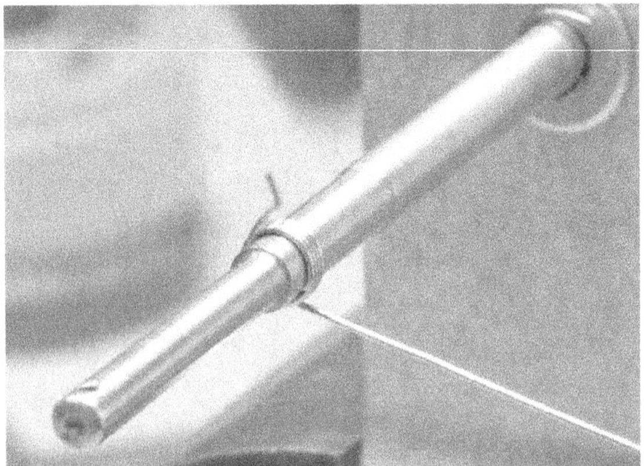

Motion Work

The term motion works refer to the additional gearing necessary to add a minute wheel/hand. The motion work is the small 12-to-1 reduction gear train that turns the timepiece's hour hand from the minute hand. It is attached to the going train by the friction coupling of the cannon pinion, so the minute and hour hands can be turned independently to set the

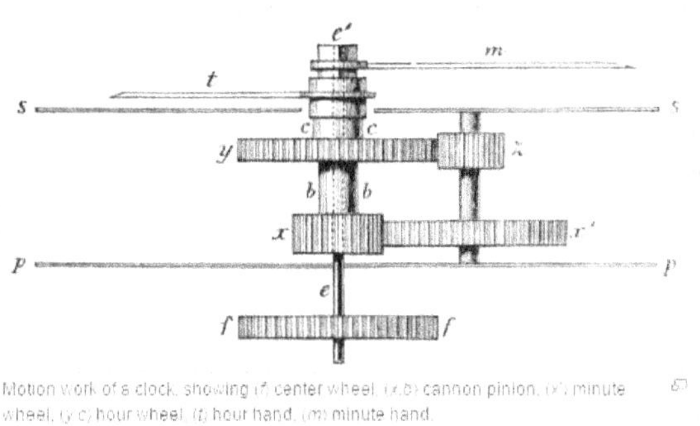

Motion work of a clock, showing (*t*) center wheel, (*x,b*) cannon pinion, (*y*) minute wheel, (*y,c*) hour wheel, (*f*) hour hand, (*m*) minute hand.

timepiece. It is often located on the outside of the movement's front plate, just under the dial.

It consists of:

Cannon pinion- a pinion with a hollow shaft that fits friction tight over the center wheel shaft, projects through the clock face, and holds the minute hand. While the timepiece is not being set, this is turned by the center wheel and drives the minute wheel. While being set, it is turned by the setting mechanism, in modern clocks, a setting knob on the back of the clock. Setting the hands is done by opening the face and manually pushing the minute hand, which rotated the cannon pinion directly.

Minute wheel- Its pinion drives the hour wheel. During setting, this is driven by the intermediate wheel, and it turns both the cannon pinion and the hour wheel, moving the hands.

Hour wheel- which fits over the shaft of the cannon pinion, and whose shaft holds the hour hand. The hour wheel rotates once for every 12 rotations of the cannon pinion/minute hand.

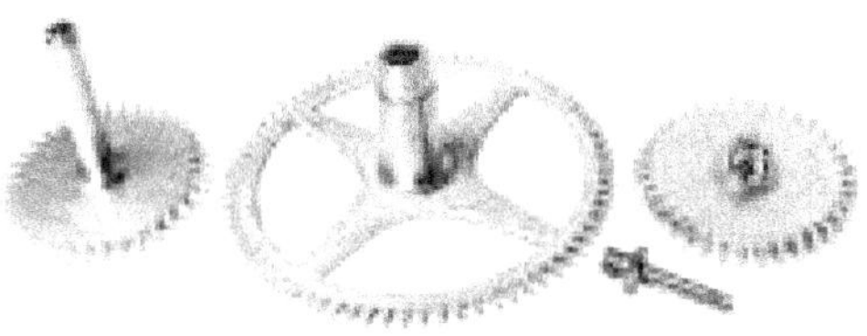

It would be possible to use only two wheels to make the gear reduction but that would leave the minute hand traveling counter clockwise. Not good.

Reassembly

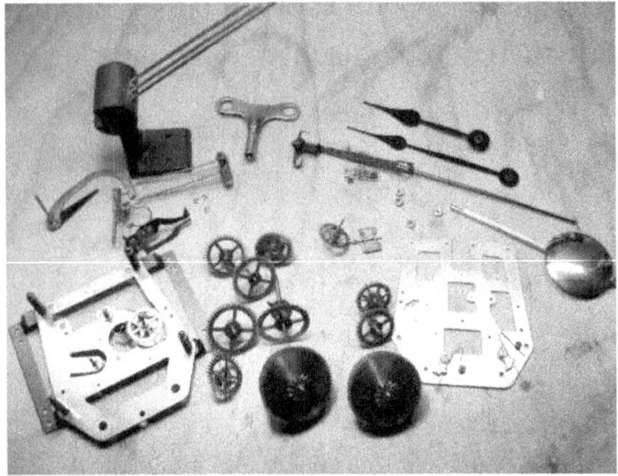

When the pivots are smooth and the pivot holes are all correct, insert each wheel in place **by itself** between the plates and make sure it spins freely, smoothly, and with a little endshake. Test the spin in several positions, top plate up, top plate down, escape wheel up, escape wheel down, looking for any possible interference. It should come to a very gradual stop, not a sudden halt. Rotating the plates up and down, the wheel should drop onto the other shoulder freely.

When all have been tested individually, insert two at a time to test the mesh of each wheel and pinion teeth. Use only light pressure to feel any roughness in the mesh at any point. Then turn them fast to observe them coming to a very gradual stop. When each pair has been

tested, insert all the wheels in the **time train only,** not including the escapement. Test that they all spin freely, the teeth mesh correctly and they come to a very gradual stop.

Look for any wobble in any wheel. Do the same for the striking train and chime train if the movement has one. **If you skip this procedure, you will likely regret it later.**

Next, do a final cleaning in a fresh solution. Then insert everything back into the plates using gloves without touching the parts with your bare hands. Or use disposable finger cots.

Place the plate that contains the pillars on your box or movement pillars. Refer to your photos, diagrams, and notes. Reset all the wheels and levers in place.

It is often most efficient to insert the wheels into the bottom plate in this order: Center wheel, third wheel, two great wheels, hammer, pinwheel, escape wheel, gathering-pallet wheel, warning wheel, and lastly, the fly.

Bring the second plate down. One by one using tweezers, locate the top pivots back into their pivot holes. Do not use pliers or anything stronger than tweezers. The pivots can bend or even be broken off very easily.

You will find each arbor is a slightly different length. Knowing this, look for the tallest and fit that first, then move on down until you get the shortest. You can add a couple of rubber bands around the front and back plates to hold it all together until everything is in the correct location.

Typically, the great wheel [home to the mainspring] is tallest with its winding arbor. Once this is in place, you can usually start a turn of the nuts on the two bottom pillars, then work up the train until you can start a turn on the other two pillar nuts. Each wheel will click in place, which I find very satisfying. When the last pivot is located, the upper plate will come down onto the shoulders of the pillars.

This can be a tricky process at first, but it soon becomes easier once you have done it several times, and you are more familiar with the parts. Be patient and be prepared that you might have to take the movement apart again and start over if fine-tuning is needed. Never force anything and take your time. Make it a habit of testing everything you add during assembly to catch any faults before you get too far. To verify a wheel is in its correct place, using tweezers, slide the arbor up and down. If it is in place, it will slide up and down freely. If it is frozen in place, it is trapped between the plates, not in its pivot holes.

For movements with a striking train, first, when you assemble the clock, make sure that the maintenance wheel is adjusted so that the count lever is in a deep notch and the maintenance lever is at the bottom of the maintenance cam. That takes care of [1] and [2]. Then, try to adjust the warning wheel so that the warning pin is about 1/2 turn away from the locking lever. The reason is that the warning wheel is spinning very fast, so it needs some "lead distance" to make sure the locking lever is down before the warning pin gets to it. [See the striking section later in this book for more information on this setup]

When you are satisfied it is all correct, tighten the movement nuts or taper pins, and wind the spring a little to remove the mainspring clamps. I recommend you use a brass pin in a steel pillar, to prevent the pin from getting stuck in a steel mating hole over time.

Occasionally you will find that once a wheel is in place and the levers fitted [especially with rack and snail] you can't access the oil sink. In that case, it is best to oil that pivot during assembly.

Rack & Snail Striking

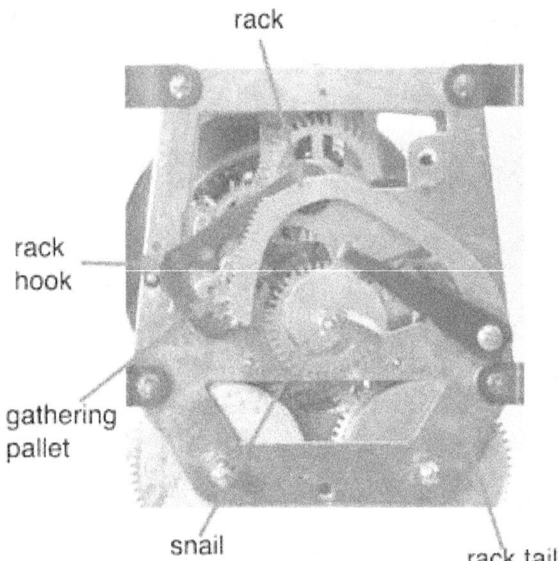

These are two common examples of Rack & Snail striking movements. This is a modern upgrade from the older more primitive count wheel system which is prone to getting out of sync.

The main mechanical components of every rack-striking clock are:
- saw-toothed rack, with a tail
- nautilus-shaped snail, with 12 steps that turn with the hour hand.
- rack hook, to support the rack
- gathering pallet, to engage the teeth of the rack

The snail, with its ever-enlarging radius, determines the number to strike and is indexed by the rack tail. The rack counts off the strike.

Things are properly adjusted when...

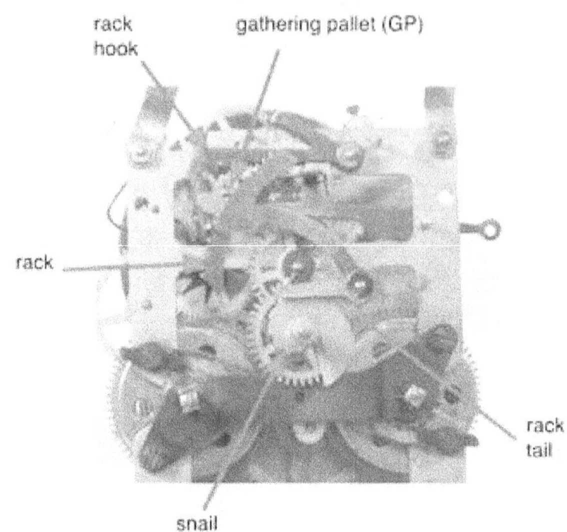

- When the rack hook is fully dropped beneath the rack,
- The warning pin is resting against the locking stub; and
- The projection on the rack hook is nestled in the dent of the bean cam.

That means the rack hook is synchronized with the warning wheel.

The cam is a pressed fit on its arbor. It can be adjusted either by twisting it on the arbor or by prying it off and repositioning it with its recess against the rack hook pin. Do this while the warning pin is against the locking flag. Observe the position of the pinwheel. There should be a little run before the next pin lifts the hammer.

Identify these parts. Each Rack and Snail striking movement will have some variation on this concept.

The Lift Cam on the minute arbor lifts the Hour Warning Lever.

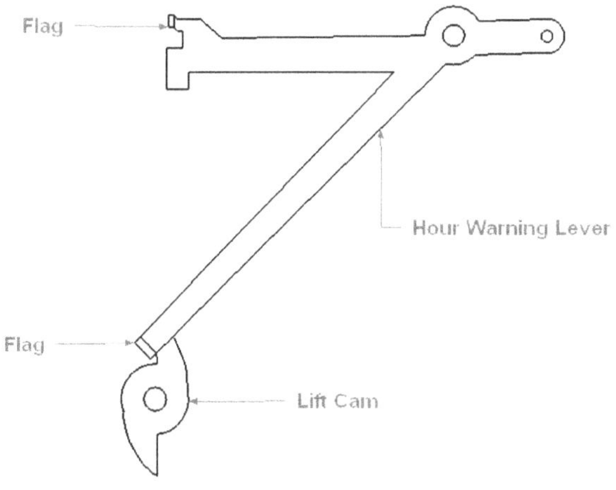

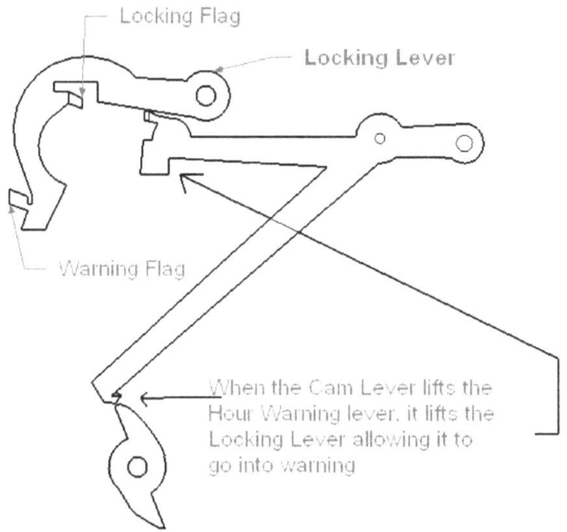

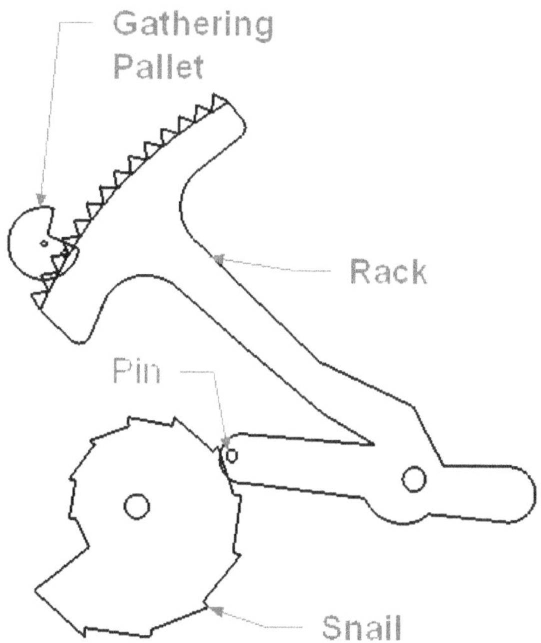

When it goes into warning, the pin on the Rack lands on the Snail to determine how many times to strike. The Gathering Pallet advances the Rack until the correct number of bell or gong strikes have sounded.

The advantage Rack & Snail has over the Count Wheel system is the striking stays synchronized with the hour hand, so it always strikes the correct hour. The Count Wheel will get out of sync if the hands are advanced without allowing the strike [and Count Wheel] to stay synchronized.

Chiming Setup

My favorite method is to take the chime count wheel off and let the chime run until it stops. That will be the auto synch position. Put the wheel back on at the 3/4 hour position and turn the chime drum at the back until you get the four or eight-note descending scale that is both the 1/4 hour and the end of the 3/4 hour chime. That will get everything working together correctly.

Congratulations, you are now **hooked.**

Lubricating the Movement

Lubricants provide a protective film that separates the two rubbing surfaces and reduces the level of friction in the two rubbing surfaces. The correct oiling of the movement is critical. There are many specialty clock oils available which you can use, but there is an ideal motor oil. Mobil 1 Synthetic– 0W-40 for pivots and Mobil 1 Synthetic 10W-60 for mainsprings. Having used this for years, I have found it does not go gummy, is not too thin to run out, and is compatible with the typical clock metals.

A fellow clock repairer used to be a chemist and studied the various clock oils on the market and their viscosity, and recommended Mobile 1 to me.

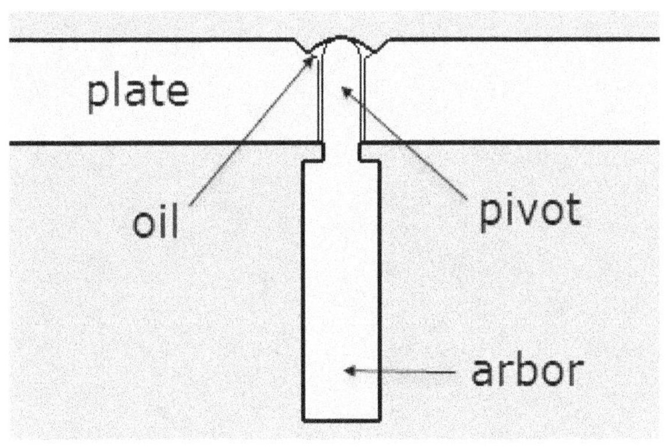

Insert only a small amount of oil in the oil sink. Oil is held in place by capillary attraction and surface tension. If you insert too much oil, the oil will be drawn out and leave it dry. No more oil should be used than is needed to coat the pivot and pivot hole.

Ideally, use a heavy lubricant for high-torque, low-speed applications [mainspring, 1st and 2nd wheel pivots] like Mobile-1 10W-40. Use a light lubricant for low-torque, high-speed applications [3rd, 4th, escape wheel pivots, balance pivots, escape wheel teeth, clock strike governor pivots, etc.] like Mobile-1 0W-40.

Approximate Viscosities of Common Materials	
Material	Viscosity in Centipoise @70F
Water	1
Milk	3
Nye Clock Oil 140B	20
Sperm Oil	52
SAE 10 Motor Oil	85-140
SAE 20 Motor Oil	140-420
SAE 30 Motor Oil	420-650
SAE 40 Motor Oil	650-900
Mobil 1 5W-30	178
Mobil 1 0W-40	215
Mobil 1 5W-40	250
Mobil 1 10W-40	325
SAE 80W-90	585
SAE 85W140	1750

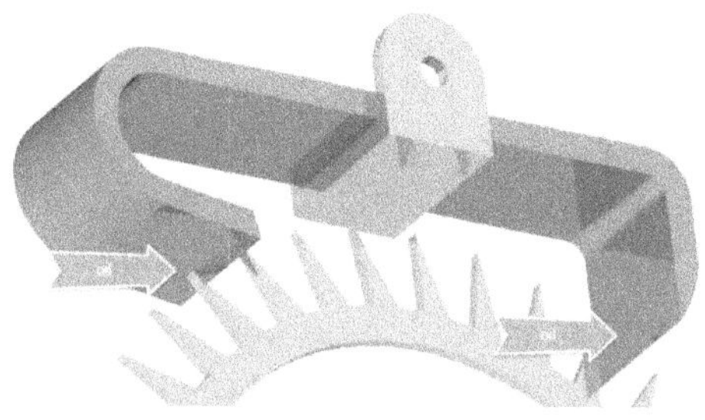

Place one drop of oil on the escapement pallet impulse faces. Do not oil any of the wheel teeth.

Place one drop on each lever post, the minute wheel post, the escapement post and on each click.

Screw the movement to a [homemade] test stand, clamped to a benchtop or table. Make sure it is level to the eye. Add the pendulum, wind it up, and start the clock to make sure it runs. Closely observe the movement and listen to all sounds. The tick and tock should be even. Adjust the pendulum crutch if it is not even. Adjust its regulation until it keeps good time.

When I say level, I find my students get paranoid about 'level.' The fact is the movement needs to be placed on the stand so it is 'in beat' [see the first chapter]. There is no guarantee the movement will be set in the case perfectly level, and the place the clock sets might not be perfectly level.

Make sure it runs for a full 24 hours before putting the movement back into its case.

The test stand below fits many movements just sitting on top. It is easy to make using ½" plywood. 12" tall, 8" wide, and 6" deep. Cut a hole in the top about 4" by 3" or to suit your movement. The pendulum [and weight chains if it has weights] fit through the hole in the top. Make a second top out of ¼" ply to fit smaller movements. An added front piece will accept movements screwed to its face. Cut a hole in it if needed.

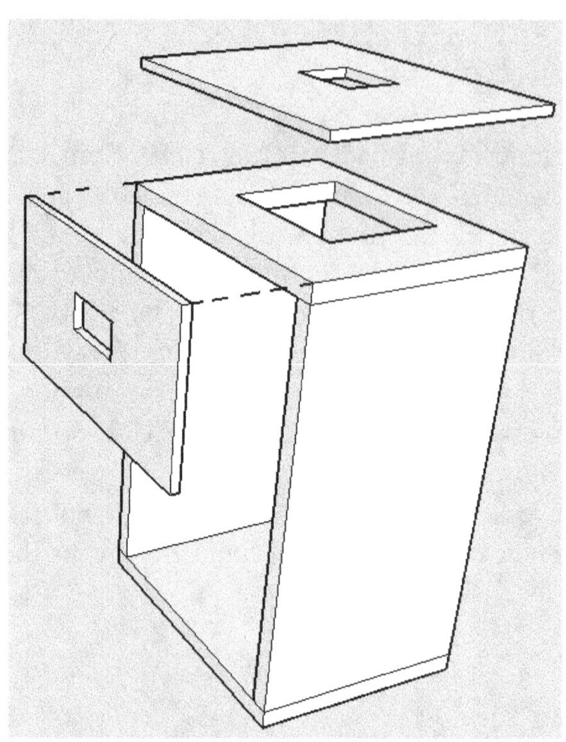

If you have a table that takes leaves? Open it just a crack for the chains, hang the weights under the table, and voila! Instant workbench. I did that a few times when I was first starting.

In a perfect world, after you have finished servicing your clock movement, it would run perfectly the first time. However, we all know this is not a perfect world. If you put your serviced movement on the test stand and it will not run, follow this process.

Assuming it runs but slows down and stops, look to see if the escapement is caught on a tooth, or swinging free of either pallet. If it is caught on a pallet/tooth, it is most likely an imperfect tooth, or the escapement needs adjusting. See above.

If it is free of the tooth, it is not getting enough power. Your work needs checking.

Try removing all but the last two wheels on the time side – i.e., the escape wheel and the next wheel down the chain. Add the escapement and hang a weight from the wheel before the escape wheel. Make sure it is pulling in the power direction. If it does not run, the problem is right there. If it does run, add one more wheel and test again with the weight on the lowest wheel. Keep testing until it refuses to run.

The wire to the pendulum rod must be close-fitting in the crutch fork. If it is loose, it will lose energy jumping the gap from one side to the other. Close the gap, so it is almost but not quite touching each side of the loop.

You may find a small notch, or at least a rough place, worn there. Dress it out perfectly smooth, or your clock will likely not work well. Small as it may seem, it stops many clocks.

Make sure the wire in this area is clean and bright and, to avoid any energy loss in the touching surfaces and provide a little oil.

High-Speed Test

One test I use quite often is a high-speed test. It is simple, lubricate up all pivots, remove the escapement lever and let the movement spin. Listen, and it should produce an even whirr sound. No pops and crackle noise. Watch the speed consistency, and any irregularities will show in unison with a particular gear rotation.

The high-speed test is useful for spotting train problems, especially in the slower gears. This test with the low-speed test [low inertia - couple clicks on mainspring or small weight and freewheeling no escapement] is a good combo diagnostic.

When doing the test, mark any suspect gear when the train stops and retest to see if the same location reappears. The idea is that low power can't overcome the problem area and becomes a pointer to the problem tooth, etc..

The high-speed test is also good for revealing bent arbor/pivot as tone/speed changes with cycling of the problem gear. The smallest arbor pivot bend is magnified and revealed by sound.

A perfect train should have an even whirr. Pops are quite often bad trundles/ pinions.

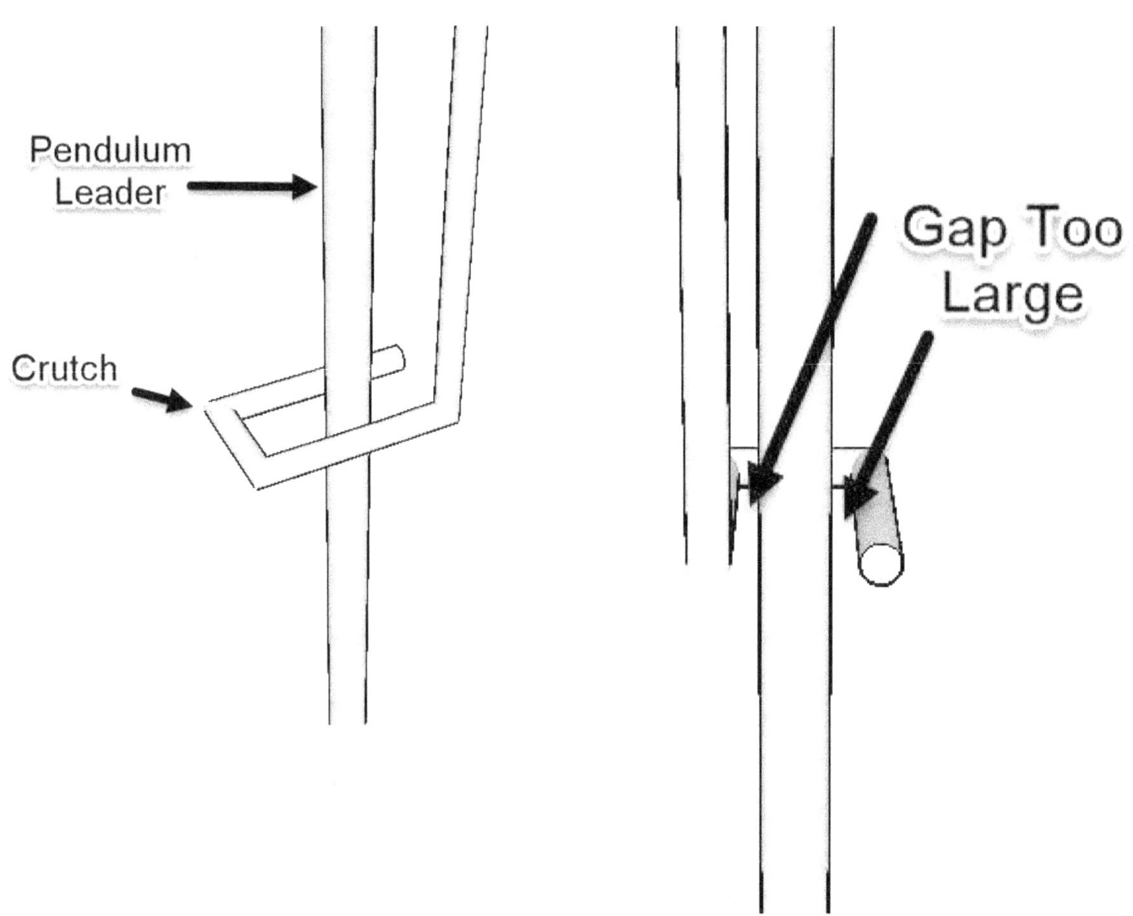

Pendulum
Leader
Crutch
Gap Too
Large

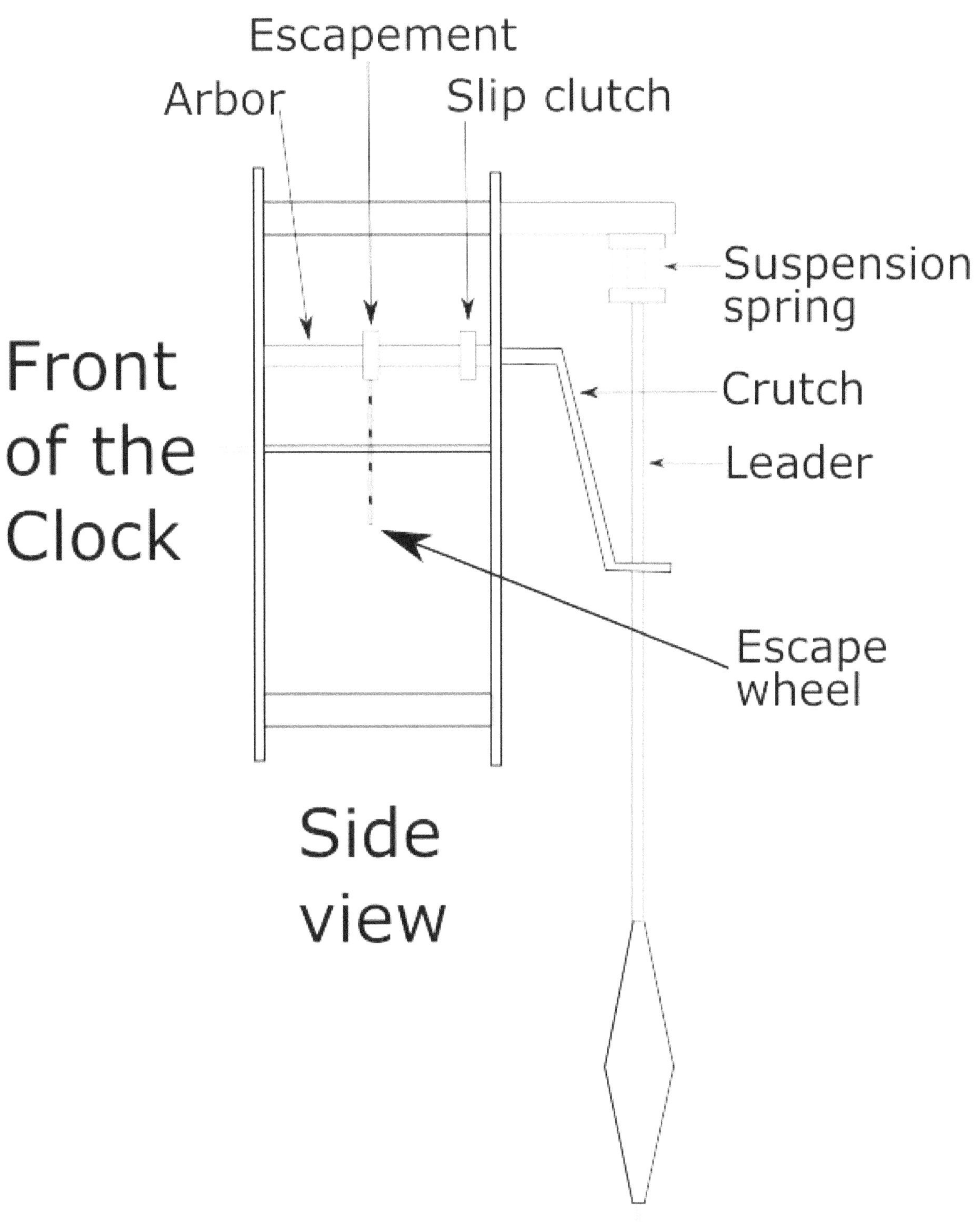

Escapement
Arbor
Slip clutch
Suspension spring
Crutch
Leader
Front of the Clock
Side view
Escape wheel

The 'cock' that supports the escapement is often friction fitted to the plate. The position of the escapement can be adjusted up or down with pliers [closer or further from the escape wheel]. Make tiny adjustments only if you are sure it is needed.

Put the Movement back in the Case

Only after you have tested the movement, made any adjustments, and tested it again for several days, you can then put the movement back in its case. Use the same screws that came out.

Reaching down into the case can be tricky, if not impossible, without the use of a slotted [not Philips] "screw holding screwdriver." They are available at many good hardware stores or online. A flashlight is helpful also.

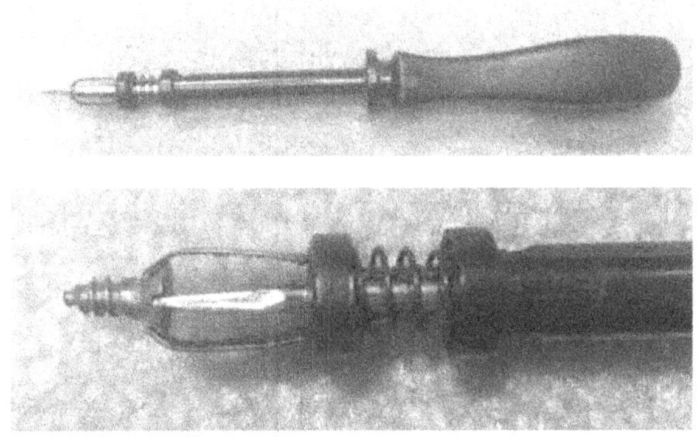

Timesavers sells a 10" Screw-Holding Screwdriver #13552 for $12.

Phillips screws were not used in the old clock, and I recommend you do not use Philips screws if replacements screws are needed. Do not be tempted to use a magnetic screwdriver. Magnetism can affect the operation of a clock, so it is normal to have a demagnetizer handy on the clock bench.

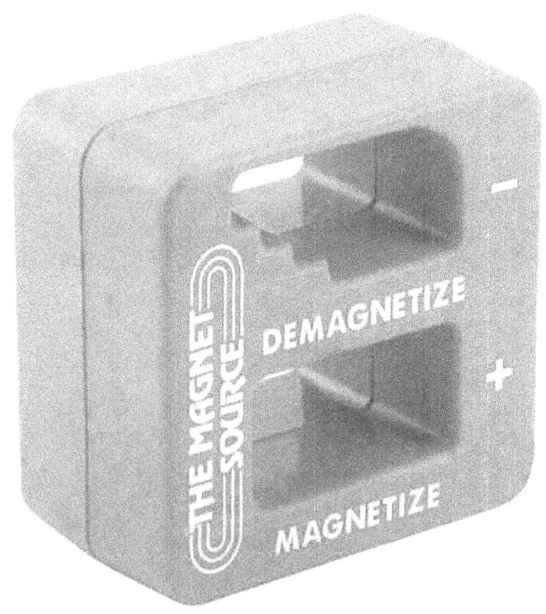

Timesavers #:*23461* $4

When installing the hands, it is very important they fit snugly so the stay in the correct alignment. If they are loose, one hand might start to catch on the other hand, the dial or the glass, which will likely stop the clock.

Make sure the minute hand is not too close to the hour hand at the arbor. This can also stop the clock and be hard to diagnose.

Install the Hands

First, put the minute hand on and adjust it forward to point precisely to 12. It usually has a square hole that fits on the square shaft. Remove the minute hand again for a moment.

Now, the hour hand is installed. It is usually friction fit onto the hour pipe. Set it to point precisely to the 12.

Next, reinstall the minute hand to the 12 o'clock position again. Both should now point precisely to the 12 at the same time. The clock is now correctly set.

If the movement includes a striking train, advance the minute hand until the clock strikes. Count the number of strikes and make the necessary adjustments to the hands. Repeat this several times to make sure it is correct.

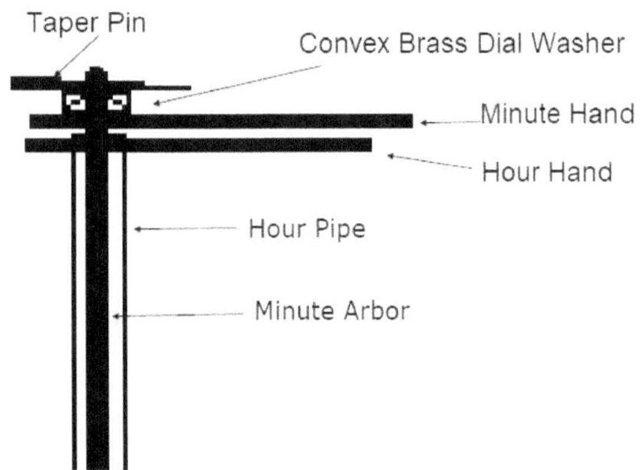

As you will note, the minute hand is very close to the hour hand, and the hour hand is very close to the clock dial. For this reason, the hands must be held firmly in place, so nothing touches each other. If the hands touch each other, the clock will stop.

The minute hand is held in place using a Convex Brass Dial Washer and either a taper pin or nut. Install a suitable dial washer, so the minute hand is held tight when the pin or nut is snugged up.

Above is an assortment of dial washers.

If you lose or break the hands, replacements are available. The length of the minute hand should just reach the chapter ring and the hour hand point to the numbers.

New taper pins are available at the parts houses or you can make your own in a minute or two if you own a lathe.

Be sure to trim the pin to a suitable length for a tidy finish.

Wooden Works Movements

Wooden works movements come in two basic varieties, American and German.

Wooden works movements were typical from the late 1700s to mid-1840s, 95% of the clocks made in America.

Servicing wood movements should be handled just like their brass counterparts.

Why wood?

Because it was plentiful and cheap.
Why not brass?
Because it was not plentiful, nor was it cheap in America at that time. Around the late 1830s brass became easier to procure for the clockmaker and from then on wood works clocks were strictly novelties.

The plates are almost always quartersawn oak while the wheels are of oak or cherry and the arbors and pinions are usually made of maple.

Bushings

Three types of bushings - bone, wood or brass.

There is always too much emphasis placed on bushings in wooden works clocks, as being the culprit for its intermittent failure. The culprit generally rests on poor gear mesh because of the 'ovalness' of wheels. If you are going to work on these clocks, you should own and use a depthing tool to test gear mesh with every wheel to pinion fit. You will find that some fit is not acceptable no matter how deep or shallow, and it's these wheels that must be either remounted or remade. As to trying to "improve" existing bushings, please DON'T!! Use only the materials that were used initially. Steel pins riding in wood provide a good bearing surface. All the improvements that have been made, are made for marketing purposes only. Study the label of the clock carefully. Some state "improvements with brass or bone" and should be replaced as such. All others should be replaced with original wood. [white oak or cherry is most common]. A plug cutter works well in fabricating bushings.

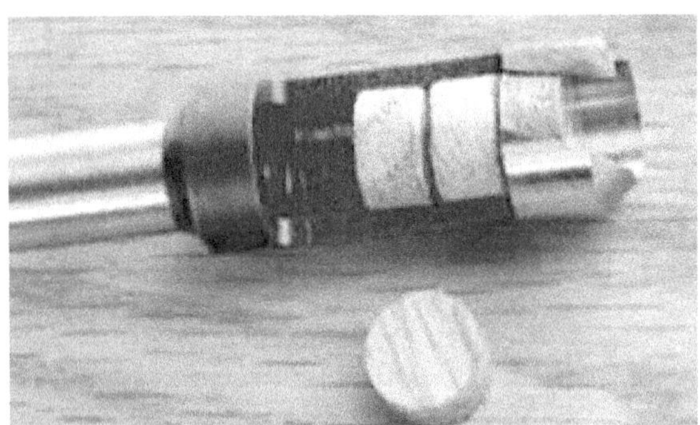

The wood plates are typically ¼" thick but the bushings should be 1/8" thick.

Using a drill press, locate the exact pivot hole position with a small drill bit about the size of the old pivot hole, then change to ¼" Forstner drill bit to drill through the plate.

Glue the new bushing into the plate, flush on the inside, using hide glue, and allow it to set.

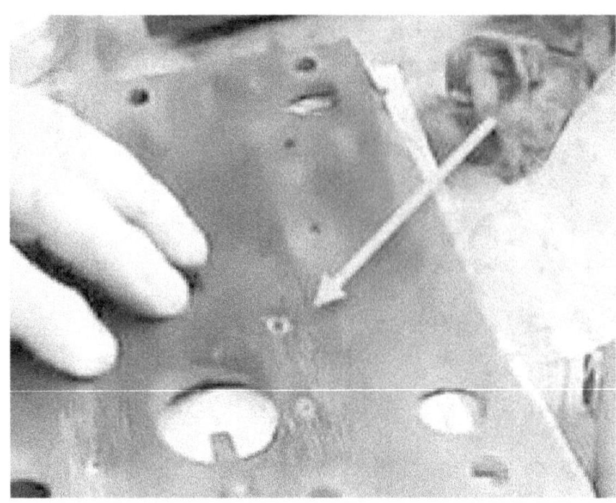

You will need to create a homemade guide bushing so you can drill the new pivot hole in the exact center of the new wood bushing.

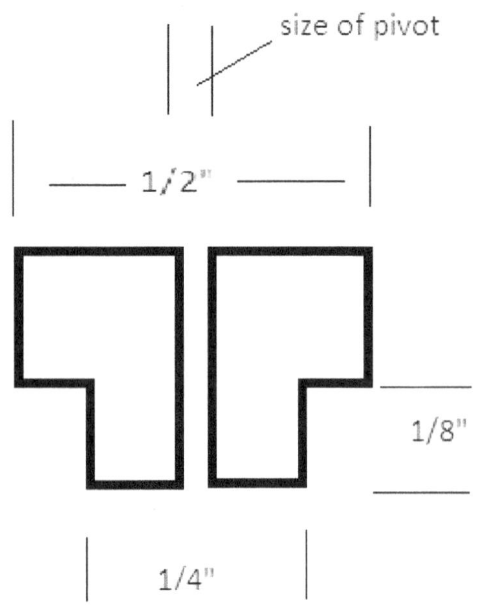

I discourage installing brass bushings unless that is what was in the clock initially and then use specialty bushings that are knurled on the outside to key into the wood grain.

Broken Teeth in Wheels

Single tooth. Before you begin the process of replacing any teeth on your wheels, get yourself a piece of scrap cherry or birch, about 1/4-inch-thick, and saw a slightly tapered slice off one side. [That tapered piece is going to be your practice tooth blanks.] Turn that slice 90 degrees and make an insert along one edge of the scrap piece, so that you have a piece sticking out from the edge. Cut off the piece sticking out and use it to do the same thing again. The object is to get the inserted pieces to fit so tightly that the joint is just a clean straight line, without using fillers of any kind. That is the most challenging part of replacing

broken teeth on wooden wheels. I know it sounds relatively easy on the face of it, but you'd be surprised how just a slight tilt of the file making that last pass can mess up the blank you were going to insert. Before I did one tooth on the clock itself, I would make at least five inserts on the practice piece. Even now, although I have done probably fifty teeth over the past thirty years, if I got one in the shop tomorrow, I'd do a practice piece, just to refresh my "muscle memory." In my head, I would hear my grandfather saying to me, "Make haste slowly." The last thing you want to do is mess up an otherwise good antique.

Multiple teeth. Cut out the bad section with a jeweler's saw making a slight dovetail at the base. Inset a piece of suitable wood. The wood is glued using hide glue, but the dovetail should be tight enough, so it is a press fit before being glued.

The tooth pattern is copied onto the blank and the teeth roughed out with the jeweler's saw and finished with a file and emery paper. After the wheel is reinstalled it should be checked to make sure it runs smoothly and there may need to be a little touchup with fine emery paper.

You can take a pattern from a good section of the wheel and trace onto the blank.

The blank can be a bit wider than the wheel and after the teeth are cut, the blank can be sanded flush with the original. The grain should be as shown in the pictures.

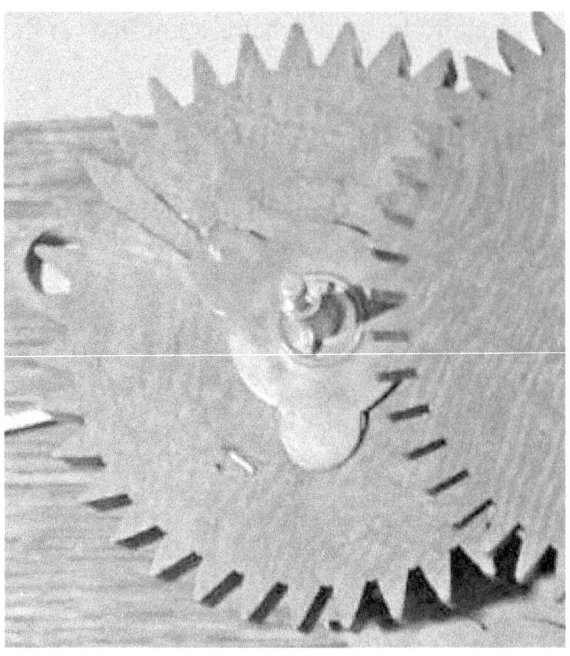

Pinion Teeth

Pinions are not as easy to repair. New teeth must be precisely formed and situated - firmly, and that is the important part - firmly in place.

Normally that there is not enough glue-able area to ensure a strong bond for the new pinion leaf.

One method is to remove the entire pinion, cut a new one, and fit it back onto the arbor. Another method, however, is to keep the existing pinion, but cut lengthwise channels where the pinions sheared off; these channels will act as a seating for the new pinion leaves once they are glued into place.

With channels cut, new leaves can be formed, fitted, and finally glued into place.

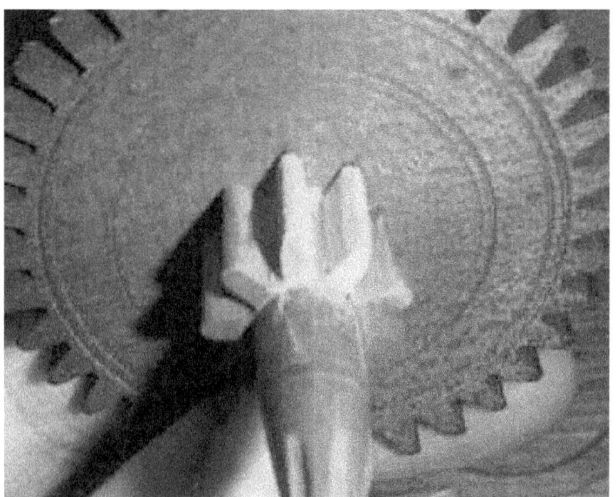

pipe cleaners [wet with mineral spirits] to clean the pivot holes in the plates.

Then, paint the movement and parts with the following mixture, 1/3 boiled linseed oil, and 2/3 turpentine. Let that dry at least 24 - 36 hours. Apply a second coat and allow it to dry fully.

Lubrication

A wooden movement should not be oiled, unless it has brass bushings [most don't]. The only lubrication needed is where there is metal-on-metal contact. This would be the escape wheel and the pallets on the escapement [which allows the pendulum rod to swing].

Cleaning

Cleaning a wooden movement, simply use odorless mineral spirits. Use an inexpensive bristle paintbrush [cut back the bristles to a short length] to apply the mineral spirits [liberally] to remove the dirt. Pour some mineral spirits into a pan and have at it. Let dry over 24 hours and then do a second cleaning to ensure a complete cleaning. Use

The Work Area

A well-designed clock shop is a tool in itself.

Having everything to hand, everything in its place, space to work on clocks is an asset, a place you want to be.

Working on clocks does not require a lot of space, at least at first. You need a clean and clear work surface about 24" by 24" to work on the clock. You also need an area for cleaning parts, a place for your lathe of whatever type nearby, and a space to run the clock while testing.

The worktop needs to be about 30" above the floor and well lit. In front of a window is nice, fluorescent light is good, giving nice even light. Two folding desk lights are also good, providing light from two directions.

It is essential the floor be clean and tidy and preferably not carpet. It won't be long before you drop a small part on the floor and it needs to be easy to find. Some people create a pull-out

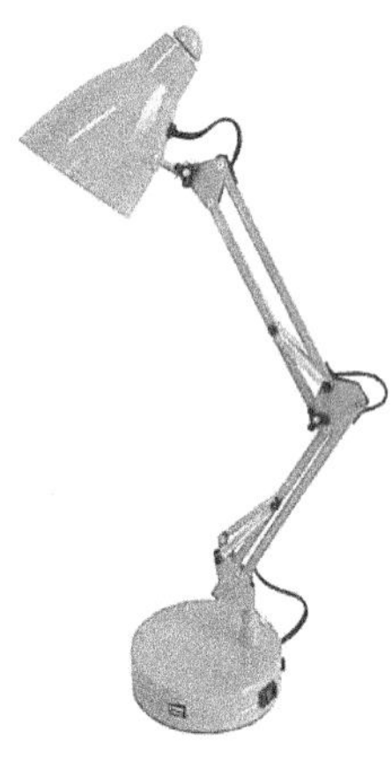

screen that comes out from the worktop to catch small items.

It is best if pets, especially cats, cannot roam on your work area that can knock things over or small children with curious fingers.

The most important thing is, all your tools be within reach.

You can start by working on your kitchen table, but as you get more serious, you will want a dedicated space. A roll-top desk or an old office desk works well.

If we want to get more technical about correctly setting up the beat of a clock, or diagnosing problems, we can introduce some electronic assistance.

The first item is a beat amplifier, available from Timesavers or Radio Shack for under $20, or your clock supply house. Using an alligator clip, attach the amplifier to the mechanism plate and turn it on. It will amplify the tick-tock sound making it much easier to get the beat accurately adjusted.

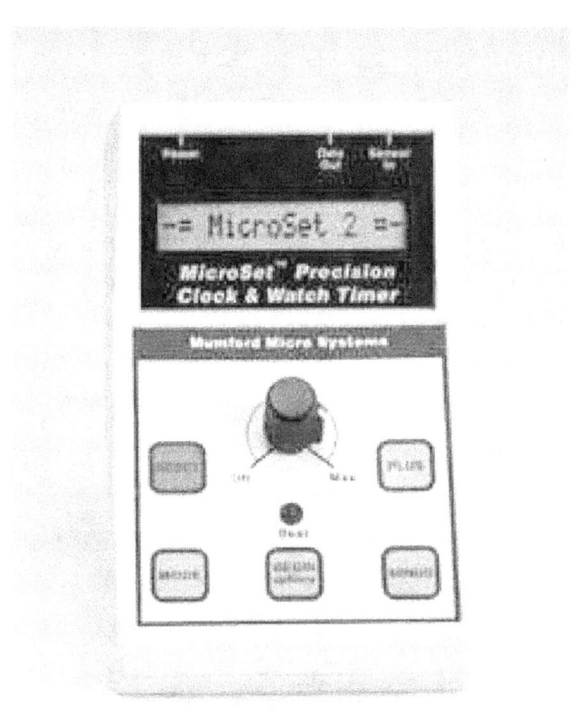

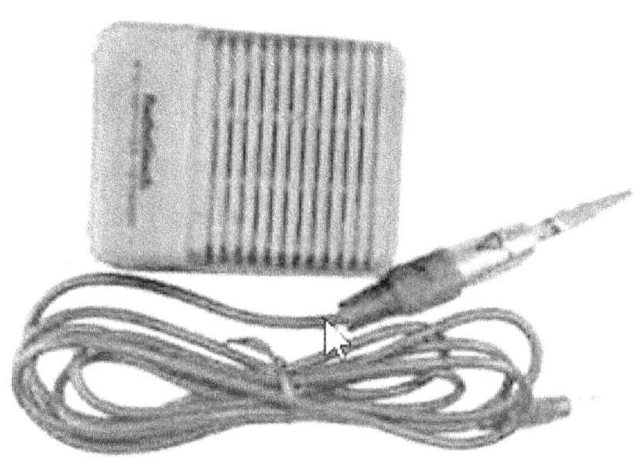

MicroSet

To get more technical, there is the MicroSet, which is a digital electronic timer.

It provides unprecedented accuracy, a resolution to a millionth of a second, an optical sensor to eliminate false readings from extraneous noise, and a powerful interface to Macintosh and Windows personal computers. The Count Mode will find the correct rate of any running pendulum clock. The Strike Mode will record the pattern of strikes over many hours to find intermittent problems. Several optional features can be added.

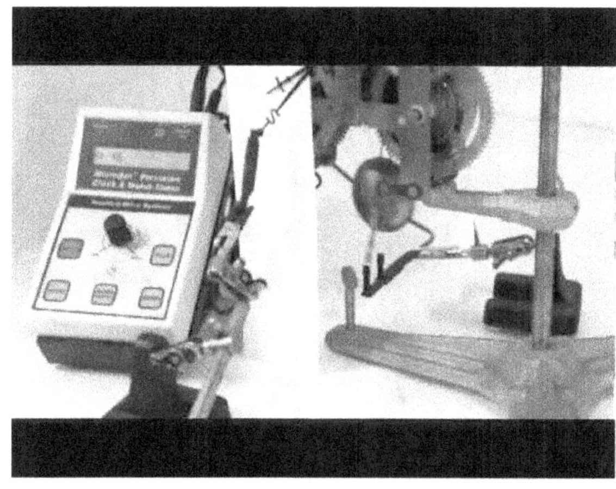

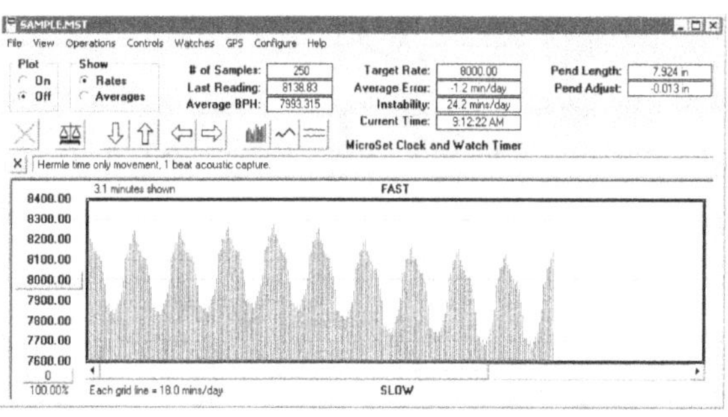

With this information, you can identify defective escape wheel teeth and put a clock in beat very precisely by reading the digital display.

Refinishing the Clock Case

Many of the clock cases you come across are very dirty, often very dark from the years of household furniture polish, and normal dust floating in the air and probably smoke. The motto "Do No Harm" means we want to restore the clock to its original state as close as possible while doing as little damage or alteration as possible.

Start by taking the case apart as much as you can: movement, carvings. Our goal is to remove the dirt and furniture polish back to the original French polish finish underneath.

Many cleaning products on the market will remove the dirt. However, most of these products will work too well and damage the original polish below over time. We learn from museum restoration practices that any cleaner with a PH above 7.0 will not only clean as you work on the clock but will continue to eat at the surface long after you have finished, damaging the original polish or shellac.

My recommendation is to use "Mr. Clean." This product happens to have the perfect PH value at just under 7.0 and removes the dirt with minimal effort. Just put some Mr. Clean on #0000 Steel Wood and using light pressure in a circular motion, clean off the dirt. You will likely see the hidden wood grain re-appear.

At this point, using a soft cotton rag and giving a little pressure to rub the surface and generate a little heat to reactivate the shellac. If the original surface has minor damage like scratches, watermarks, or 'alligatoring' [a series of cracks grouped in one area], you can use an "Amalgamator" from Mohawk. Used carefully, it will reactivate the shellac a little and blend it to create a newly restored finish.

Any loose veneer can be reglued using "Hide Glue." This is the type of glue used by the original case maker, and we still use the modern version from Titebond because it can be unglued using vinegar, and re-glued after repairs and restoration had been completed.

Once all the dirt is removed, you need to "feed" the wood again. For this, it is recommended you use Howard "Feed-n-Wax" orange oil, which is readily available. This will stop the pores from completely drying out and give life back to the wood.

The final step is to protect the clock case with Bri-Wax to give a mat shine that resembles the original hand-rubbed French Polish.

If the original finish is too severely damaged, use a good-quality stripper to remove the old finish. Do not use a water-based stripper or it will likely harm the veneer. Make sure 100% of the old finish is removed. Use gloves and eye protection. Let the stripper sit for at least 15 if not 30 minutes to allow it time to do its work. Repeat the stripper if necessary.

When all the finish is off, wash the case with mineral spirits to remove any residue.

Sand all the bare wood, starting with 300 grit, working up to 800 grit. Wipe clean with a tack cloth.

Staining the case is optional. Some feel it enhances the natural wood grain. I like Minwax. After staining, use #0000 steel wool and wipe clean with an old t-shirt.

Others prefer to see the woods natural color without stain.

Next, use a wood filler. Not to fill holes but to fill the wood pores. Wipe on, leave for 15 minutes, and buff off with burlap.

Lastly, add a seal coat. Varnish is suitable but takes days to dry and picks up any dust in the air. Do not use Polyurethane.

The best choice is Tung Oil. Plan on 6 to 10 coats, letting each coat dry overnight and rubbing with #0000 steel wool and a t-shirt before applying the next coat. You will be delighted with the finish, and it is foolproof.

The Lathe

Why a lathe?

One of the most expensive ~~toys~~ tools we use is a jeweler's lathe. However, used lathes are often available on eBay for a few hundred dollars.

I am going to give a general description of a lathe and what it is used for.

A jewelers' lathe is a small lathe suited to the clock and watch repair. It consists of a:
Bed – the general base and horizontal support
Headstock – holds and drives the work
Tailstock – can support the end of the work or hold tools
Tool rest – to support tools that do the cutting
Motor – to drive the headstock using a belt and controlled by a footswitch
Cutting tools – gravers, drills, files, etc

Lathes come in different sizes. 8mm is most common, but some use a 10mm size. The size refers to the size of the collet it takes.

The 'work' is most commonly held in a collet rather than a chuck.

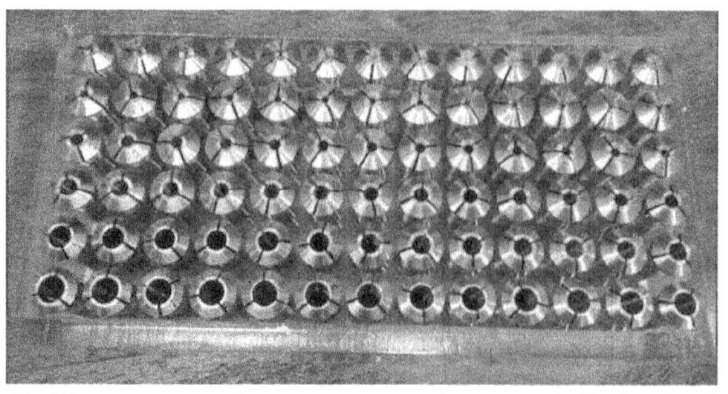

Collets come in sets, and the work is held in the collet the same size as the work it holds. This set is 3 to 80, with no gaps. A good beginner set of collets could consist of:
10, 12, 14, 16, 20, 25, 30, 35, 40, 45, 50
and this will cover most items.

The correct size collet must be used as described below.

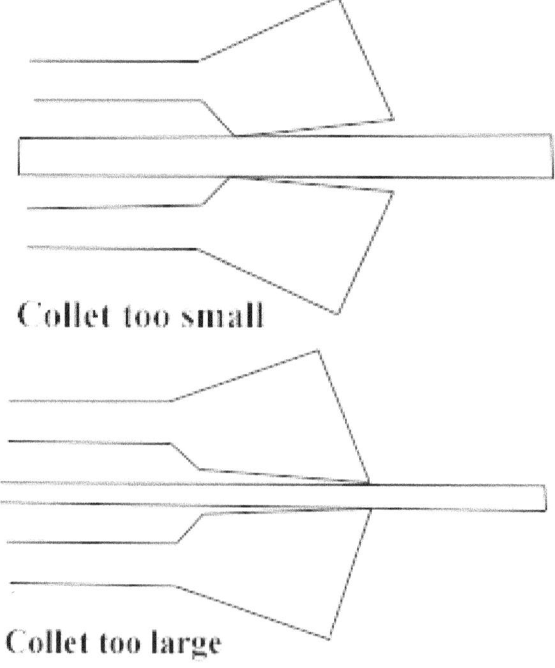

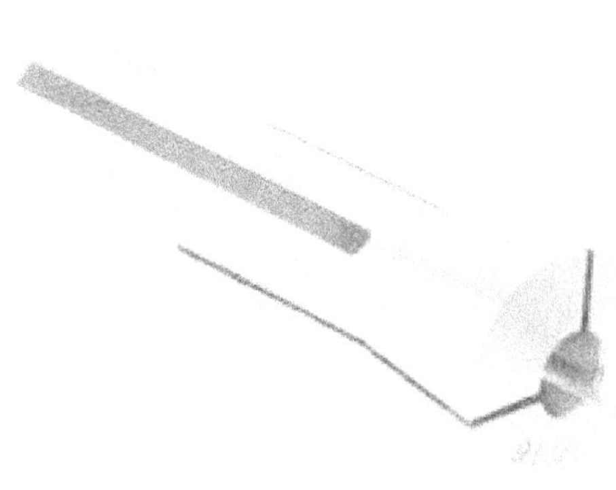

The collet must be the same internal diameter as the work it holds, so it grips the work its entire length keeping the material very stable.

If the collet is too small or too large, the inside of the workpiece can be unstable and wobble, making the cut inaccurate. It might mark the work also where it grips.

It is nice to have a way to hold drill bits - either collets or small Jacobs chuck in the tailstock.

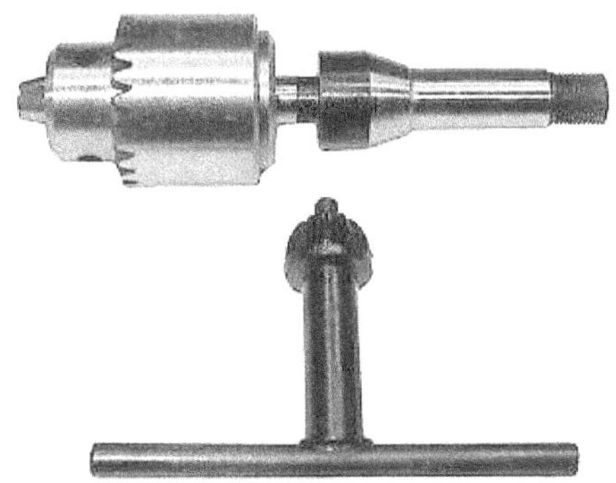

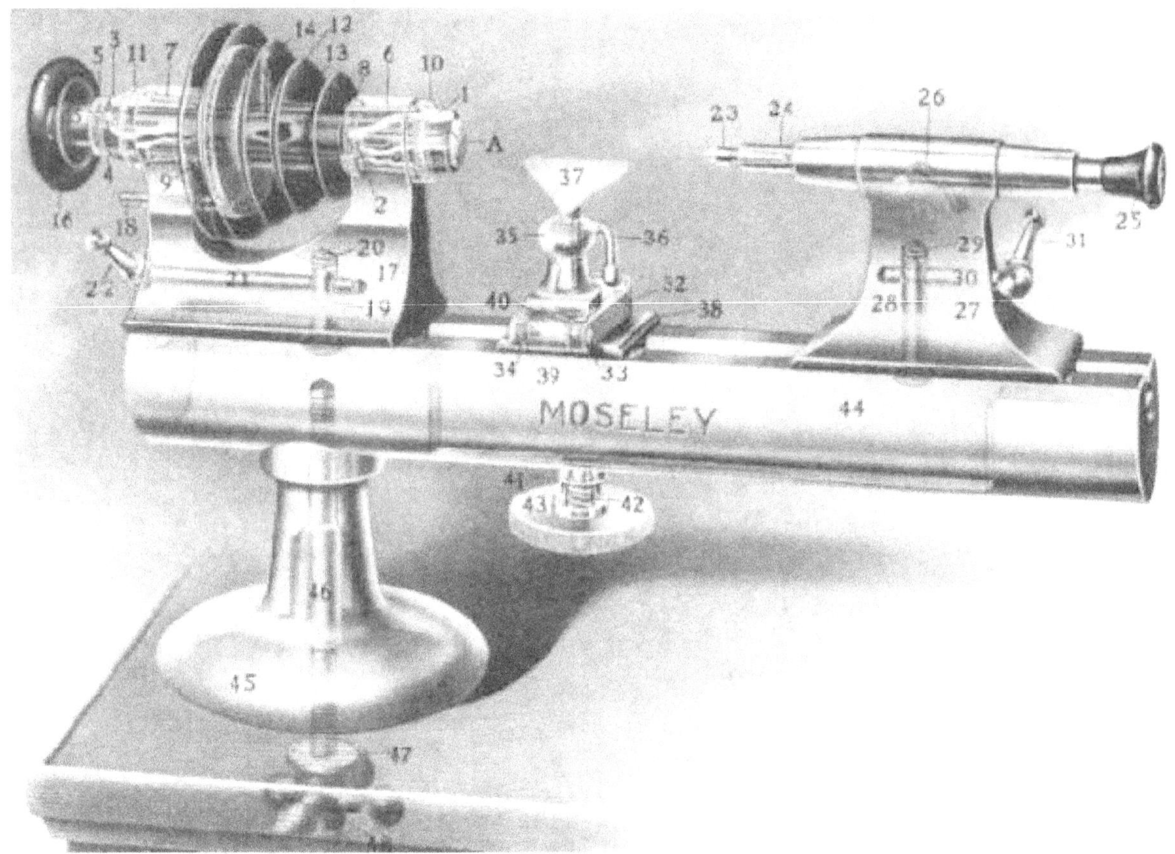

An early American-made Moseley lathe of the "WW" type with parts as annotated by the maker.

1. Headstock Spindle	2. Throat pin	3. Loose bearing	4. Loose bearing pin
5. Adjusting nut	6. Front bushing	7. Rear Bushing	8. Front inside shield
9. Rear inside shield	10. Front outside shield	11. Rear outside shield	
12. Pulley	13. Pulley Hub	14. Pulley screw	15. Draw-in spindle
16. Draw-in spindle wheel	17. Frame	18. Index pin	19. Bolt
20. Spring	21. Eccentric	22. Lever	23. Pointed Centre
24. Spindle	25. Spindle Button	26. Spindle Binder	27. Frame
28. Bolt	29. Spring	30. Eccentric	31. Lever
32. Slide	33. Pivot Screw	34. Pivot Screw	35. Post
36. Lever	37. T graver rest	38. Shoe	39. Shoe bolt

The work that can be performed by a lathe:
Polishing pivots
Pegging
Re-pivoting [broken off pivots]
Straightening bent pivots
Making replacement clock and watch parts
Make your own bushings and taper pins
Repairing parts

But the best part is you can make your own
tools.

Micro Drilling

The system that I used is simple and self-explanatory in the following photos. The tailstock spindle was replaced with a mild steel spindle and fine threaded on one end [40 TPI] to hold a threaded sleeve and threaded plastic ball. Spindles for the major brands are generally 5/16" or 8MM, and stock is available from metal suppliers for about $2.00 per ft. The large round item in the photo is a 3" neoprene fender washer. It is friction fitted to the threaded spindle sleeve. Everything but the spindle stock and fine thread Taps/Dies are available at Hardware stores. The next photo shows everything assembled and ready for use.

To place in use, first spot drill, then drill a drill shank size hole in the new spindle where the drill will be inserted. This assures highly accurate drill alignment. Also, micro drills usually come in a single standard shank size for many drill sizes, such as circuit board drills as an example. As such, two or three spindles will cover most of one's needs.

In operation, you apply continual light forward pressure gripping the ball at the rear of the spindle. At the same time, you slowly rotate the 3" disc allowing the drill to slowly advance. Spot drilling before drilling and mechanical controlled feed rate is the key to protecting a drill from breakage. On items of value, especially with carbide drills, I do not advance the drill greater than the diameter of the drill every two minutes or so. Thus the 3" disc. 1500-2000 rpm should be Max.

With this setup, a person with no experience can successfully drill a hole down to about .002" [.05 mm] or about half the balance staff pivot size in the photo on their first attempt. All that is required is steady tension on the tailstock spindle and slowly rotate the 3" disc no more than a 1/4 turn every two minutes.

Clock wheels that fit into the Lathe can be drilled for pivots or whatever in the same manner per the last photo.

To protect micro drills, mount them in a collet in the lathe headstock with the shank out. Then move the tailstock spindle over the shank installing the drill. Removal is done in the same way.

The shanks on micro drills are quite long, thus the hole should also be equally deep. If quality drills are used, the hole fit to the shank will offer far more resistance than drilling these small holes.

Organizations like the NAWCC hold annual marts where dozens of fellow members and clock hobbyists set out tables of clocks, practice movements, tools, books, and materials for sale at reasonable prices. A swap meet dedicated to clock repair. These sellers hold a wealth of knowledge and can be a sauce of local mentors or support. There are often classes held at the same time. Contact the NAWCC to find an upcoming local mart.

In this section, I will provide some miscellaneous problems and their solutions.

Problem getting into beat.

If you have trouble getting a movement into beat and it has a regulator, a **very slight** amount of "slop" or movement in the Chops or the part of the regulator assembly which raises or lowers the suspension spring through the chops could be the cause. The bottom line: Don't forget to evaluate the regulator assembly for wear or looseness critically. Even a very slight amount of looseness there can rob enough energy to cause seemingly random stalling problems.

Slop in the pallet arbor and/or the escape wheel pivots will create some lost motion, as will excessive clearance between the crutch loop and the pendulum rod. These will reduce the pendulum arc, sometimes to the point where the clock won't run reliably or at all. Note that often pallet arbors with seemingly insignificant side-play can cause a remarkable amount of trouble; I often bush these even if they seem fine.

Lost Weights

If you have a clock without weights, one trick I learned is that you can use a fish weighing scale. You tie one side to the clock cable and the other side to a large weight. As the clock runs and the weight touches the floor, the clock will continue running until the scale spring stops pulling hard enough to make the clock run. When the clock stops, the scale points to the minimum weight required to run.

Round up the value to make it a little more robust.

From teaching my clock repair class, I can give some feedback that many students fail to learn the first time around. I will use this feedback to provide you with a heads up and an essential recap of things to pay extra attention.

Many students seem to have a problem with the importance of pivot and pivot-hole polishing. It is vital that whenever a movement is dismantled, **ALL** the pivots and pivot holes be re-polished to a very high standard. Not just cleaned in soapy water, or even a good quality clock cleaning solution, not just making a dull pivot a little shinier. Not just removing grooves, but making the pivot very flat, smooth, and glass shiny so you can see reflections in it.

Before putting the movement back together, test each wheel **individually** between the plates to make sure it spins very freely. Then check **two wheels** together and finally the complete train [without the 1st wheel or escapement], and make sure everything runs smoothly. I have countless times tried to help a student where the clock will not run when put back together. Invariably they have not followed this procedure and must take the movement apart again to make small adjustments.

The escape wheel teeth must be in **perfect** condition for a clock to run. The slightest deviation to any tooth and the clock will stop or skip when the escapement gets to this tooth. I have yet to see a successful replacement of an escape wheel, even if the mating pallets are obtained with it.

Many students skip the step of making diagrams, especially noting the position of levers and pins. Or they lose the diagrams and or photos. It comes back to haunt them on assembly.

Clean all the parts as soon as you have dismantled the movement, but re-clean everything immediately before re-assembly, and this time do not touch the pieces with your bare hands.

Always use the correct, well-fitting screwdriver for each screw. Take pride in keeping the screws in perfect condition.

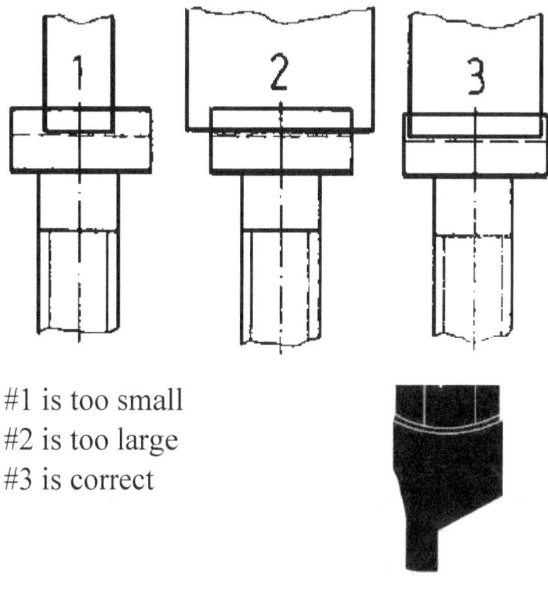

#1 is too small
#2 is too large
#3 is correct

Never, never, never open up a movement without capturing the mainspring, especially when adjusting the escapement or striking.

Clocks have only one known predator – the well-meaning hobbyists. Respect the clock, work slowly, and methodically. Use the correct tools.

Conclusion

Caution, **clock repairing is addictive**.

This introduction is just the beginning of your learning curve. Before you know it, you will be buying old clocks that don't run and making them work. You will be able to repair clocks for family and friends or even to make extra money.

If you have been following along with a project clock, you have been performing engineering at the highest level, making repairs and adjustments to $1/1,000^{th}$ of an inch.

Please bear in mind, the clockmakers of the past served a five-year apprenticeship under the direction of a master clockmaker to learn and master the techniques, then another 5 years working for the master at fine-tuning and perfecting their skills. Then they could call themselves a Horologist. I feel privileged to work on these masterpieces. I urge you to work hard, enjoy the journey, and have fun in your apprenticeship.

You are not alone. I strongly urge you to join a local clock club i.e. NAWCC or AWCI. Attend clock marts. Watch YouTube clock videos. Buy more books. Practice, Practice, Practice.

At the very least, monitor the free message boards at
www.mb.nawcc.org
www.awci.com/forum

There are many fine historical and modern timepieces in daily use, and we need more people to service and maintain them.

National Association of Watch and Clock Collectors [NAWCC]
717-684-8261
www.nawcc.org

American Watch-Clockmakers Institute [AWCI]
513-367-9800
www.awci.com

British Horological Institute [BHI]
 [01636]813795
www.bhi.co.uk

Clock Supply Houses

TimeSavers [tools, parts, and supplies]
Box 12700
Scottsdale, AZ 85267
800-552-1520
480-483-3711
www.timesavers.com

S. LaRose Inc. [tools, parts, and supplies]
3223 Yanceyville St.
Greensboro, NC 27405
888-752-7673
336-621-1936
www.slarose.com

Norkro Clock Supplies [tools, parts, and supplies]
2209 NW Mill Pond Rd.
Portland, OR 97229
800-566-7576
www.norkro.com

Player Piano Co., Inc. (Durrel Armstrong)
704 East Douglas
Wichita, KS 67202

316-263-3241
Raw material for cuckoo hands they sell simulated ivory which is the same thickness (.045") and coloring as real ivory, and with a fake marbelized grain structure, for piano restoration. Available in white (No. 1244) or yellowed (No.1245).

Empire Clock [tools, parts, and supplies]
1295 Rice Street
St. Paul, MN 55117
800-333-8463
651-487-2885
www.empireclock.com

Merritts Antiques Inc. [tools, parts, and supplies]
1860 Weavertown Road
P.O. Box 277
Douglasville, PA 19518-0277
610-689-9541
www.merritts.com

Mile Hi Clock Supplies [Manufacturer of Keystone Tools and Mainspring Lubricants]
877-906-1200 Order Line
303-469-1220 Assistance
www.milehiclocksupplies.com

Butterworths clocks [supplier of Hermle, Urgos, Kieninger Herr cuckoo, etc. movements]
5300 59th. Ave. West
Muscatine, IA 52761
563-263-6759
www.buttersworthclocks.com

Meadows and Passmore
[Brighton England]
www.m-p.co.uk

Sherline Products Inc. [lathes, mills, and accessories]
3235 Executive Ridge
Vista, CA 92081-8527
800-541-0735
760-727-5857
www.sherline.com

P.P. Thornton LTD [clock wheel cutters]
The Old Bakehouse
Upper Tysoe
Warwickshire
CV35 0TR United Kingdom

TimeTrax [clock timing machines]
Can be purchased at www.merritts.com
Makers of TimeTrax www.adamsbrown.com

MicroSet [clock timing machines]
805-687-5116 www.bmumford.com

Horological Book Sellers

Clock Watch Books
www.ClockWatchBooks.com

Arlington Books
http://www.arlingtonbooks.com
US Books www.usbooks.com

Recommended Books
My Clock Won?t Run….D. Rod Lloyd
The Clock Repair First Reader.... P.E. Balcomb
The Clock Repair Primer.... P.E. Balcomb
The Top 300 Trade Secrets of a Master Clockmaker. J.M. Huckabee
Clock Repair Basics.... Steven Conover
Clock Repair Skills.... Steven Conover
Chime Clock Repair.... Steven Conover
Clock Repair Tips.... B.C. Tipton

Practical Clock Repairing.... Donald DeCarle
Clock Design & Construction

I think I overwound the clock. It's wound all the way, and the clock won't run.

In actual fact, it is almost impossible to overwind a clock. Once the coils of a flat mainspring are in firm contact with one another, the spring cannot be physically wound any tighter. The only way to truly overwind a clock spring is to turn it so tightly that the spring actually breaks. The most likely problem is that the lubrication on the mainspring has failed due to age.

As lubricant ages, its viscosity slowly rises [it gets thicker]. Eventually, a lubricant no longer acts as a lubricant and gets tacky. This causes the coils of the mainspring to physically stick together. In actual fact, it's time for a cleaning /overhaul to remove old lubricant and accumulated dirt and replace it with fresh oil specially designed for clocks.

My clock use to run a full week on a winding, but now it will only run for a day or two.

The same answer as above. A clock that only runs a few days on a winding when it should run a week, likely has lubrication problems, although not usually the mainsprings. It is likely that the lubricant found in each bearing surface of the gears has failed and likely, there is a buildup of dirt and grime attracted by the lubricant. It is time for a cleaning. Alternatively, the spring might have become "set" or has lost its elasticity. It is time for a new spring.

My clock was just cleaned, and it won't run for more than a few minutes, even when fully wound. Also, I checked it with a level, and it is level on the wall/mantle

My first suspicion when I hear this comment is to question whether the clock is in beat. A clock being in or out of beat has nothing to do with a clock being level. First, to explain what "in beat" means. A clock is in beat when ticks and tocks occur with the same time interval between each tick and tock. You can listen to a clock's ticking and make a pretty close approximation of an "in beat" condition.

If you have trouble hearing the difference between in and out of beat, purposely tilt the clock slightly left or right off level. It's easier to hear different time intervals when the out of beat condition is exaggerated. Sometimes, a clock can be knocked out of beat by over swinging the pendulum. Also, moving a clock from one location to another without immobilizing the pendulum can knock a clock out of beat. Some wall clocks have a degree's scale attached to the clock behind the tip of the pendulum. In such cases, I will set the clock up to be in beat when the tip of the pendulum is centered on this convenient scale.

My clock stops once an hour

Does the clock stop every time the hands are overlapping? If this is the case, then the most likely cause is that the hands are interfering with one another. It could also be a striking problem.

I was winding my clock and I heard a loud bang and now the clock won't wind.

In this case, the problem is usually related to one of two possible causes. Either the mainspring has broken, or, the ratchet pawl on the mainspring has failed. The ratchet mechanism is responsible for preventing the mainspring for unwinding as you wind a clock. It is the clicking that you hear as you wind. It is important to check out the rest of the mechanism after an explosive release of a mainspring, as there is often other damage that occurs. Bent arbors and bent or missing teeth are the most common problems seen when a mainspring or ratchet fails.

I'm interested in going into the clock repair business. Where can I go to get training?

AWCI is the only establishment in the US that certifies professionals. They have home study courses, in-house training at their facility in Ohio, and professionals who travel around the country and do training. BHI, based in England, also certifies professionals and has a home study course as well as in-house training. Both institutes turn out some of the finest professionals in the business but their course studies are demanding.

The NAWCC's School of Horology is another resource for education. Although not able to professionally certify their students, it is a wonderful training ground for those interested. The school's disclaimer reads "The Avocational courses and the Specialty courses do not fall under the School's accreditation with ACCSCT. These courses are strictly taken as hobbyist courses or courses to further enhance the knowledge of people working in the industry." The NAWCC also has field suitcase courses which are organized through local NAWCC chapters around the country.

There are a number of books available if you are unable to afford to take classes and would like to be self-taught. The best books are DeCarle's "Clock Repair" and Goodrich's "The Modern Clock". These are available online from Arlington Books.

The only other way to learn the trade is to become an apprentice to a clockmaker. Ask around and see if there is anyone willing to train you but don't be disappointed if you don't find someone. Persons who are qualified to take on an apprentice, and have the time to do so, are few and far between.

How do I transport my clock?

If you're moving a clock that has a pendulum, please make sure you remove the pendulum from the clock and wrap it to keep it from damaging the movement or your case. If you cannot get the pendulum off by yourself, you can cushion and wrap it with towels or some other material to keep it from swinging wildly as you move it.

Why did my clock stop after running perfectly for so many years?

Clocks work great…until they stop. Over the years, the holes in the movement plates become worn and elongated, therefore misaligning the gears and wheels, causing the amount of force required to run the clock to be so great as to stop it. The oil dries up and becomes gummy, causing the clock to work dry and have excessive wear. Even with regular oiling, every clock will eventually wear out and stop working. Without regular oiling, they wear out even faster.

My clock is over 100 years old. Can you still get parts for it?

As you might guess, parts for antique clocks are not always available. Most clock repair shops do not have the expertise or equipment to fabricate or rebuild worn and damaged parts that were manufactured in the 18th or 19th centuries.

How do I reset my clock?

Since there are some older antique clocks whose hands cannot be turned backward, there is a common misconception that you must never turn the hands backward on any clock. It is okay to move the hands backward on all modern clocks and most antiques. If you try to move the hands backward and you feel resistance, don't force them. It is always okay to move the hands forward, waiting at each hour, ½ hour, or ¼ hour for the chimes & strikes.

Is my clock worth repairing?

I cannot answer this question specifically since each clock and clock owner is different, but I can share with you, what I feel is the best way to come to a decision.

There are two kinds of clocks we will consider here. The first type is a clock that has no emotional value to a person at all; it is simply a functioning clock that no longer works. In this case, the replacement value of the piece should factor into the decision. If the clock is going to cost as much or more to repair than it is to replace, you might as well replace it. An honest clockmaker will inform his customer when this is the case.

The other kind of clock is one that has either been passed down to its current owner through a family member, the current owner intends to pass it on to their children or the clock holds some special sentiment or meaning to the individual. In this case, the most important factor is not its replacement value, but its emotional or sentimental value. Because this type of clock is "one of a kind" and essentially irreplaceable, it is well worth whatever the cost of a proper repair would be.

Most of the time when dealing with a quality clock, even a complete overhaul of the clock movement is going to cost less than the clock's actual value. On some of the more common antique clocks, the cost will frequently come very close to or perhaps be a little more than its actual value and the more unusual or rare pieces will have a repair cost that will fall well below. Unless the clock has been purchased for "investment" reasons or for resale, the clock's emotional value should be considered first.

Should I replace my worn clock dial?

Many early American clocks had dials that were nothing more than a printed piece of paper glued to a metal dial pan. As these paper dials aged many of them have become extremely dirty and or worn badly.

Many times, the customer will ask whether anything can be done about this and if it will affect the clock's value. The first thing I do is ask them if they are planning to sell the clock. If they are not, then the value of the clock after a dial replacement is not a factor.

In the case of most common clocks, if the value of the clock is an important consideration in making the decision to replace or not, I will usually tell them that they have lost either way. If the clock's dial is in bad enough condition to consider a replacement, then some of the clock's value is lost already. Whether the dirty, badly worn dial is left in place or the dial is replaced, when it comes time to sell the clock, the purchaser will likely want to pay less either way. If the purchaser is an investment style collector he will be less interested either way because he will only be looking for clocks in original and mint condition.

Therefore, unless the clock is rare or has great antique value I tell them they should do what they think will please them the most when they look up at their clock sitting on the shelf or hanging on the wall.

Should I refinish my clock case?

The answer to this question is essentially the same as the last one. However, I'll add this. Many people now watch the "Antique Roadshow" on TV. They have heard the appraiser's comments about how a particular item's value has been diminished due to refinishing. This certainly can be true. A very rare piece is often worth more even if the original finish is in very bad condition. Notice I said very rare! Most clocks that people are bringing in for repair and considering the "refinish question" have clocks that are only worth several hundreds of dollars and although quite old are not rare at all. Frequently, the antique furniture in question on the "Antique Roadshow" is worth thousands and thousands of dollars, not a few hundred.

For most of my customers, the sentimental value far outweighs any antique value. Therefore, they are repairing, refinishing and or replacing dials for their personal satisfaction, not for some future investment return.

Each clock owner must decide this question for themselves.

How often should my clock be oiled?

Manufacturers recommend oiling every 2 to 3 years, with a professional cleaning every 5 to 7 years. To get the most years out of your clock's movement, you should follow this advice.

Why does a clock have to be cleaned and oiled?

The movement or works of a clock is a mechanical device with gears moving in contact with other gears. These gears are made of steel. These steel axles [pivots] are positioned between two brass plates. The brass plates are usually coated with lacquer to prevent oxidation [tarnish]. The holes in the brass where the steel axles rotate are NOT covered with lacquer. Tarnish will form in those areas unless protected by oil. This tarnish [oxide] breaks off in abrasive particles. It is like putting sand in a mechanical engine. These abrasive particles cause both the steel axles and the brass hole to wear out. The holes become egg-shaped, and the gears no longer mesh properly, causing premature friction and wear. This is what kills a clock movement.

In addition, the fresh oil acts as a lubricant. The pendulum of a mechanical clock oscillates anywhere from 3,600 beats per hour to over 10,000 beats per hour. This goes on 24 hours a day, seven days a week for years. Can you imagine running your car or your sewing machine without oiling it? I have seen newer clocks be completely shot in 17 years without oiling. Older clocks will last longer due to thicker brass plates. At any rate, it appears that with proper oiling and cleaning the clock movement will last for 10 additional years or more.

How do I set the time? It strikes 4 times on the half hour and once on the hour, and the time is not set right, and the hour hand is wrong.

Assume your clock is right and your hands are wrong. At least 90% of all cuckoo minute hands have a large round hole in them. If you get the hand off and it has a square hole in it just remove the hand and replace it in the next quarter or half hour. For the majority that does have the large round hole in them here is what you do. All the real adjustment takes place with the minute hand. Loosen the nut and remove the minute hand.

Stuck on the hand is a round piece of brass called a hand bushing. It has a square hole in it. This piece of brass needs to be turned one direction or the other and then just set the hand back on the clock. If it looks about right, put the nut on and tighten it and rotate the hand clockwise to see if it strikes the hour and half hour at the correct time. It probably won't be quite right the first time around. It rarely is for me. Be patient, adjust again.

Hold the minute hand still while you tighten the nut with a pair of pliers in the other hand. Once you get the minute hand striking where you want it to, then just move the hour hand to the last hours struck. The hour hand is a press on fit. Just turn it in either direction, then use your thumbnails to push down on each side of the hand near the shaft.

My clock runs for 3 or 4 minutes and then stops. What do I do?

First, make sure the clock is level on the wall. If it still doesn't run move the base slightly to the left and listen for an even tic-tic sound. Try running it again and if it still doesn't run move it slightly more to the left. If the tics don't even out and the clock still doesn't run then go back to level and repeat all the above by moving it to the right. Don't worry if the clock looks a little off level, right now we are trying to see if it will run. It may be out of beat and still be able to run. You won't know unless you try this first.

My chain has come off the gear. What do I do?

First, we want to avoid the other chains coming off while you are fixing this one. Take a twist tie or a piece of string and capture the other chains together right at the base of the clock. Put the twist tie or string inside the links and tie it. If you put it around the chain, they sometimes slip down the chain. This will keep those chains from coming off.

Now take the back off the clock and turn the clock upside down and give the loose chain a little slack. What you are trying to do is allowing enough slack to make a loop that you can hook around the gear sprocket.

It may take a few tries, but if you can see it, there is a good chance you can do it. Use plenty of light. Some clocks have more room in them than others. If you succeed hold onto the chain while you upright the clock. Hang it on the wall and then remove the ties on the other chains.

My clock runs and keeps time, but the cuckoo bird won't come out?

Check and see if the shipping latch above the cuckoo door is open so the door will operate freely. If the clock is new or has been shipped back to you be sure you have removed the clips that hold the bellows together. Newer cuckoos may have a night shutoff feature. Some have a shut-off lever coming out of the side or a black heavy wire with a loop on it that comes out of the bottom of the clock. Move the lever down or pull the loop down and try the cuckooing again.

I've been told by others that my movement is worn out and needs replacing. Is that the only answer and how can I tell the difference?

Here is how to tell if your clock has significant wear that is causing it to stop running or cuckooing. Caution: do not lay the clock on its back or turn it over because the chains are only held on their sprockets by gravity and will come off. While looking in the back, pull up and down on one chain. In other words tug back and forth on the winding chain and the weight chain of one wheel.

Watch the back plate where the pivots come through the plate. Particularly the 2nd gear up from the bottom. If that steel pivot rod is jumping back and forth in the hole then you have significant wear.

Keep doing it and look at the other holes as you go up each train as you are pulling. If your case is big enough to get your hand in there just wiggle the bottom gear that the chain rides on. You will get the same effect.

Usually, the wear starts on that second gear but it is normal to have 2 or 3 gears worn that much on a clock that has been run a lot. The wear causes the gears to start separating and they don't mesh well. That causes it to lose power all the way up the train of gears. Try the time side also to check for wear. If one side is worn, it is likely that the other side isn't far behind.

How does the clock operate the music box?

Notice, this is for information only, pretty please don't try to fix this yourself or you will need me or someone else for sure. I always advise people to stay away from these and don't bend anything, but some are going to anyway and at least this gives them some idea of how they work. I'm going to try to tell you how the music box works. It may not be exactly what you have, but all are similar and will give you somewhere to start. There should be 2 connections from the movement to the music box. On some movements, both wires come from the same spot. On others, there is a flat strip of metal coming from the right-hand corner of the clock and a straight wire coming off the back center of the clock.

The flat strip of metal is hooked to a linkage that pulls a locking pin out of the music box at the top of the hour.

The music box tries to play but the fan is immediately stopped by the straight wire coming off the back of the clock. That wire will move back and forth as the clock cuckoos and when it finishes it is supposed to drop away just enough to let the fan rotate freely and the music will play and will lock itself back down. That is how it is supposed to work. Getting it to do that is extremely tricky. I sometimes spend as much as a whole day on adjusting one music box. Others may take me 10 minutes. There is only one sweet spot where everything will work.

A collection of meanings of common clock terms.

Alarm

Sound a clock makes to awaken the sleeper at a certain time. They come in various sounds: bell, double bell, chirp, beep, buzz, melody, etc.

Analog

The traditional look of time told by the angular positioning of hands on a dial.

Anniversary Clock

The name comes from the fact that when it was first invented, it needed winding just once a year on its anniversary [approximately 400 days]. Characterized by a glass dome and a rotating pendulum. Also known as a "400 Day Clock".

Arabic Numerals

Most common number style [1, 2, 3, 4, etc.] used on clock dials.

Arch

The curved part of a clock case that resembles a door arch.

Beat

Term to describe the tick-tock of a mechanical timepiece. A clock is said to be in beat if the spacing between the tick and the tock are equal. If they are not equally spaced, the clock is out of beat and will generally stop after a short run.

Beveled Glass

The glass used in the clock case with an angled surface beginning about 3/4" from the edge.

Big Ben Gong

The deep-sounding chime that announces the hour. Modeled after the large bell clock in the tower of the House of Parliament in London.

Bim-Bam

Chime which only counts the hour and announces the half-hour.

Bob

Round, weighted end of a clock pendulum. Often made of brass.

Bow Top

A decorative feature found in certain mantel and wood case wall clocks. Characterized by a curved top section.

Bracket Clock

A term used by the British to indicate a table or shelf clock. Characterized by a square case with a handle on top, as it was designed to be carried from room to room.

Balloon Clock

Mantel or tabletop clocks shaped like hot-air balloons of the late 18th Century.

Burl

The decorative pattern in the wood grain caused by a series of irregularities that add to the character of the wood.

Cable Driven

A mechanical movement powered by weights hanging on cables wound with a key or crank.

Case/Cabinet

That which contains the clock, the housing or containment for the works [movement]

Carriage Clock

A small portable clock, usually has a brass case with glass sides and a decorative handle on top.

Center Shaft

The shaft that the minute hand is attached to, geared to make one revolution every 60 minutes.

Chain Driven

See also Weight Driven

Traditional cuckoo clock movement. It is driven by weights hung from chains with engaged sprockets.

Chapter Ring

A decorative ring on the clock dial upon which the hours are indicated. A feature of many traditional style mantel clocks. Also a prominent feature of clocks with skeleton movements.

Chime Melody

A tune played by the clock on the hour. A 4/4 Chime plays music and counts the hour, quarter-hour, half-hour, & three-quarter hour.

Chime Rods

Tuned rods which, when struck by small hammers powered by the clock movement, produce the chime melody and strike the hour. A component found in mechanical chime mantel and wall clocks.

Chip

Small silicon square onto which integrated circuits are imprinted. An integral part of the quartz movement.

Cornice

Topmost molding of a clock case. The 833-W is a great example of a well-defined cornice.

Crystal

A flat or convex piece of glass that covers the dial. Usually fitted into a brass bezel.

Day Ring

Divided ring on a lunar dial that indicates the days in the 29 1/2 day lunar cycle.

Dial

The face of a clock on which the hours are located.

Digital

Time display that uses no hands but shows the time in numbers and readout screen.

Drop Case

Wall clock with a lower case, which usually houses a swinging pendulum such as a Schoolhouse style clock.

Escapement

A means by which the pendulum allows the going train to operate at a regular interval, thus controlling the passage of time. It usually consists of an anchor and escape wheel.

Etching

A process used to create a design in metal by the action of an acid. A feature found on the metal dials of many German Anniversary Clocks.

Finial

The spires, turnings, or decorative points on top of a clock case. Maybe wood or metal. Sometimes removable. Some are called "ball and spike", "urn", "acorn", etc.

Finish

Process and materials used to create an attractive wood surface. Examples include deep cherry, medium oak, mahogany, antique walnut, etc.

Grandfather Clock

The correct name is Long Case Clock [in Britain] or Tall Case Clock in the USA.

Hands

Used to mark hours, minutes, or seconds on a clock dial. Made of metal or plastic.

Inlay

Thin layers of wood are applied to form a decorative pattern.

Keywound

A spring-driven clock that is wound with a key or crank.

Liquid Crystal Display [LCD]

Most frequently used in quartz alarms. Time is continuous, displayed in digital form.

Light Emitting Mode [LED]

Number telling the hours and minutes light up on a readout screen.

Lunar Dial

See also Moon Dial

An additional dial on a clock face that indicates the phase of the Moon each day.

Lyre

An ornamental feature on a pendulum resembling the ancient Greek instrument.

Marquetry

A type of decoration on wood made by inlaying wood veneers in elaborate designs.

Minute Track

Square or circular track divided into 60 equal segments. It may appear on the outer perimeter of the dial or in the dial center.

Moon Dial

See also Lunar Dial

An additional dial on a clock face that indicates the phase of the Moon each day.

Movement

Timekeeping mechanism of the clock, which also produces the strike and chime. Comes in quartz [battery], key-wound, or weight-driven.

Pediment

The decorative top of a case, above the cornice.

Pendulum

A suspended, swinging rod and weight [bob] that regulates the clock movement in key-wound/mechanical clocks. The pendulum in quartz [battery] clocks is purely decorative; the clock does not need it to properly function.

Pilaster

A decorative feature used to create the effect of columns on the clock cabinet.

Pinch-Waisted

Traditional clock style with the crown and case wider than the part of the clock enclosing the pendulum.

Quartz

Electronic transistorized movements that work on battery energy and require no winding or plug-in electricity. A tiny quartz crystal, vibrating at a high frequency, allows the clock mechanism to perform with extraordinary precision.

"R-A" Regulator

Slang term for wall regulator with "R-A" on the pendulum. "R" stands for retard by turning the adjusting nut toward R to lower the pendulum bob. "A" stands for advanced by turning the adjusting nut toward A to raise the pendulum bob.

Regulator

The mechanism that can be adjusted to make the clock more accurate. Sometimes the word "Regulator" is printed on the clock's glass, usually on Schoolhouse clocks.

Roman Dial

A dial with Roman numerals [I, II, III] frequently used in traditional style carriage, mantel, wall, tabletop, and anniversary clocks.

Rotating Pendulum

A feature found on both key-wound and quartz [battery] anniversary clocks. Characterized by decorative balls in crystal or metal finish.

Schoolhouse Clock

Traditional wood cabinet wall clock with a round or octagonal clock case and lower pendulum cabinet. Said to be true Early American Design. This style was most commonly found on classroom walls in American Colonial days.

St. Michael Chimes

Chimes originally installed in the St. Michael church steeple in Charleston, SC in 1764.

Scroll

A decorative ornament resembling a partially rolled scroll of paper.

Straight Sided

A style of clock cabinet in the same width from crown to base.

Strike

Chime or gong that indicates the hour.

Tambour

Style of clock case sometimes referred to as "Napoleon's Hat".

Tempus Fugit

Latin phrase meaning, "Time Flies". Sometimes engraved on a decorative panel on the clock dial or a plaque attached to the clock case.

Time train

The series of gears in the clock movement that operates the minute and hour hands [and second hand where applicable]. The time-train is responsible for activating the chime in the movement.

Triple Chimes

Movement that plays 3 different chimes: Westminster, Whittington, St. Michael

Tubular Bell Chime

Long hollow tubes which, when struck by small hammers powered by the clock movement, produce the chime melody and strike the hour.

Verge

An escapement belonging to the Foliot and Verge. Not all escapements are verges.

Veneers

Thin layers of wood chosen for their attractive grain and permanently applied to a core material. The same material and method are used in making violin and guitar cases.

Weight Driven

See also Chain Driven

Traditional cuckoo clock movement. It is driven by weights hung from chains with engaged sprockets.

Westminster Chimes

The most popular tune used in chiming clocks. This famous tune originated in the Victorian clock towers in the House of Parliament in London.

Whittington Chimes

Chimes originally rang in the church of St. Mary Le Bow in London. Legend has it that a young boy running away from his master thought he heard them call out his name, telling him to turn back. Dick Whittington did and eventually became the Lord Mayor of London.

Other Books for sale that I have written that might interest you – available at my website

www.ClockWatchBooks.com

or on Amazon

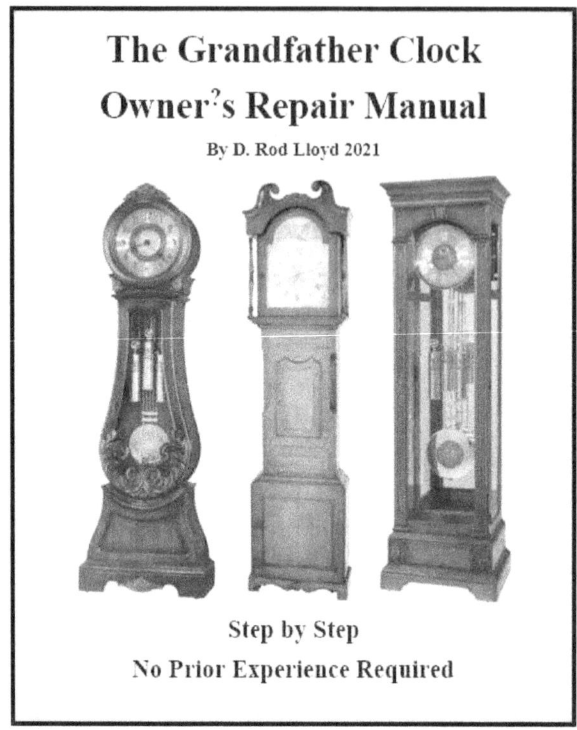

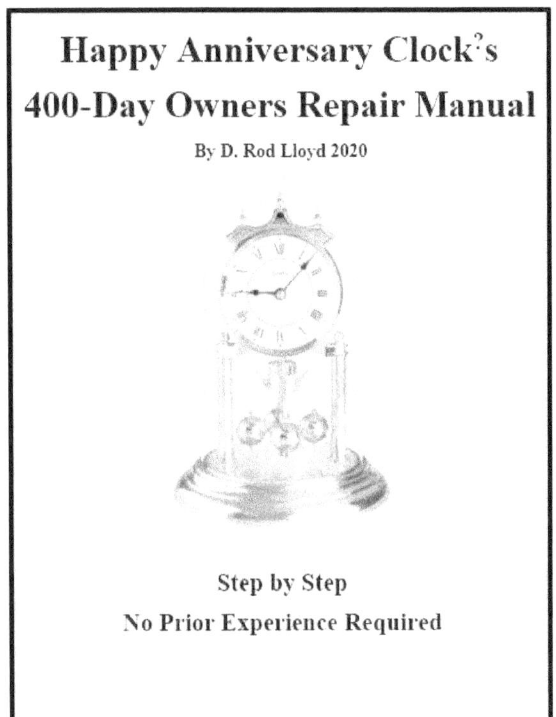

The Grandfather Clock, many think is the king of clocks, standing tall and stately with their impressive case like a fine piece of furniture.

Many not only tell the time, but they also strike the hour and even play a heartwarming tune to continually remind you of their presence.

The Anniversary Clock is somewhat similar to Cuckoo Clocks in that they are a unique style and many, many sit on the shelf not running, just because the owners have not taken the time to understand them and keep them running, even though many have sentimental value.

Not many people are aware of the Atmos clock. It is a perpetual motion clock that was ahead of its time when created in the 1930s and still is today. The Atmos clock is a true masterpiece of a timepiece. No other clock demands such pride of ownership. No batteries, no winding, no power cord.

The power to run this clock comes from changes in the atmosphere. An internal bellow expands and contracts with small temperature changes. One degree temperature rise will run this clock for two days.

This book is the most comprehensive clock repair book, covering a wide range of clocks. Everything you need right at your fingertips.

You would need to buy a dozen other clock books to get all the information contained in this comprehensive manual.